Mentorship:
The Essential Guide for
Schools and Business

Jill M. Reilly

Published by Ohio Psychology Press, P.O. Box 90095, Dayton, Ohio 45490. Copyright © 1992

Library of Congress Cataloging-in-Publication Data

Reilly, Jill M.
  Mentorship: The essential guide for schools and business / Jill M. Reilly.
        p.   cm.
  Includes bibliographical references and index.
  ISBN 0-910707-18-9
  1. Education, Cooperative—Minnesota. 2. Mentors in education—Minnesota. 3. High school students—Employment—Minnesota.
  I. Title.
  LB1029.C8R45   1992   91-42116
  370.19'31—dc20   CIP

Dedication

To Peg Schaefer

Who devoted herself to establishing and maintaining first-class mentorships for students and professionals, and who thoughtfully and caringly mentored me;

And to all the Mentor Connection students, mentors, staff, and advisory members—past, present, and future — who, I know, benefit from her efforts.

Jill Reilly
February 5, 1990
Minneapolis

Acknowledgements

With deepest gratitude to:

My dissertation committee at the University of St. Thomas: Karen Ristau, my Chair, Bob Brown, and Karen Rogers who made this project possible for me and whose insights added to its content.

Karen O'Brien for giving me the outstanding opportunity to shape the program; Doug Webster for listening and his willingness to help; and all the staff at Dakota County Secondary Technical Center and Intermediate District 917 whose broad range of talents constantly aid and amaze me!

The Dakota County Mentor Program Advisory Boards for years of advice, service, support, and expertise.

All the students past and present whose presence and insight guided me.

Elizabeth Jenner, Linda Silrum, Jeanie Pullen, Dorothy Welch, and Carol Kronholm for all of their contributions to Mentor Connection and this project. They add class and stature to all they do!

Jim Boesen, Marsha Besch, and Chuck Erickson for their assistance in developing the Apple Valley High School model and to the entire Apple Valley staff for their inspiring example of what educators should be.

Bonnie Featherstone who believed in me to begin with.

Geri Masson who has been a friend across the distance.

Kristin Thomas and Trista Patterson for input into this project as former students, consultants, and cheerleaders.

The University of St. Thomas Doctorate in Educational Leadership Cohort 3 who have so enriched my perspective.

The Metropolitan Service Unit of the Twin Cities, the *Minneapolis Star & Tribune,* and Les Suzukamo and the *St. Paul Pioneer Press* for permission to reprint materials.

Beth Franks, Theresa Palmersheim, Jean Wincek, and Don Poplau for their assistance in preparing the manuscript.

Jim Webb and Pat Kleine for all the TLC given to the publication of this book—and me.

Chris Adams who has become my trusted colleague.

My husband, Patrick, and my children, Elizabeth, Joseph, and Heather, who supported me in all kinds of wonderful ways.

TABLE OF CONTENTS

MENTOR PROGRAM PLANNING GUIDE

WHAT	WHO	WHEN	
12 PLANNING FOR NEXT PROGRAM CYCLE	Instructor Faculty Contacts Steering Team	Analyze results of last evaluation and plan accordingly	STEERING TEAM (Informed of all phases of the program) — Composed of Instructor, School Personnel, Mentors, Parents, Students. Meets 3–4 times during the school year
11 EVALUATION	Mentors/Students Instructor/Faculty Contacts Steering Team	Forms completed and analyzed at end of term	
10 RECOGNITION	Mentors/Students Instructor/Faculty Contacts Steering Team Parents/Public	1 day at the end of shool year	
9 BEGIN FIELD EXPERIENCE	Mentors/Students Instructor Faculty Contacts	12–30 weeks, 10 hours per week	
8 BEGIN MENTOR SEMINAR	Students Instructor Faculty Contacts	Approximately 60 hours of instruction: 1 hour period, 12 weeks or 2 hour period, 6 weeks	
7 SELECT PARTICIPANTS	Instructor Screening Committee	1–4 months prior to Seminar	
6 INTERVIEW APPLICANTS	Instructor Screening Committee	1–4 months prior to Seminar (1–2 weeks prior to selecting participants)	
5 REVIEW AND RATE APPLICANTS	Instructor Screening Committee	1–4 months prior to Seminar (Approximately 2 weeks prior to interviews)	
4 CONDUCT INFORMATIONAL MEETINGS	Instructor Former Students	2–4 weeks prior to application deadline	
3 ANNOUCE APPLICATION DEADLINE AND REQUEST APPLICATIONS	Instructor Counselors Teachers Students	2–5 months prior to Seminar	
2 IDENTIFY STUDENT'S NEED FOR MENTOR PROGRAM	Students Parents Teachers Counselors		
1 DEVELOP PROGRAM AWARENESS MATERIALS	Instructor Steering Team		

WHAT	**WHO**	**WHEN**

START HERE!

Introduction

America's education revolution will come from the personal involvement of parents, teachers, principals, and the community—working together to remove barriers of change.

— Louis V. Gerstner, Jr.
Chairman and CEO
RJR Nabisco Incorporated

Much has been written about the failures of the United States' educational system, specifically the failure of high schools to graduate students capable of entering the business sector. Former Secretary of Labor Elizabeth Dole (1989) announced that "America's workplace is in a state of unreadiness . . . unready for new jobs, unready for new realities, unready for the new challenges of the '90s." The situation challenges not only education, labor, business, and the government but "the very foundation on which America is based." Dole recommended to educators that :

. . . we first need to understand that the connection between educational excellence . . . and business success is fundamental. Closer ties between education and business must be formed.

At the educational summit held in 1990 in Charlottesville, North Carolina, President George Bush and the Governors of the United States responded to the charges of a nation educationally at risk with The National Goals for Education (1990): "America can meet this challenge if our society is dedicated to a renaissance in education. We must become a nation that values education and learning."

To achieve a "renaissance in education," the National Goals demand that "sweeping, fundamental changes in our education system must be made. Educators must be given greater flexibility to devise challenging and inspiring strategies to serve the needs of a diverse body of students."

A Contribution to the Solution

A mentoring program for high school students meets the requisites specified by both Dole and the National Goals for Education. It provides flexibility to educate beyond the traditional time, location, and method constraints. A mentoring program unites education and business to best meet the interests of individual students. Mentors and students interact one-on-one as they develop a plan to integrate the knowledge, skills, and abilities the students need and desire. As students gain experience in the workplace, educators continue to provide educational, social, and emotional support.

The gains for student and mentor alike are documented and extensive. Many articles have been written to define the meaning and roles of a mentor and mentee for gifted students (Boston, 1978; Mattson, 1980; Runions, 1980; Torrance, 1984), to affirm the need for the gifted to study in-depth and with some degree of autonomy (Betts, 1986; Gallagher, 1975; Renzulli, 1977) and to document the benefits mentor and mentee derive from a mentorship in a variety of settings (Cox & Daniel, 1983; Cox, Daniel, & Boston, 1985; Feldhusen, 1985; Lambert & Lambert, 1982; Seeley, 1985; Shapiro, 1988; Torrance, 1984). Two recent books provide suggestions on how to develop a mentoring program for gifted and talented students (Haeger & Feldhusen, 1989; Nash & Treffinger, 1986).

But while much has been written on mentoring in schools and in business, the literature does not include a detailed description of the design, structure, operations, and curriculum of school-based mentoring programs. The literature also lacks a comprehensive look at a specific mentoring program.

I wrote *Mentorship* in an effort to fill this gap. In addition to documenting the philosophy, operations, and successes of a specific mentoring program, I have tried to provide a complete "how-to" manual for readers to consider and use. It also offers an in-depth synthesis of the effects of mentoring programs on high school students, staff, and their schools, as well as on mentors and their businesses. This book is for anyone who wants to know more about mentoring or who wishes to develop or participate in a mentoring program. I also hope that this work will stimulate additional research.

In particular, I wish to show that mentoring programs are indeed "doable." To make the most of the opportunity, however, high school students need training in specific skills. Unfortunately, many of these skills are not currently addressed in high school classrooms. I would like to see more of this training happen.

In my experience consulting and speaking across the country, I have observed a surge in interest in mentoring programs. I've also seen enthusiastic proponents of these programs stifled due to a lack of time, dollars, and encouragement. Change does not come easily. When mentoring programs are established, too often they are perceived as simply asking someone in the workplace to mentor a student while offering minimal orientation, training, or follow-up for either mentor or student. This occurs not because people don't care, but because of the same lack of time, dollars, and encouragement.

Meet the Mentor Program

In the Twin Cities region of Minnesota, the Mentor Connection program has successfully allowed hundreds of high school students to prepare for and participate in advanced-level learning with professionals, or mentors, working in fields of interest to each student. This book will fully explore the *Mentor Program* which derives from and expands upon the Mentor Connection. The *Mentor Program* presents an educational option which may benefit other communities seeking innovative educational alternatives.

The information presented in *Mentorship* has been obtained from my experiences over the past twenty years, particularly the work I have done with educators, students, parents, and the community at large to join forces in educating our young. My work with the Mentor Connection, and as creator and developer of the *Mentor Program,* have most greatly influenced the contents of this book. In addition, I have consulted with schools across the country on this topic and have gained a great deal from these encounters.

Consistent with the program's slogan, "real life, real people," the students discussed and quoted are all real people who participated in mentorships and shared their stories. This book provides documentation of their experiences; the educational outcomes resulting from these partnerships truly make a difference in students' lives. Students not only learn about their field of study, but they unlock inner resources, gain competence, discover links between their formal education and the worklife that extends beyond them. In Dole's words, they become "ready."

Mentorship speaks to the effectiveness of a mentoring program for high school students. The first chapter addresses the question: When does a student really need the help of a professional mentor? Following chapters will examine the "how to's" and underlying principles of the *Mentor Program,* so that readers can apply the information to create or support an educational opportunity for the students with whom they have a personal connection. Chapter 8 provides ammunition for persuading a reluctant teacher, guidance counselor, businessperson, administrator, or parent to become involved or to institute a mentoring program. It considers when and where a mentoring program might be deemed appropriate in the context of current educational research and presents the qualitative and quantitative data to support the information and outcomes presented. The final chapter provides an inspiring example of one student's growth—and professional success—as a direct result of his experience in the *Mentor Program.*

By definition alone, mentorships provide obvious benefit to adolescents: new experiences; a role model; support to learn and grow; and transition into adulthood. Those who have been affiliated with high school mentorships have observed the results first-hand. To add depth and credibility to the argument for mentorships, it is important to review what others have observed and to hear what high-school-age mentees say when reflecting upon their own experiences.

Throughout this book, I've quoted students who participated in the *Mentor Program.* Unless otherwise noted, the student quotations cited are responses to the *Mentor Program Graduate Survey* (Reilly, 1990), also referred to as the *MPG Survey.* The *MPG Survey* was administered to all students completing the *Mentor Program* during the five years from 1985 through 1989. The *Mentor Program* graduates cited here responded to the two questions :

1. Please list which skills, abilities, activities, insights or other gains you felt were most valuable to you as a result of participating in the *Mentor Program* and why?

2. How, if at all, have you continued to use the knowledge and skills you gained in mentor class and/or in your mentoring?

In a sense *Mentorship* was born with my experience as a student-teaching supervisor while I pursued a graduate degree. I observed students from twenty to sixty-five years old shaping and reshaping their careers—an unhappy lawyer who became a gifted teacher; a home-maker who became a teacher after educating her own children. While trained in literature, oral and written communications, and teaching methods, few of my students had insights into the inner workings of a classroom, much less a school. They had spent at least sixteen years in school but could not truly grasp what it meant or what was needed to work at the front of the classroom. Those with desire deserve the opportunity to explore their passions *and* their options long before they enter the workforce—and they must come to the workforce better prepared.

With today's educational crisis, it seems clear that students' natural interests and talents must be cultivated with the full force of our nation's resources. The community beyond the classroom can offer much to our young. Mentoring has proven an effective means of channelling those resources. *Mentorship* thoroughly describes one model for others to test, modify, perfect, and utilize. If the book generates interest on the part of educators, businesspeople, or parents, it may also engender experimentation. Then others can share new and even better educational ideas upon which we can build.

References

Betts, G.T. (1986). *Autonomous learner model.* Greeley, CO: Autonomous Learner Publications and Specialists.

Boston, B. O. (1976). *The sorcerer's apprentice: A case study in the role of the mentor.* Reston, VA: Council for Exceptional Children.

Cox, J. & Daniel, N. (1983). The role of the mentor. *G/C/T,* 29, 54-61.

Cox, J., Daniel, N., & Boston, B. O. (1985). *Educating able learners: Programs and promising practices.* Austin, TX: University of Texas Press.

Dole, E. (1989). *State of the workforce address.* Washington, DC: Department of Labor.

Gallagher, J. (1975). *Teaching the gifted child.* (2nd ed.). Newton, MA: Allyn and Bacon.

Gerstner, L.V., Jr. (1990). School CEOs must take risks. *The School Administrator,* 19.

Haeger, W. W, & Feldhusen, J. F. (1989). *Developing a mentor program.* East Aurora, NY: D.O.K. Publishers.

Lambert, S. E, & Lambert, J.W. (1982). Mentoring a powerful learning device. *G/C/T,* 25, 12-13.

Mattson, G. (1979). The mentorship for the gifted and talented: Some practical considerations. *G/C/T.*

Nash, D., & Treffinger, D. (1986). *The Mentor.* East Aurora, NY: D.O.K. Publishers.

A nation a risk: The imperative for educational reform. (1983). Washington, D.C.: National Commission on Excellence in Education.

Office of the Press Secretary. (1990). *National goals for education.* Washington, DC: The White House.

Reilly, J.M. (1990). *Fifth-year survey of Mentor Connection graduates.* Unpublished.

Renzulli, J. S. (1977). *The enrichment triad model.* Mansfield Center, CT: Creative Learning Press.

Runions, T. (1980). The Mentor Academy Program: Educating the gifted/talented for the 80's. *Gifted Child Quarterly,* 24(4), 152-157.

Seeley, K. (1985). Facilitators for gifted learners. In J. F. Feldhusen (Ed.), *Toward excellence in gifted education* (105-133). Denver, Co: Love Publishing.

Shapiro, G. (1988). Ethical leadership. *University of Minnesota Focus,* <u>4</u>(1), 1-2.

Torrance, E. P. (1984). *Mentor relationships: How they aid creative achievement, endure, change, and die.* Buffalo, NY: Bearly Limited.

CHAPTER 1

When Does a Student Need a Professional Mentor?

Understand that a talent is something given,

that it opens like a flower, but without exceptional energy,

discipline, and persistence will never bear fruit.

— May Sarton
World of Light

As a high school senior, Chris possessed a keen intellect which he shared with his friends. However, he saw school as a "game I can observe and easily win." Little truly involved him except for art classes. At home, he loved to play his guitar and draw on his computer. Clearly Chris had more energy and skill to offer than he expended in school.

Dave languished in the bottom third of his high school class, and his test scores ranked at the bottom third as well. "School just doesn't interest me," Dave said. "Oh, I turn in all my work, but I just can't seem to make myself do well." His teachers and his supervisor at a local office supply store regarded him as a "responsible, good kid." When asked what he truly loved, Dave responded enthusiastically, "Clay animation and sports." Dave's high school offered a wide variety of art classes, but they only mildly interested him. After all, the art classes did not show him how to animate clay characters.

Jenny had loved writing ever since she learned to form letters and words. When she was in third grade, a fifth grade teacher who shared Jenny's passion volunteered to read her writing and to help her develop it. That year, Jenny's parents also began taking her on field trips to enhance her writing awareness and skill: trips to libraries, theatre productions, literary readings, and a repository for original manuscripts and illustrations of children's literature.

When she was in sixth grade, Jenny's school recruited a high school composition teacher to assist the budding science fiction writer. By her junior year in high school, Jenny's skill and need surpassed the resources her school could offer. At this point, Jenny wanted to develop her writing skills more than ever.

Shannon attended a small high school with no advanced science courses. She, like Jenny, actively sought additional resources and support to further her life-long interest in natural science, particularly animals. During the summer of her junior year, she paid hundreds of dollars to participate in an intensive animal research program to get the "hands on" experience she passionately desired. After completing the animal research program, Shannon had exhausted all the science course options her high school offered, yet she wanted more.

Chris, Dave and Jenny, and Shannon each had the opportunity to participate in a mentoring program at a critical point in their education. Chris's interest and energy were tapped as he worked with the owner of a graphic arts firm and her employees. Within a few months, Chris assumed responsibility for creating materials for real clients. Meaningful and challenging learning ignited Chris' intelligence and drive. As a result he produced prolifically and professionally, and was subsequently hired by the firm.

Dave's passion for clay animation was fulfilled by the two owners of a special effects firm. They immediately identified with Dave and recognized the isolation he felt at having no one with whom to share his interest. The men mentored Dave through the complete artistic and financial processes of creating his own clay-animated film. After finishing the mentoring program, Dave, like Chris, became employed by his mentors.

Jenny's writing talent and drive were rewarded as she developed her own adolescent novel with a well-known writer. When she displayed her work at a mentoring program open house, a book publisher noted her work and requested an immediate meeting.

Shannon's interest in animals provided intrinsic motivation for advanced learning both in researching the breeding problems of the bacteran camels at a local zoo and working as an interpretive naturalist. In the later capacity, although quite shy, Shannon taught groups of youngsters how to tap a maple tree, how to handle reptiles, and ways to identify birds native to the area. Her mentors became her friends. She wrote:

> *This has been the best of my high school years! I have learned so much from the* **Mentor Program**. *I'm so happy that someone like you cares about young people and their dreams! I know now that I will be able to achieve at least part of my huge dreams because of all your support and help. Please don't ever stop the* **Mentor Program** *because it's the best thing that happened to me—Thank you [personal communication, June 10, 1990].*

Mentoring programs can offer expanded options and renewed enthusiasm for students like Chris, Dave, Jenny, and Shannon. Chris, Dave, Jenny, and Shannon are real people, although their names have been changed to protect their privacy. For educators and business people seeking innovative solutions to students' needs, high school mentorship may provide one promising possibility for advancing students' learning and preparing them to assume their roles in society.

What Is Mentorship?

Mentoring is a buzz word in educational and professional circles. But what exactly does it mean?

The term mentor is derived from Greek mythology when Odysseus entrusted his son, Telemachus, to the care of his wise advisor, Mentor.

Mentor assumed the role of guiding Telemachus into young adulthood in his father's absence. Athena, the goddess of wisdom, also assumed the form of Mentor when she appeared to Telemachus urging him to initiate a mission to find his father and to gain a fuller understanding of himself.

Examples of mentorships emerge from real-life situations and the literature throughout the ages: In United States government, Vice President Hubert Humphrey mentored Walter Mondale; in the Star Wars movies, Ben Kenobi mentored Luke Skywalker; psychoanalyst Sigmund Freud mentored Carl Jung; and Socrates mentored Plato. In recent times, both business people and educators have advocated mentoring as a means to help develop an individual's cognitive and psycho-social potentials, particularly the capability to function more effectively in some aspect of society.

The Jewel Corporation, a Chicago-based chain of food stores, provides an example of mentoring as means of perpetuating exceptional corporate leadership in a highly successful business. Interviews with three of Jewel's chief executives, Frank J. Lunding, George L. Clements, and Donald S. Perkins in a 1978 article, "Everyone Who Makes It Has a Mentor," demonstrate how the corporation's leaders successfully cultivate younger protegees to move into high-level management. Frank J. Lunding, former Chief Executive Officer of the Jewel Corporation, expressed his basic philosophy of managing a successful company. What Lunding calls the "first assistant philosophy" essentially is one way in which to define mentorship. He says:

> It is simply that executive responsibility involves assisting the people down the line to be successful. The boss in any department is the first assistant to those who report to him. You've got to live your life in a worthwhile way. This is a worthwhile philosophy. It doesn't hurt people, it helps them; and after it helps them, it helps the business (p. 90).

"Serving," "living life in a worthwhile way," "helping," these words echoed by all three of the Jewel chief executives interviewed not only describe Jewel's management style, but they also help define mentoring. In the Jewel Corporation, mentoring is defined and clearly institutionalized. Mentoring as a philosophy, then, can fit into the business world as well as into education.

Other definitions vary depending on the field or perspective of those offering the definition. Whatever their orientation, however, each emphasizes the relationship between the mentor and mentee and the positive values derived from the relationship.

Consider the psychoanalytic overtones in Burton's (1977) definition of the mentoring dynamic in the context of a therapeutic setting: "The mentor is an adult companion who stands as the model not of rebellion, but of a socially useful and fully creative life" (p. 118). Here Burton emphasizes emotional growth into adulthood. Through mentoring, the mentees see a model that counters destructive or rebellious behavior. The mentor shows the way to a more purposeful and satisfying maturity. Burton also defines mentoring as connected to both work and love.

At the same time Burton wrote about mentoring as a means of assisting an adolescent's growth into adulthood, Boston (1976) studied the role of mentoring and its implications for gifted students. Cox and Daniel (1983) cite Boston's plea to regard mentorship as "a special and privileged relationship" (p. 54) that should not be confused with other varieties of individualized and practical education.

Phillips (1977) speaks to the role of mentors in the career development of women managers and executives. She says that mentoring in business and industry derives from a caring personal relationship. Phillips defines primary mentors as individuals who contribute time and effort, even make sacrifices, to help their protegees because they care personally about them.

Notions about Mentoring Adolescents

Noted psychologist Erik Erikson (1963, 1980) describes adolescence as a period of transition when youth meld their individual personalities and cognitive abilities with their ability to identify with others. The purpose of the melding is to form an image of how youths fit into the adult world. As Burton (1977) describes, mentors can model that image.

Levinson (1978) and other researchers note that mentors generally enter people's lives during times of transition or change. Adolescence is, of course, a transition period fraught with great change. Mentoring can play a key role in easing students, particularly eleventh and twelfth graders, through developmental stages. Burton (1977) suggests that mentoring allows adolescents to move beyond a parent-to-child relationship as their main contact with the adult world and adult expectations. He argues, "Adult adjustment, therefore, not only depends upon a proper mother/child relationship base but a proper peer development in young adulthood of which mentoring is an important component" (p. 117).

Subotnik (1987) builds on this critical notion of adolescent identification with adults in her study of the role that mentoring plays for the gifted young winners of the National Westinghouse Science Talent Search. She concludes, "There may be a critical time in adolescent development during which an apprenticeship serves the adolescent even more richly than independent exploration" (p. 19).

Boston (1976) argues that mentoring goes beyond teaching or guiding; mentoring shapes the individual's perspective or outlook on life. Kram (1985) notes a distinction between instrumental mentoring which allows mentees to change their social circumstances through teaching, advising, coaching, or sponsoring, and psychosocial mentoring which facilitates personal changes in mentees through confirming, counseling, and supporting. In instrumental mentoring, the changes or rewards are extrinsic or environmental in relation to the mentee. In the instance of psychosocial mentoring, the mentees change within themselves. In a high school mentoring program, either instrumental mentoring or psychosocial mentoring may result; in most cases, both occur simultaneously.

In the study of *The Season of a Man's Life* (1978), Levinson, et al. found that a mentor:

> . . . *fosters the young adult's development by believing in him [or her], sharing the youthful dream and giving it his [or her] blessing, helping him [or her] to define the newly emerging self in the newly discovered world, and creating a space in which the young man [or*

*woman] can work out a reasonably satisfactory life structure that con-
tains the Dream (pp. 88-89).*

This parallels Shannon's thank you note, cited earlier in this chapter. Both Levinson, a researcher, and Shannon, a *Mentor Program* student, perceive a mentor as someone with more experience who
supports a young adult to do for herself, to strive to attain what was previously a dream.

High School Mentoring Defined

Synthesizing many elements of mentoring noted here, Flaxman,
Ascher, and Harrington (1988) define mentoring in their book, *Youth
Mentoring*. Their definition of mentoring will stand for the purposes of
this book. It provides a consistent fit with the model for mentoring utilized by the *Mentor Program* and a basis for understanding what the program seeks to achieve. Mentoring is:

> *A supportive relationship between a youth or young adult and some-
> one more senior in age and experience, who offers support, guidance,
> and concrete assistance as the younger partner goes through a
> difficult period, enters a new area of experience, takes on an impor-
> tant task, or corrects an earlier problem. In general during mentoring,
> mentees identify with, or form a strong interpersonal attachment to,
> their mentors; as a result, they become able to do for themselves what
> their mentors have done for them (p. ii).*

The *Mentor Program* derives from and expands upon the Mentor
Connection, a highly successful mentoring program which serves more
than fifty high schools in the Twin Cities region of Minnesota. By working with mentors in fields of their choice, students learn skills that
could not be taught at such a challenging level in their high schools.
The students also experience personal gains in confidence, persistence,
personal empowerment, self-efficacy, self-knowledge, knowledge of a
field, interpersonal skills framed within the "adult world;" a sense of
autonomy; educational and career path awareness; friendship and support; research and critical thinking skills; and connections between

other areas of study and their own interest area. One college senior illustrated this point when he intimated, "In all areas where a great deal is expected of me as an individual, I continue to draw upon the experience I gained in Mentor Connection" (Reilly, 1990). Much data has been collected and results documented about the *Mentor Program* and Mentor Connection (Bathke, 1990; Beck, 1989; Hess, 1984, 1985, 1986; Nathan, 1990; O'Connor, 1989; Reilly, 1990; Suzukamo, 1987).

The *Mentor Program* consists of two separate, sequential classes. The first class, *Mentor Seminar*, prepares students for advanced-level learning with a mentor. Then in the second class, *Mentor Field Experience*, the class instructor/coordinator connects students with a professional mentor in the student's chosen field of interest. Students are ready for mentorship only after they have studied their individual interest areas and developed a repertoire of additional skills which help make the experience valuable for themselves and their mentors.

Mentoring Is Not Always the Answer

Years ago, I received a telephone call from a neighboring school district's volunteer coordinator. She asked if I could help her find a published writer to mentor a promising student. When I requested more information about the student, the volunteer coordinator told me about Jenny, a third grader, who loved to write. Jenny's writing accomplishments had surpassed the other students in her grade.

A youngster with a passion—and a need—I thought. But does a third grader really need a professional to help her develop her talent? I asked how Jenny's teacher had helped with her writing up until this point.

The volunteer coordinator replied, "Only through the district's third grade writing curriculum. Jenny's skills go beyond that, but her teacher feels uncomfortable with teaching writing beyond the lessons in the curriculum."

"Have you or her teacher considered specifically what type of help Jenny needs to advance her writing skills?" I asked. "Does she understand how to write a paragraph, what a plot is, or a little about developing characters? Can she write dialogue? Does she need more encouragement?"

The volunteer coordinator paused. "Well, let's see. Jenny is writing more detailed stories while her class is learning to write a simple paragraph. Her teacher says the stories consist of a few imaginative paragraphs with more advanced vocabulary than most third graders use—and Jenny wants to write *on her own*."

"On My Own"

When a student says she wants to work "on my own," the phrase may have several interpretations. Generally, it sends a signal that a learner has an unmet educational need. Sometimes, teachers and other school personnel confuse a student's need to learn "on my own" with the need for a full-scale, ongoing mentorship. "On my own" can have several interpretations besides "I need a mentor." A mentorship is not the only answer. Nor is it always the best one.

Before they can accurately determine if a mentorship best fulfills a student's learning needs, teachers and parents must probe further to discover the nature of the student's educational needs. Students like Jenny may be asking to study a topic at a more advanced level or in more depth than her peers. Another interpretation may be a desire to study a topic of interest which is not covered in school, as exemplified by the fourth-grade student who wanted desperately to study waterfowl. Obviously students do not receive substantial instruction on waterfowl in grades kindergarten through twelve.

Other students may desire a more rapid—or more relaxed—pace when they ask to study on their own. "On my own" may also be a plea for more individual control over the approach to learning, such as working individually instead of in a group or "hands on" versus "pencil and paper." The student may also wish to change a required end product: "Instead of writing a description of a pioneer's home, I'd like to build a model." "On my own" can also mean "I want to see the connections between what I am learning and how it applies in the 'real world.'" Whenever "on my own" crops up, wise teachers and parents respond in two steps. Step one: probe for an interpretation. Step two: search for solutions.

Many times, the solution may extend beyond resources available within the classroom and, perhaps, the school—particularly if the student's goal is to study at a more advanced level or an unusual topic. Before considering a mentor, teachers and parents can seek existing resources and research materials that, with encouragement, creativity, and a little instruction, the student can use to work "on my own." These resources might include independent study, at-home projects, or activities like a trip to an exhibit, an informational interview, or an afternoon's shadowing experience which demand a limited amount of time and supervision from adults. Each new endeavor will allow the student to stretch himself, test his interest, and prepare for a mentorship should that option become necessary over time.

Answers for Jenny

The discussion about Jenny's needs continued and we planned an approach to the problem.

The volunteer coordinator had just described Jenny's ability to write a few paragraphs and her advanced vocabulary. I wanted to help find resources for Jenny, but believed there were more suitable alternatives for her than an extended commitment from a writer. I continued the discussion: "What kind of stories is she writing? Are they tales about children her age? About animals?"

"I think her teacher mentioned they were fantasies."

I suggested that maybe the best help for Jenny would be to encourage her to read fantasy stories that fit within her reading and writing levels, then someone could talk with her about how the writer makes the story interesting. I suggest "reading *and* writing levels" because she may be able to read books by a science fiction writer like Madeline L'Engle, but a third-grader will surely become frustrated if she tries to write like her.

After this discussion, Jenny's teacher and her parents could also encourage her to expand her current stories or write new ones from ideas she got while reading. When she has a few stories written—which might be months or even next year if her interest persists— perhaps either the volunteer coordinator , the teacher, or her parents could locate someone within her school to give Jenny a few suggestions to develop her writing. That person would only need to take a few minutes to read Jenny's stories and provide suggestions. At Jenny's age, she will need much more work on basic skills even if her writing ability far exceeds that of her peers.

The volunteer coordinator agreed that this might be a good plan. I still had questions and thought about other options: "Do you think Jenny's teacher would allow her to work on her own writing project while the other students continue their paragraph instruction? And are there other times during the school day when Jenny could have time to read and write? She's going to need support to develop her talents."

The volunteer coordinator responded, "I imagine that would be possible. I'll make a note to ask her teacher."

"Are her parents involved with this request?" I asked.

"I know they are interested and willing to help. I don't know if they initiated this request."

I explained that Jenny's parents could also be a real resource to her. I had noticed that the public library in Jenny's community was hosting a noted children's fiction writer for story hour. I suggested that Jenny might enjoy hearing him read his own stories. If it were possible to arrange, a brief chat with him could teach her, too. "I'm sure you, her teacher, and Jenny's parents can brainstorm many other ideas to help develop Jenny's interest and potentials," I concluded.

"Of course we can. We'll talk about it . You've given us a lot to think about," the volunteer coordinator responded. She thanked me and asked if she could call again with any further questions. I agreed.

Jenny is fortunate to have a teacher, parents, and even a volunteer coordinator who are frontline supporters and nurturers of her potential. When Jenny's needs surpassed the traditional curriculum for her grade level, these caring adults sought nontraditional ways for her to learn at an appropriate level and pace—and they willingly followed through with a plan to help her. These people have been directly involved in improving Jenny's education and in paving the way for other students like her.

You may have guessed that this is the same Jenny as the one mentioned at the beginning of the chapter. When she reached high school, she was ready for a mentor. She distinguished herself in her work and hoped to continue to develop her writing career.

"America's education revolution will come from the personal involvement of parents, teachers, principals, and the community— working together to remove barriers of change," (1990, p. 16) predicts Louis V. Gerstner, Jr., Chairman and CEO of RJR Nabisco Incorporated and a leader in Nabisco's 30 million dollar Next Century Schools program. Jenny and those who care about her are at the forefront working together for change.

When Is a Student Ready for Mentorship?

In American society, schools have the primary responsibility to educate children. Schools have many resources, although at times seemingly insufficient, to accomplish this mission. Before educators can ask the business community to provide long-term experiences for students, they must guide students and their parents to other available resources. Students should certainly understand their topics, work hard at learning independently, and strongly desire the mentoring opportunity they request before undertaking such a relationship.

In fairness to prospective mentors, this philosophy mandates that mentorships are suitable only if the student has exhausted other resources and is ready for and capable of sustaining a long-term commitment. That way students take best advantage of a professional's time. If students become effective, independent learners prior to mentorship, they also can better gauge when they can find answers on their own and when they truly need a professional's help.

From an educator's perspective, two questions require thought: How or when can teachers ask other professionals to take time to explain basics when students can easily learn them from other sources? How can students learn effectively in a fast-paced professional setting if they are not eager and self-directed?

While this book deals primarily with high school students and their needs, Jenny's story has merit here. The issue of finding resources beyond the classroom emerges long before students reach high school, and the strategies suggested in this chapter have also been proven successful with elementary school children. The remainder of this chapter will examine the resources available to students prior to seeking the assistance of a professional. This course of action allows students to become more ready for mentorship, or to become what George Betts describes as "autonomous learners: independent, life-long learners who have developed the appropriate skills, concepts and attitudes for growth" (1990, p. 4). When schools develop autonomous learners, they develop more than students' intellectual abilities; they develop desire and an understanding of how to obtain the resources they need. As John L. Clendenin, Chairman and CEO of BellSouth Corporation notes (1990), "As is the growing trend in business, education must develop the personal potential of each individual, not just his or her educational skills" (p. 20).

Think again about Jenny as she might progress as a writer. How might she continue to develop her potential? If Jenny's interest and skill in writing continue to develop through fifth or sixth grade, a junior or senior high communications teacher might provide her with more sophisticated feedback. Later, as she masters plot and character development and skillfully writes short stories or begins a novel, Jenny's needs may exceed the skill and time any teacher can reasonably devote to an "extra" student.

At this point, Jenny's writing will be skillful and specialized enough to warrant the expertise of a writer. Jenny may even know what fiction category best suits her skills and interests. **Now** Jenny needs, deserves, and most likely will find a willing mentor. When a school representative contacts a writer, he or she can say that their school has made every effort to help Jenny develop her writing skills. Jenny truly has exhausted the resources available to her. Knowing this, most business people are willing, if not delighted, to help. Gerstner of Nabisco comments:

> *If school administrators dare to encourage fresh ideas and the entrepreneurial outlook, they can transform our schools. If they do that, I believe they'll find the business community willing to move from the sideline cheerleading and sniping to become resourceful partners (1990, p. 17).*

How to Assess Readiness for a Mentor

In the *Mentor Program*, students may seek a mentor when they have exhausted the resources of their school; when they need to move beyond what can be offered within their school district; or when their pace in learning greatly exceeds the classroom instruction available to them. Students best demonstrate their readiness for mentorship if they can form clear questions that only a professional can answer and can provide concrete examples of what they have already learned. *If these primary criteria have been met,* a student might also seek a mentor to further understand the realities of the professional world or obtain the social and emotional support or one-on-one attention that a mentor can provide.

Assessing readiness for a mentor is a judgment call at best. A teacher or parent must balance the student's needs and readiness with concern about the request for a professional's time. The information presented in Figure 1-1, **Identifying and Using Resources,** may generate ideas to enrich the student. Start at the *bottom* of the flow chart and work your way up. Don't move up a level until you have exhausted the potential of the current one. Reaching the top of the chart indicates readiness for a mentor.

The following discussion provides further explanation of how to identify and use the resources suggested in Figure 1-1. The discussion begins with the bottom level of the chart and moves upward toward mentorship.

Who will help?

The first step in obtaining resources for a student is to decide who should be involved in the decision-making process. This choice may depend upon several factors including the student's interest, availability, age, grade-level, maturity, and parental involvement. The organizational structure of the school, job descriptions, and staff availability will affect who will represent the school. The most likely participants include the student, the student's parents, a gifted coordinator, a classroom teacher and/or interest-area specialist. Depending on the situation, students, a parent, or school personnel can assume the facilitator's role.

Fig. 1-1

MENTOR PROGRAM IDENTIFYING AND USING RESOURCES

START AT THE LOWEST LEVEL THAT WILL SERVE THE STUDENT.

11 Arrange for a mentorship or internship, a long-term commitment from both the student and the expert. Best done during school time or during the summer so the experience is not tacked on to the end of a full day.

10 Arrange for the student to meet with experts at their workplace. Meeting can be a short conversation and/or an observation, or shadowing, experience.

9 Ask a specialist to visit the classroom to offer enrichment to all students while directly serving the one with a more in-depth need. Some programs arrange for specialists to visit schools regularly over a span of time.

8 Ask a specialist within your school district to assist the student. With minimal inquiry, you will be amazed at the range of expertise within your district.

7 Ask someone within the student's school to help the student one-on-one.

6 Brainstorm possible activities and resources that will allow the student to advance his learning as independently as possible. Consider public libraries or specialized libraries located within museums, wildlife centers, or even businesses; community education classes; zoos, art, history and science museums or galleries and/or their classes; local theatres and public park systems and/or their classes; private lessons such as dance, musical instruments or voice, theatre, foreign language or computer instruction. Local colleges and universities, businesses, human service agencies, clubs, or organizations may also offer resources for students from preschool through high school. Television and videotaped programs may offer information, culture, or a perspective on an issue. They are also helpful to those who prefer alternatives to reading.

5 Add a list of what the student has already accomplished to your student profile. Include courses, clubs, books read, related activities, independent research, and work experiences.

4 Ask parents how they have helped the student to date. Inquire about their availability and willingness to assist the student in pursuing new opportunities. Can they provide transportation? "Field trips"? Supplies and appropriate equipment? Space? If parents can't, who might be able to provide these resources?

3 Find out what the student's needs are. What does he want to learn? How does she think would be the best way for her to learn? How much time and energy can he devote? Develop a student profile.

2 Who perceives the need for additional enrichment? The student? The parent? The teacher?

1 Decide who should be involved in the process of identifying the students' needs and planning for further learning and development.

START HERE!

Don't move up a level until you have exhausted the potential of the current level. Remember this chart has been designed to give you ideas. There are additional levels and opportunities not shown!

• • •

Who sees the need?

Teachers often observe talent that would flourish with further development much sooner than the student even realizes he or she has talent. Parents, of course, have the obligation and vested interest to nurture their children's growth whether through monitoring their progress in school or finding additional resources outside it. However, the best test of the appropriateness of your assessment is to ask the student what she or he would be interested in doing and to what level of intensity. How much time and energy is the student willing *and able* to commit to advanced learning beyond his everyday school work?

What are the student's skills and needs?

Next, consider the student's intellectual needs. What is his or her current level of expertise? What has the student already done to advance her skill in the interest area? In addition, consider the student's other needs such as learning style preferences, personality, level of maturity, social and emotional development or needs. A student profile should become clear.

Identifying opportunities and resources

After listing what the student has already done, look for other easily accessible resources. Brainstorm a list concentrating on what the student can do independently. Jenny read five fantasy stories and improved the stories she had written. Soon she wrote two new stories. Jenny's activities entailed trips to the school library; she also needed paper, pencil, and a place to write. A few months later, as her interest persisted, she received personal attention from a teacher.

Other community resources available for students might include public or specialized libraries located within museums; wildlife centers; businesses; community education classes; zoos; art, history and science museums or galleries; local theatres; or public park systems. These places can offer more in-depth and specific resources not commonly found in schools or public libraries. I've learned that there are periodicals on just about every possible topic if you look in the right places, and they are a wonderful source of up-to-the-minute information.

These same facilities might also allow their personnel time to share information with the public. What better way for an industrious student to gain helpful pointers than to ask a professional? The best way to approach an informational meeting is to inquire in advance about the possibility, then schedule a brief appointment.

Other resources might include private lessons in such areas as dance, musical instruments, voice, theatre, or computer programming. Any of the above resources might also offer classes for interested learners, or the classes may be more informal. An advanced and interested high school or college student can be a wonderful teacher. Television and videotapes also offer gems of information, culture, or a perspective on an issue. In addition, they are a relief to those students who experience difficulty with reading.

Local colleges and universities may also offer resources for students from preschool through high school. Sometimes local businesses, human service agencies, clubs, or organizations may also offer opportunities. In the Twin Cities metropolitan area, several clubs and organizations have offered to help schools locate appropriate resources for students whether within their membership or outside of it. If your school employs a volunteer coordinator or if a voluntary action center has been established within your community, their staff members might also assist you.

Ready for one-on-one

By working independently, students are respectful of those who may later be asked to assist them. They also advance their own knowledge and skills as well as their personal commitment to the topic. The more students understand, when they seek additional help from others, the more rewarding the experience will be to both students and those assisting them.

When a student has worked independently using existing resources, a one-on-one relationship is in order. When seeking someone to provide a few minutes of encouragement, start within the student's school. The meeting can be scheduled on a weekly, biweekly, or even monthly basis. In Jenny's case, another teacher in her school who enjoyed writing provided the encouragement and instruction Jenny craved for twenty minutes each week. After several months, the teacher expressed concern that Jenny needed more than she could offer. What a gem! She helped where she could, then was wise and confident enough to know when *her* resources were exhausted. Every school has supportive staff like this if someone seeks them out. The staff has much to gain in these endeavors, too.

When a student exceeds the expertise within a school, look to a specialist at the next level on the chart for help. For Jenny, a junior- or senior-high communications specialist or a teacher whose avocation is to write fiction for literary magazines might meet her needs. Most teachers are willing to assist a student who is enthusiastic, requests a limited amount of time, and has the skills to work independently between meetings. Teachers are also more willing to assist if the student can meet at the teacher's work site.

As a next step, ask a specialist to visit the classroom to offer enrichment to all students while directly serving the student with more in-depth needs. For example, a local artists-in-residence or writers' workshop might delegate a fantasy writer to work with all students in Jenny's sixth-grade class (assuming Jenny's interest remains and her skills have developed). After group sessions, the specialist might spend a few minutes individually with Jenny. This type of service can be arranged as a one-time-only event or as service to students over a longer period of time.

An informational interview and/or shadowing

If the student's interest continues to develop, arrange for a one-time-only visit with a professional in the workplace. During the initial contact, explain as clearly and specifically as possible the student's age, grade, current level of expertise, and what he or she has already done to develop this interest. This information helps the professional to understand the student's commitment and skill level. Also explain what the current learning needs are and how you hope the professional will help meet those needs. Sometimes the student needs only to discuss his learning with the professional and to obtain more informed suggestions for continued growth. In my experience, most professionals willingly allot one-half hour to any student, and an hour if they feel the need is pressing.

Often students will desire or need to observe the professional at work and to see the equipment or facilities available in the workplace. This would be particularly true if the work requires complex equipment such as a sophisticated laboratory, a mainframe computer, or an industrial kitchen. Ask the professional if the student might spent time observing or "shadowing" him or her.

Whoever requests the opportunity for a student should be prepared not only to clearly and specifically discuss the student's needs for the visit, but to listen carefully to what the professional might and might not be able to offer. To a teacher, a visit to a research lab with state-of-the-art equipment is clearly a wonderful experience for the student. However, corporate security might forbid it. The student may want to attempt certain crystallizing techniques, but the company safety officer may view that as too great a liability risk. With some patience and effort, teacher and professional should agree upon a situation that will benefit the student and also be comfortable for the professional and the company.

Finally, the person who arranges the visit needs to assume responsibility for preparing the professional *and* the student so the visit will be productive and positive for both. Besides knowing the student's level of expertise and needs for further learning, the professional should know a little about the *person and the situation.* Will the student come prepared with questions? Is the student shy or outgoing? Will an adult accompany the student? School personnel should also ask the professional about her expectations. How would she like you to prepare the student to take best advantage of this opportunity?

The student should be briefed on where he is going, with whom he will meet, and his agenda for the meeting. He needs to be informed about appropriate etiquette and behavior for this visit, and how he can best prepare for it. He might obtain a little bit of information about the company from the library or by telephoning the company to request it. He should prepare a list of questions to ask the professional. He might also bring his samples of his best work and a current reading list—both neatly written—to help the professional more completely assess his level of expertise and to provide topics for conversation. Students need to be reminded that they are being given a special opportunity so they need to show respect and appreciation to those who offer it. Equally, thorough preparation for the visit will earn the respect of the professional.

What if the student changes her mind?

The student's focus of interest can take many interesting twists and turns along the way. For example, in third grade Jenny thinks she wants to write short stories. This may become an ongoing interest area, or her interest may stem from the fact that her level of skill will not allow her to write anything else. Also, in third-grade Jenny is probably unaware of many other forms of writing such as feature-writing for newspapers or magazines, or public relations or advertising pieces.

Through her schoolwork—or even her writing—Jenny may also become aware of other interests and talents that seem even more significant to her than writing. For example, let's assume that in her freshman year Jenny wrote a science-fiction story that required additional knowledge of lasers. Through her research on the subject, Jenny came to understand how lasers significantly improve medical treatments.

As is the case for many gifted students, Jenny's science teachers appreciated her excellent skills in *that* area and encouraged her to continue to take science courses. After careful consideration and discussion, Jenny believed that through laser research and development, she could make a more significant contribution to humanity than she could through writing fiction. She decided to channel her motivation in a new direction.

Is all the time and energy spent on developing Jenny's writing ability wasted? Absolutely not! Jenny now knows much more about how to learn autonomously. She needed far less assistance to develop her knowledge of lasers. She has become a better communicator and has several options open to her because of her writing skills. She can become a technical writer for science-related issues, be better able to publish her own laser research, or even continue to write publishable science-fiction as a hobby. Haensly and Roberts (1983) state that chang-

• • •

ing topics is not whimsical, but part of the creative process. Regardless of the path she chooses, Jenny has indeed developed her unique personal potential.

It Takes Time, But It's Worth It!

Arriving at the need for a mentor can take a period of months or even years! Not everyone shares my opinions about the school's role in the process. Regardless, this process requires energy from others beyond the student's own initiative and some costs in terms of staff or parent time and additional resource materials.

Helping to meet a student's educational needs can unite parents, students, schools, and the community in the student's best interest. What would happen to Jenny's talent, and the talent of millions of others like her, if means aren't offered to help her develop it?

Gerstner offers this challenge: "Educators need to become as impatient as are business leaders to get real results . . ." (1990, p. 17). When students arrive at the need for mentors through the process I have suggested, they are independent learners who can readily justify their need for business participation and can take fullest advantage of the opportunity offered through a mentorship. This process—and it's just one model—helps to justify why businesses should "become resourceful partners" in the education of our children.

When students have identified and used the resources suggested in this chapter, they should be ready to apply to a mentoring program. The next chapter presents methods for checking students' readiness for a formal mentorship.

References

Bathke, J. L. (1990). *Mentor Connection: Students' perspectives.* Unpublished master's thesis, University of St. Thomas, St. Paul, MN.

Beck, L. (1989). Mentorships: Benefits and effect in career development. *Gifted Child Quarterly,* 33(1), 22-28.

Betts, G. T. (1990). Understanding the profiles of the gifted and talented. *Counseling&Guidance,* 1(3), 4. (Available from Counseling and Guidance Division, National Association for Gifted Children. Washington, D.C.).

Betts, G. T. (1986). *Autonomous learner model.* Greeley, CO: Autonomous Learner Publications and Specialists.

Boston, B. O. (1976). *The sorcerer's apprentice: A case study in the role of the mentor.* Reston, VA: Council for Exceptional Children.

Burton, A. (1977). The mentoring dynamic in therapeutic transformation. *American Journal of Psychoanalysis,* 37, 115-122.

Clendenin, J. L. (1990). Reform through human resource planning. *The School Administrator,* 20.

Cox, J. & Daniel, N. (1983). The role of the mentor. *G/C/T,* 29, 54-61.

Cox, J., Daniel, N., & Boston, B.O. (1985). *Educating able learners: Programs and promising practices.* Austin, TX: University of Texas Press.

Erikson, E. H. (1963). *Childhood and society.* (2nd Ed.) New York: W.W. Norton.

Erikson, E.H. (1980). *Identity and the life cycle.* New York: W.W. Norton.

Flaxman, E., Ascher, C., & Harrington, C. (1988). *Youth mentoring: Programs and practices.* NY: Eric Clearinghouse on Urban Education.

Haensly, P. A. & Roberts, N. M. (1983). The professional productive process and its implications for gifted studies. *Gifted Child Quarterly,* 27(1), 10.

Hess, K. M. (1984). *Mentor Connection first year evaluation report.* Minneapolis: The Educational Cooperative Service Unit of the Twin Cities Area.

Hess, K. M. (1985). *Mentor Connection second year evaluation report.* Minneapolis: The Educational Cooperative Service Unit of the Twin Cities Area

Hess, K. M. (1986). *Mentor Connection third year evaluation report.* Minneapolis: The Educational Cooperative Service Unit of the Twin Cities Area.

Levinson, D. J., Darrow, C. N., Klein, E. B., Levinson, M. H., & McKee, B. (1978). *The seasons of a man's life.* NY: Alfred A. Knopf.

Nathan, J. (1990). Mentor program makes big connection. *St. Paul Pioneer Press Dispatch,* 1DW.

O'Connor, D. (1989). Student getting down-to-earth start in aviation. *St. Paul Pioneer Press Dispatch,* 1-2DW.

Phillips, L. L. (1977). *Mentors and proteges: A study of the career development of women managers and executives in business and industry.* Unpublished doctoral dissertation, University of California, Los Angeles.

Reilly, J. M. (1990). *Fifth-year survey of Mentor Connection graduates.* Unpublished.

Renzulli, J. S. (1977). *The enrichment triad model.* Mansfield Center, CT: Creative Learning Press.

Subotnik, R. F. (1987). Mentoring winners of the National Westinghouse Science Talent Search. *International Journal of Mentoring,* $\underline{1}$(2), 17-19.

Suzukamo, L. (1987). Mentor may have learned more than student in program. *St. Paul Pioneer Press Dispatch,* 1E.

CHAPTER 2

Screening Students for Successful Experiences

Many practitioners search for the gifted *child, not for* signs *of*

giftedness, of potential. They typically pay little attention to

diagnosing children's particular strengths or talents.

— John Feldhusen
"Synthesis of Research on Gifted Youth"
Educational Leadership

In the first chapter of *Mentorship,* Dave was introduced as the responsible, good kid with limited successes in school. Throughout junior and senior high school, Dave's standardized tests scores never exceeded the 30th percentile. At the end of his junior year, his class rank was 320/510 or the 37th percentile, and Dave had a C grade average. However, Dave had a passion—he wanted to create clay animation. His high school did not offer art instruction in this area, so Dave sought other options. He decided to apply to the *Mentor Program.*

When Dave applied, his acceptance was questionable. His academic credentials were weak, although he had pursued a variety of art classes and averaged B work. His recommending teachers described Dave as "very responsible and a pretty good artist." They had never seen any of his work creating clay figures or in producing animated films, so they could not comment on the activity that Dave loved most.

When interviewed, Dave spoke of his quest for information on clay animation and his ongoing correspondence with animators across the United States. He described the projects he created on his own. He wanted help desperately. His parents had even taken him to Disney World to observe animation there. Dave had strong commitment to the task, above-average ability in his field, and could work independently. Were these credentials enough for a successful mentoring experience?

Application and Screening: Toward a Successful Experience

The *Mentor Program* seeks motivated, academically capable students who have identified and documented needs for advanced learning. In order to assess whether students are ready for mentorships, they submit written application materials and participate in an interview.

This process verifies that prospective mentees have prepared in-depth for the program, fully utilized their school's resources, and, with preliminary research and training, will form questions that only a mentor can answer. It also helps staff to ensure that students do not use the *Mentor Program* to simply explore careers or to satisfy idle curiosity. However, the most important reason for careful individual screening is to ensure a successful learning experience for each student.

The application and screening procedures described in this chapter facilitate both the instructor's understanding of the student's individual needs, desires, and personal traits and the student's understanding of the program. The screening process also allows students and teachers to assess more accurately the opportunity offered through preparation for, and participation in, a mentorship, to decide if a student is ready for mentorship, and, ultimately, to determine if this option would be a good one for the candidate.

For the gifted and talented?

A good portion of the information about high school mentoring programs presented in the literature stems from research and programs for the gifted and talented. The questions often arise, "Is your program for gifted and talented students?" and "How do you determine a students' gifts or talents?" Even among Mentor Connection and *Mentor Program* instructors, answers to these questions would vary. However, the way giftedness is defined and used within the program will determine who may have access to the opportunity and how well professionals can serve as appropriate resources.

To begin the discussion, consider the current United States Office of Education (USOE) definition of giftedness (Marland, 1971) which states:

Gifted and talented children are those identified by professionally qualified persons who, by virtue of outstanding abilities, are capable of high performance. These are children who require different educational programs and/or services beyond those normally provided by the regular school program in order to realize their contribution to self and society.

Children capable of high performance include those with demonstrated achievement and/or potential ability in any of the following areas, singly or in combination:

1. general intellectual ability;

2. specific academic aptitude;

3. creative or productive thinking;

4. leadership ability;

5. visual and performing arts;

6. psychomotor ability.

Public Law 95-561 deleted psychomotor ability from the definition leaving only five areas. Joseph Renzulli (1978) noted that the definition "has served the very useful purpose of calling attention to a wider variety of abilities that should be included in a definition of giftedness" (p.181). Indeed, specific areas of giftedness in the USOE definition cannot readily be identified through one standardized test—or even a group of them. Yet school districts often rely on a standard intelligence test, which measures verbal and nonverbal capacities only, as the primary means of identifying gifted children. The identification process often qualifies or disqualifies students for additional opportunities like a mentoring program.

The *Mentor Program* opts not to rely on standardized tests such as intelligence or college admissions tests as part of students' evaluations. However, they may be considered as supporting evidence in a student's profile. Similarly, the *Program's* steering team strongly recommended that a school district's means for identifying gifted students not be the only criteria for allowing students to participate. Several other approaches to identifying students with the motivation, ability and self-management traits necessary to a successful mentoring experience have been incorporated in the screening materials and procedures.

Renzulli (1986), for example, offers another approach to identifying gifted students. He depicts the "ingredients of giftedness" as three interlocking clusters of traits: Above-average ability, task commitment, and creativity. Gifted students demonstrate all three traits. These criteria fit well with the goals and objectives of a mentoring program although they may not provide an all-encompassing measure of readiness for a mentorship experience. Measuring each component of the triad also presents some difficulties.

Certainly, *Mentor Program* candidates apply because they are motivated to learn beyond the high school curriculum. The primary purpose of the *Mentor Program* is to fulfill that motivation. If students have truly exhausted the resources available to them and they *still* want to know more about their interest areas, their task commitment becomes apparent.

Obviously, the mentor's time and professional expertise would be wasted on a student without desire to learn about the field. The application and screening process for a mentoring program must probe for task commitment; this is essential to students and mentors. If students have not shown task commitment and prepared themselves well, they can be directed to return to the process described in Chapter 1 and continue to identify and use resources. They may reapply to the program after they have demonstrated their commitment to task.

A second component of Renzulli's triad, creativity, helps potential mentees master their new environments. Flexibility, originality, and analytical skills all help young adults to cope with the risks inherent in a new situation. Creativity, then, is an asset in a mentoring situation. However, it is very difficult to determine how much creativity is necessary for success in a mentoring situation. In addition, while formal measures of creativity exist, many schools do not administer them. It would be prohibitive for a mentoring program to use these measures in screening.

Even if the instruments measuring creativity were utilized, the individual skills and traits associated with a successful mentoring experience may not be assessed. To screen for creativity, the designers of the recommendation form (Figure 2-9), Linda Silrum and Jeanie Pullen, identified the individual creativity traits most relevant to a successful mentorship. Through the recommendation form, they opted to ask for adult observations of each candidate's personal creativity.

Pinpointing above-average ability again presents problems. Obtaining sufficient background to become ready for mentorship warrants above-average ability in that field. The student's and the mentor's success with a mentoring program depends on the student's ability to grasp more advanced concepts and techniques. However, it is difficult to prove ability through even standardized ability tests, particularly in certain areas. Standardized tests may establish ability in verbal, mathematical, or spatial skills, but not in all areas recognized by the USOE definition. For example, standardized tests of ability in the visual or performing arts remain elusive. In addition, standardized tests attempt to measure potential. They do not measure knowledge in specific fields such as waterfowl breeding or clay animation. Students may score poorly on a standardized test, yet astound a listening adult with their knowledge and understanding of a field. So, gauging ability may be elusive in less traditional fields.

Since the USOE definition of giftedness was published, Harvard University professor Howard Gardner (1983) has developed another theory about intelligence. Gardner's theory further validates the difficulties in rigidly defining giftedness. The theory of multiple intelligences suggests that each person possesses seven different intelligences which include linguistic or spoken, logical/mathematical, spatial, musical, kinesthetic or bodily, interpersonal, and intrapersonal or self-awareness intelligence. Gardner believes that an individual's personal blend of these competencies produces a unique cognitive profile, his or her intelligence. A person can be gifted in one or several of these areas, yet not appear gifted on a standard scale of intelligence nor will the intelligence quotient (IQ) reveal Gardner's more complex conception of a cognitive profile. Depending on their fields of interest, students who apply for a mentoring program may be gifted in one of Gardner's intelligences, yet not meet the USOE's definition nor their district's standards.

Robert Sternberg (1986) also veers away from traditional measures of intelligence. His triarchic theory of intelligence defines intelligence differently than the other notions presented in this chapter. Sternberg defines intelligence as applied to the way we live: "mental activity involved in purposive adaptation to, shaping of, and selection of real-world environments relevant to one's life" (p. 33). The three components of Sternberg's triarchic theory of intelligence are "schoolhouse," "creative," and "practical" intelligence.

In a mentoring program students apply all the skills of practical intelligence to their experience. They *select* an appropriate environment for their mentorship. They *shape* their environments as they discuss with prospective mentors their learning needs and desires. Once they begin work with a mentor, the mentees *adapt* to the workplace environment by trying to fit into the place they have chosen. Successful mentoring requires practical intelligence applied to "real life and real people," the *Mentor Program* slogan. Practical intelligence also addresses those self-management skills so elusive in ability testing. While Sternberg is currently developing an instrument to measure his triarchic theory of intelligence, it would not be the sole factor for successful mentorships. Even if students are "gifted" in schoolhouse, creative, and practical intelligence, they still might not have the defined giftedness in a field nor the task commitment. The difficulty in defining and assessing a candidate's giftedness and aligning that with readiness for mentorship becomes ever more apparent.

To complicate matters further, much of the literature which discusses mentoring programs for gifted and talented students fails to describe the criteria for identifying students appropriately "gifted" for mentorships. However, the staff of the Learning Activity Mentor Programme (LAMP) in New Zealand did describe their population of gifted thirteen- and fourteen-year-old mentees (Beard & Densem, 1986). Their profiles include students with very high ability across the board; those with specific talents in a field which requires a differentiated course of study; very able, divergent students; and students lacking in self-esteem.

Each of the four categories of gifted Learning Activity Mentor Programme students presents a different definition of giftedness. Those with very high ability across many areas could readily be identified with standardized IQ testing and the USOE definition. Within Gardner's theory of multiple intelligences, these students would probably show signs of giftedness in more than one of the seven areas. The students with specific talents in one field would fit within the USOE definition, Gardner's theory, and depending on the field of their ability, these students may surface as gifted on aptitude or ability measures. The very able, divergent thinker might also be identified through creativity measures.

The student lacking in self-esteem may also be an identified or unidentified gifted underachiever. Terman and Oden (1947) noted the major characteristic differences between underachieving individuals and effective achievers are a lack of self-confidence, the inability to persevere, a lack of integration of goals, and feelings of inferiority. They also found that the role modeling a mentorship can provide helps underachieving children whether of average or gifted ability.

In the article, "Educating the Gifted and Talented: An Agenda for the Future," Parke (1989) proposes that we "intensify our efforts to discover a broader range of students' abilities." If standard techniques for identifying gifted and talented students are used for a mentoring program, the program risks overlooking unique talents or potentials that should be cultivated. It also risks accepting students who do not have the requisite practical intelligence, motivation, and creativity to successfully develop a mentoring relationship.

Because *Mentor Seminar* and *Field Experience* focus on the individual, each student gains differentiated curriculum tailored to his or her own abilities. Burger and Schnur's experiences (1981) concur with those presented here: "Individualization through student-mentor matching seemed to accommodate the needs of the regular as well as the gifted students" (p. 30). Again, however, they do not define "gifted" or "regular" students. The process that follows was designed to ensure selection of candidates who could most benefit from a mentoring experience and to ensure them an opportunity to develop their own unique potentials regardless of whether they are in some way identified as gifted. Through a written application, two recommendations, grades, class rank, and a recent aptitude score, the screening committee seeks to identify students with the ability, motivation, and self-management skills necessary to a successful mentorship.

Developing Understanding of the Program

The nontraditional course structure can baffle students, faculty, and parents. So, the first step is to cultivate an awareness and understanding of the program. This will be an ongoing task during the first few years of the program. Eventually, through the steps described here and word-of-mouth recommendations from former participants, the program will require less and less explanation and promotion.

Building awareness of a mentoring program begins prior to registration when the school distributes registration information. As the first step toward student enrollment, mentoring program staff place a course description in the school's registration guide. The description may be listed under advanced learning, honors or advanced placement, gifted or high potential programs, or as a separate course in each department. Sample course descriptions might read:

Mentor Seminar
Grades 10-11-12

In this course, prepare to learn at an advanced level with a professional in a field of interest to you. With the instructor, each student will formulate a personalized educational plan for further investigation of the student's interest area. A faculty member in the student's specialty area will also be available as the student prepares a project related to this field of interest. Classroom instruction is designed to improve the student's communication and independent learning skills, to assist them in in-depth learning, and to help them develop a focus and readiness to continue their learning with a mentor. (Apple Valley High School, 1990, p. 83)

Mentor Field Experience
Grades 11-12

*This two-credit course will immerse you into the real world of advanced learning in a field you select. You will observe, converse with, and work with a professor and/or business professional in your field of interest. This person will be located for you by the **Mentor Program** staff. With your mentor you will complete a project that provides an opportunity for in-depth research and experiential learning. This course offers academic challenge and requires a high level of student responsibility. You must provide your own transportation to and from the mentorship site. (Reilly & Schaefer, 1989, p. 3)*

In contrast, the message can be as simple as:

This program is designed for juniors and seniors who have advanced knowledge in a particular field of study and would like to work with a professional, a mentor in that field. (Apple Valley High School, 1990-91, p. 5)

To gain additional program awareness, use of the school public address system and/or radio stations for announcements is beneficial when application time approaches. Some schools place articles or notices in district- and school-wide newsletters or counselor's bulletins. Often the local press will run an article and/or announcement if asked. A graphic arts student in the *Mentor Program* designed a sophisticated, contemporary poster to pique interest.

As a course project, another innovative student and his mentor developed a short video (Glenn & Pullen, 1987) featuring actual students and their mentors. As they say, "A picture is worth a thousand words;" a video condenses the time staff must spend explaining the program while it presents clear and interesting information. This video is available for check-out to interested students in their high school guidance or career centers and is used for informational meeting with students.

A mentoring program differs enough from other courses in that students will respond most favorably to a more thorough explanation either from a guidance counselor or teacher who recognizes a student's talents, or a *Mentor Program* instructor. Several high schools ask teachers and counselors to recommend students who have exhausted their school's resources in a field as one method of informing students (see sample letter of request, Figure 2-1).

When the program instructors or steering team members receive the teacher recommendation forms, they send each student a letter stating that they were recommended for the program and by whom. The students also receive a program application in the packet. Students are invited to attend an informational meeting and to apply for the course (see letter sample, Figure 2-2). This method works best in identifying the appropriate students and in helping them become familiar with the opportunity. It also gives them a familiar person with whom to discuss the possibilities.

Even if students are not interested in the course, they receive a delightful ego-boost when teachers recognize their talents. The *Mentor Program* wants to help students develop their potentials and the letter itself may be a student's first formal notice that someone sees his or her

Fig. 2-1

MENTOR PROGRAM MEMORANDUM

To: Faculty Members

From: [Mentor Program Coordinator]

Re: Mentor Program Enrollment

We need to find those students who would be interested in and benefit from the Mentor Program for next year's class.

Students who will be accepted into the Mentor Program do not necessarily have to be gifted but should have a strong interest and ability and be highly motivated in a certain area. I have included a list of students currently in the program to give you an idea of their variety of interests.

Last fall your recommendations were the strongest factor in identifying students for the Program. I would appreciate your help again. Please suggest current 10th and 11th graders who might benefit from this program. Please return the form to me by [date].

Name   Grade

_____   _____

_____   _____

_____   _____

_____   _____

_____   _____

MEB/kk
xc: Principal   [Teacher's Name]

• • •

Fig. 2-2

MENTOR PROGRAM STUDENT NOTICE

[Date]

Dear [Student],

[Teacher's Name] has recommended you as a prospective student in the Mentor Program. The Mentor Program is designed to immerse students into the real world of your chosen area of advanced learning.

If you are chosen for the program, you would enroll in a one-credit preparation course called Mentor Seminar next spring. The following year you would have an opportunity to work one-on-one with your mentor at the work site.

For more information about the program, I encourage you to attend an informational meeting on [date] at [time]. Both meetings will be held in [room number].

If you have questions or cannot make the meeting, contact me at [location and phone number].

[Signed]

capabilities. I remember one young woman hopping up and down with pleasure because Ms. Jones thought she had writing talent!

Recently a mother told me that she felt that same letter changed her daughter's life. When I thought about it, she may not have been exaggerating. Her daughter, Heather, had been intensely involved as a volleyball player, but was not physically talented enough to make the "A" team. Heather was very bright and an exceptionally hard worker. The coach had told me he felt Heather needed to redirect her energies into an area where she could truly shine—fashion. So he recommended her for the *Mentor Program.*

Heather loves fashion. She created a "shining" fashion scrapbook for her *Seminar* project in spring; took a college-level course in fashion coordination during the summer; was responsible for selecting garments and accessories in two shows with a local mall; obtained employment in a local "juniors" store; and by winter of the following year gave up being cheerleading captain to enter into a mentorship with a fashion director of the largest department store chain in her city. Currently, she's debating the merits of moving to New York City for college with her parents. Needless to say, Heather feels very glad that she received that recommendation and that she followed through and applied to the program.

Informational meeting

Once their interest is aroused, students want to understand the intricacies of a mentoring program before they apply. They have questions about scheduling, how their mentors will be selected, and how colleges will regard this course when they apply for admission. Students frequently express surprise when they learn that they may leave their high school campus during the school day or that they will receive grades and credit for participating in this adventure.

Logically, the mentoring program instructor conducts the informational meeting, but the involvement of a partner—a counselor, administrator, or other teachers—can help add interest and credibility to the meeting. Two sessions—one meeting before school and another after school on two different days—offer students adequate flexibility to attend if they wish. Sometimes program instructors also visit classes where several students would be interested in hearing about the course.

The same format applies to either situation. Allow approximately thirty minutes per meeting. An informational meeting agenda might cover a brief description of the program and application procedures, as well as time for other questions. Gear how the following information is presented to the needs of the audience.

What Is the Mentor Program?

The *Mentor Program* consists of two separate, sequential classes. The first class, *Mentor Seminar,* prepares students for advanced-level learning with a mentor. *Mentor Seminar* expands the preparation opportunities for students through additional instruction and more time to research their own areas of interest. It is structured like any traditional class, a one credit course offered one hour per day for a term.

The objectives for the *Seminar* classroom instruction include:

1. *Developing* independence and responsibility for the student's own learning. This includes student recognition and articulation of individual learning styles, personality preferences, and the mentor's likely expectations of him or her.

2. *Enhancing* oral and written communication skills necessary to successful functioning in the adult world. This includes skill building specific to initiating contact, assertively expressing learning needs, interpreting nonverbal communications, using the telephone in business situations, scheduling and executing an informational interview, and writing a business letter and resumé.

3. *Improving* research and practical problem-solving skills. Most mentor students have exhausted the resources of their local libraries. They are taught to efficiently use university and professional libraries and resources.

They are also encouraged to tap community resources
such as museums, professional organizations, or
individual faculty members who share a similar interest.

When students successfully complete the *Seminar,* they may enroll
for *Mentor Field Experience* and receive mentoring both from a professional and from the class instructor. Students are released from school
to learn with a mentor during the last two class periods four days per
week. Students meet as a group during the same time one day per week
to receive support and instruction from their teacher and peers.

Students do not pay any fees to participate in the *Mentor Program,*
but they pay their own transportation and related expenses. Neither
student nor professional receive pay for their work during their *Mentor
Program* experiences. Because of the advanced nature of the course and
the independent learning skills required, *Mentor Seminar* students must
be enrolled in tenth grade or beyond. Because they must transport
themselves to a work site, *Mentor Field Experience* students should be
eleventh or twelfth graders. By successfully completing the *Field Experience,* students earn grades and credits toward graduation equivalent to
two high school classes each term. They may enroll for a minimum of
one semester to a maximum of one school year.

Also, in the informational sessions we try to cover how college
admissions offices view this kind of experience. They generally regard it
very favorably— appreciating not only the advanced-level learning that
results but also the strong motivation and independent learning skills
which mentoring program students develop. In fact, several students or
their parents claim that admissions offices commented that the mentoring program formed a strong basis for students' acceptance. For example, Anna conducted genetic research on the RSV virus connected with
AIDS. While an outstanding student by any measure, a nationally prestigious science and technology institute admissions officer told Anna that
she was accepted on the basis of her mentoring program work.

"Tips for a Successful Mentorship," Figure 2-3, makes a good handout for interested students or for an informational meeting. The information presented reminds students of the attributes a mentoring
relationship requires. When they distribute this article during an infor-

mational meeting, presenters can stress how important it is for students to consider the demands as well as the benefits of mentorship before they decide to apply for the program. Other possible resources to add "pizazz" to an informational meeting may include a video, brochures, copies of newspaper articles or former students.

How do I apply?

The *Mentor Program* application packet includes an introductory letter, an explanation of the qualifications of the program, an explanation of how to complete the application process, an application form for the student to complete, and two recommendation forms (see Figures 2-4 through 2-9). A teacher must complete one recommendation. The second may be completed by a teacher or other adult who knows the student well. Students must also submit a high school transcript.

Ideally, students register for the mentoring program along with the rest of their classes and thus avoid scheduling conflicts. But sometimes registration occurs too early in the school year to adequately inform students about the option or for students to recognize an emerging field of strong interest. The *Mentor Program* screening procedures also may require too much attention at a very hectic time. So, in order to plan staffing and budget effectively, students submit their completed application packets by April 1 at the latest for entrance into the program during any term of the following school year. This arrangement allows students more time beyond the standard registration deadlines to consider the *Mentor Program* option, yet still allows them adequate time to register prior to the end of the school year.

When the *Mentor Program* receives application materials, students are notified about what has been received and what remains for their applications to become complete (Figure 2-10). When the file is complete, students are again notified and scheduled to attend an interview (Figure 2-11).

After April 1, a screening committee forms. The committee consists of one *Mentor Program* instructor and two steering team members who are part of the high school staff. One of the three should be a counselor or administrator who can advise students about planning their schedules. The screening committee reviews and rates applications, conducts interviews, and decides which students meet acceptance criteria.

In the past, the *Mentor Program* also included representatives of the business, professional, and academic communities in screening applicants. These people added a new dimension to the process. If students' interests matched the interviewers', the professionals could better advise students in depth. However, participating in interviews demanded valuable time from professionals which they decided was better used in direct service to mentees. At the same time, high school staff could best advise students about fitting the *Mentor Program* into the rigorous demands of high school life and about which faculty members could serve as preliminary contacts for students enrolled in *Mentor Seminar.* So we discontinued this practice.

Evaluating Written Materials

As the screening committee receives completed applications, at least one member completes a screening form for each student (see Figure 2-12.). To ensure reliability in scoring, several applications may be reviewed by both screeners so their ratings can be compared and discussed. Students are rated on a scale of one through four on the following criteria:

1. Clarity of intent, expectations, motivation.

2. Depth of background preparation for the experience.

3. Recommendations submitted by two adults.

4. Ability to learn: grades.

5. Ability to learn: class rank.

6. School attendance.

7. Aptitude score, if relevant and available.

Fig. 2-3

1 A mentorship takes **curiosity**. What do *you* want to know about? Are you willing to spend weeks or months learning? If you're not curious – if you're not interested – then there's no point in wasting your mentor's time (or your own).

2 A mentorship takes **motivation**. Don't do it unless *you* want to.

3 A mentorship takes **planning**. Can you find time in your busy schedule? Can you find transportation?

4 A mentorship takes **work**. If you've already proven that you're academically capable – that you can handle responsibility, do research, complete assignments, and think – then you'll probably do well in a mentorship. Then again, if you haven't done well in school, maybe it's because you're the type who thrives in a work setting instead.

5 A mentorship takes **maturity**. Are you grown-up enough to handle a working relationship with an adult? Can you dress, walk, talk, and act in ways that fit the workplace? Can you accept failure as well as success, and learn from your mistakes? Can you ask for help when you need it?

6 A mentorship takes **courtesy**. Always remember that your mentor has invited you into his or her workplace. Speak politely and listen respectfully.

7 A mentorship takes **commitment**. If a professional agrees to work with you, be on time and be prepared! (The same goes for your mentor, of course.) Go the extra mile (or five, or ten) when it comes to assignments. Don't just skim the top of what you're supposed to be learning. Dig deep.

8 A mentorship takes **communication**. Listen carefully, don't interrupt, and ask the kinds of questions that show you've been paying attention. Remember, you're there to learn, not to show off. Nobody wants to mentor a "know-it-all" who isn't interested in listening to advice and acting on new ideas.

REMEMBER!

A mentorship isn't necessarily over when it ends. If you establish a good relationship with your mentor, stay in touch with him or her after the experience is over. Mentors are interested in your progress. Keep them informed and they will likely be willing to help you again and again throughout your career.

Fig. 2-4

MENTOR PROGRAM STUDENT APPLICATION

Dear Student,

The Mentor Program is designed to immerse you into the real world of your selected area of advanced learning. This course provides an opportunity for in-depth research and experiential learning. You will observe, talk with, and work closely with a professor and/or a business professional in a field you select. (This person will be located for you by the Mentor Program staff.)

You will also learn new and challenging technical concepts. You can define and produce a meaningful project under the guidance of your mentor. You and your mentor will assess your learning experience. Your Mentor Program instructor will guide your progress and assign a grade for the credits earned by you through the Mentor Program.

But before you get into a one-on-one Field Experience in your senior year, the Mentor Program will prepare you for meeting your mentor and will help you to explore the opportunities in your field of interest. In the spring of your junior year, you will attend the Mentor Seminar, a class in effective research and communication, and you will develop a personalized educational plan. You will also explore your chosen field through advanced level reading.

Now sophomores and juniors can register for the Mentor Seminar to be offered in the Spring Trimester for one credit. Students who complete the Mentor Seminar may register for their Mentor Field Experience next year. The Field Experience will be a two-credit class. You must provide your own transportation for the Field Experience.

The Mentor Program can give you a challenging learning opportunity. If you want to get involved, read on! Then complete the application process. If you have questions, please contact [Instructor Name or Place and Phone Number].

Fig. 2-5

IF YOU ARE

- Motivated by challenges
- Creative
- Willing to work hard
- Looking for advanced learning
- Able to provide your own transportation
- Willing to minimize your outside of school work hours
- Willing to complete this application
- Acceptable to a screening committee
- Willing to complete a meaningful learning project

YOU CAN RECEIVE THESE BENEFITS

- Advanced Learning
- Improvement of interpersonal skills
- One-on-one time with a professional in your field of learning
- Hands-on learning
- Access to professionals or experts in your field
- Involvement in a meaningful research project

FOR MORE INFORMATION CONTACT

Your Guidance Counselor or
[Instructor]
[Program Name]
[Address]
[Phone]
[Hours]

Fig. 2-6

MENTOR PROGRAM SELECTION PROCESS

APPLICATION

To apply for the Mentor Program, you must:

1. Complete the application form. Include the necessary signatures. Applications for _____ are due by _____ .

2. Have two adults, at least one of them being a teacher, complete the RECOMMENDATIONS for you and return them. A brief description of the program is included with this packet for them to read.

3. Include a copy of your high school TRANSCRIPT (a record of your high school grades) with the application. You may obtain a copy from your Guidance Office.

SCREENING

After your application is received, you will receive confirmation. The application will be reviewed by a screening committee who will evaluate all application on the following criteria:

- Background preparation for the experience
- Ability to learn: grades, achievement
- Clarity of intent, expectations, motivation
- Recommendations submitted by two adults

INTERVIEW

The committee will be looking for evidence of perseverance, high motivation, good background and ability, and creativity. You will be invited to an interview after an initial screening.

SEND APPLICATION TO

[Name]
[Title]
[Address]

Fig. 2-7

MENTOR PROGRAM STUDENT APPLICATION FORM

DATE

NAME   HOME TELEPHONE

ADDRESS   CITY   ZIP

GRADE   AGE   BIRTHDATE

AREA OF INTEREST FOR ADVANCED LEARNING

What has stimulated your interest in this area?

What activities have you undertaken to explore this field of interest?

What do you think are your next steps in learning? How do you see a mentor involved in that process?

Fig. 2-7 cont'd.

MENTOR PROGRAM STUDENT APPLICATION FORM, cont'd.

Which classes have you taken that have helped you want to learn more about your field of interest?

....

....

In which activities have you been active both in school and outside of school?

....

....

If you have any work experience, please list it.

....

....

What are your other interests and hobbies?

....

....

• •

I have explained the program to my parents and they have indicated their permission for me to participate in this program by their signature below.

I am applying for the Mentor Program _____ trimester/ semester of _____ year

....
STUDENT SIGNATURE   DATE

....
PARENT SIGNATURE   DATE

TO:
[Instructor]
[Address]

• • •
47

Fig. 2-8

The Mentor Program allows high potential eleventh- and twelfth-grade high school students from across the metro area to learn firsthand the skills and responsibilities associated with a profession. The program relies heavily upon the willingness of university, business, and community people to be mentors to the juniors and seniors who participate in the Mentor Program.

Program Goals
1. To give students the opportunity to learn beyond the limits of the available high school curriculum.
2. To give students access to resources and facilities not available within the high school.
3. To give students access to professional leadership role models in the community.
4. To raise student awareness of education and career options and assist them in making decisions concerning these options.

Screening
Students who wish to participate in the program must complete a comprehensive application sequence. Included is the requirement that the student must obtain two recommendations from adults (one must be a teacher). Those applicants who show evidence of perseverance, ability, creativity, and who have identified and pursued an area of advanced learning are selected for the program. The screening process has been designed to help ensure a high-quality, successful experience for the students.

Program Content and Expected Outcomes
The program is divided into two phases, *Mentor Seminar* and *Mentor Field Experience*. Activities in each phase are tailored to the needs of the individual student. The following general content descriptions and outcome expectations hold true for all participants:

Mentor Seminar
Orientation. Each student meets individually with the Mentor Program Instructor to formulate a plan for further investigation of the student's interest area. From the results of this research, a learning focus is reached and the search for an appropriate mentor begins. Potential mentors meet with the student and instructor to determine an advanced project for the student.

Preparation Lab. Students meet as a class with the instructor to prepare for their interaction with mentors. Instruction is designed to improve the student's communication and independent learning skills.

Mentor Field Experience
Each student works at least eight to ten hours each in the work setting of his/her mentor. The instructor visits the site to determine that the experience is beneficial to all participants. Student, mentor, and instructor determine an advanced project which the student will complete. Students also spend up to two hours each week in class discussion with the instructor and other students.

Fig. 2-8 cont'd.

MENTOR PROGRAM PROGRAM SUMMARY, cont'd.

Summation. Students meet as a class to evaluate their learning experiences. Each student finishes an individual display product which is completed for an open house. All students' work is exhibited for public review at the Annual Open House. Student learning is assessed by the student, the mentor, and the instructor. The instructor then uses the three assessments to assign a grade for academic credit.

Class Location and Transportation
Mentor Program classes may include students from several schools or school districts. Classes meet at [Location] . Each student works with a mentor at the mentor's workplace. STUDENTS MUST PROVIDE THEIR OWN TRANSPORTATION.

Further Information
The Mentor Program is open to any junior or senior high school student who has identified and documented a need for advanced learning. Program information can be obtained from either the Mentor Program instructor(s) or the contact person(s) in your high school:

Mentor Program Instructor(s):

High School Contact Persons:

MENTOR PROGRAM RECOMMENDATION FORM

TO BE COMPLETED BY STUDENT

NAME

HIGH SCHOOL   GRADE

To Student Reference:

This student is applying to participate in the Mentor Program. Your recommendation within the following areas is useful in helping determine if this is a good learning match for the student.

Please read the statements below and place the appropriate number after each characteristic according to the following scale:

x Teacher has not had the opportunity to assess
1 Student **never** demonstrates this trait
2 Student **occasionally** demonstrates this trait
3 Student **consistently** demonstrates this trait

Motivation

___ Persistent

___ Strives for perfection

___ Assertive

___ Organizes/ structures situations

___ Evaluates events

___ Good attention span

___ Finishes activities/ assignments

___ Responsible

___ Sets high standards for self

___ Bored with routine tasks

Creativity

___ Elaborates on ideas

___ Displays imagination

___ Criticizes constructively

___ Accepts constructive criticism

___ Flexible in new situations

___ Sense of humor

___ Is able to revise

___ Uses various forms of expression

___ Original

___ Risk-taker

Learning

___ Uses an advanced vocabulary

___ Possesses a large storehouse of information

___ Processes information quickly

___ Reads a great deal

___ Displays curiosity

___ Generates many ideas

___ Independent

___ Deals with abstract ideas well

___ Enjoys research

___ Interested in high-level problems

If you wish, please include additional written comments in a letter of recommendation which accompanies these ratings. Thank you.

Signature   Position

Please return to: [Name, Title, Address]

Fig. 2-10

Dear [Student Name],

Thank you for applying to the Mentor Program. I have received part of your application packet. However, I still need the item(s) checked below for your application to be complete.

__ application form

__ application form is here, but is not complete

__ recommendation(s)

__ transcript

__ other _____

I will notify you when I have received everything necessary for your application to the Mentor Program. You will be contacted regarding your interview at a later date.

Please contact me at [Phone Number] if you have any questions.

Sincerely,

Instructor/Coordinator
Mentor Program

• • •
51

Fig. 2-11

MENTOR PROGRAM INTERVIEW NOTICE

[Date]

Dear [Student Name],

Thank you for applying to the Mentor Program. I have received your completed application packet.

Your interview has been set for [Time, Date, Place]. Please make every effort to attend this important interview, which has been scheduled with three or four other students.

During the interview, you will have the opportunity to become more familiar with what the Mentor Program offers you and with other students who may become your classmates. You will also be asked to share ideas related to your field of interest and the activities that have been part of your personal experiences.

If you are unable to attend the interview or have any questions, please contact me at [Phone Number] during the day, or at [Phone Number] in the evening. I look forward to meeting with you.

Sincerely,

Instructor/Coordinator
Mentor Program

Fig. 2-12

MENTOR PROGRAM SCREENING FORM

STUDENT NAME	SCREENER

Read the student applicant's file and rate each piece in the file according to the criteria listed for the item. Circle the appropriate number rating.

APPLICATION FORM	Unclear		Goal Oriented	
Look for a clear understanding of the interest area, goal-orientation to learning in that area.	1	2	3	4

BACKGROUND PREPARATION	Limited		In-Depth	
Look for depth of learning about interest and range of experiences related to the learning – both within the classroom and, particularly, outside it.	1	2	3	4

RECOMMENDATIONS	Low			High
Look for high scores in totals. Calculate total number of responses x 3, divide student total points by total possible to obtain percentages.	60-69%	70-79%	80-89%	90-100%
Recommendation 1	1	2	3	4
Recommendation 2	1	2	3	4

GRADES	Low			High
Look for high ability (A's) in the area of interest. Also note advanced courses.	1	2	3	4

CLASS RANK	Low			High
Class place – total in class.	60-69%	70-79%	80-89%	90-100%
	1	2	3	4

SCHOOL ATTENDANCE	Low			High
Number of days attending.	1	2	3	4

PSAT SCORE	Low			High
Verbal _____ Nonverbal _____	1	2	3	4

Please comment on any extraordinary observations or notes from file. Are there any other more appropriate programs to recommend for this student?

....

....

....

Clarity of intent

All students should demonstrate a clear understanding of their interest area and the initiative to learn more about it. Applications should reflect students' intentions and expectations as well as their motivation to pursue topics independently prior to obtaining mentorships. In short, students should be goal-oriented and have plans to achieve their goals.

Preparation

In reviewing applications, the screening committee also considers the student's depth of preparation. The student most ready for mentorship would have completed the process described for Jenny in Chapter 1. While not all students can realistically receive the support and assistance given to Jenny, the strongest candidates for mentorship have in some way independently sought experiences to further their background knowledge in their interest areas. Some examples include the correspondence, trips, and animation I mentioned in the beginning of this chapter which Dave had accomplished prior to his application to the *Mentor Program* or the summer zoological research program which motivated Shannon (Chapter 1) to seek new resources in this area.

Recommendations

The recommendation form developed by Linda Silrum and Jeanie Pullen synthesizes much information and research on gifted education and mentorships. It is designed to evaluate the traits which will assure student's readiness and needs for mentorship. The form meshes both the model for Renzulli's triad of above-average ability, creativity, and task commitment with those specific traits regarded as most helpful in a mentoring situation. Figure 2-9, the recommendation form, lists ten specific traits for each category.

Students are required to submit two recommendations from adults with at least one from a teacher. With each recommendation form, the application packet also includes a program description for students to give to each of the two recommending adults. This way recommending adults better understand the program for which they are assessing the student.

One trait is *not* tabulated in rating the recommendation: "Bored with routine tasks." If students are bored with routine tasks, they may indeed need the new and challenging learning that a mentoring program provides. That is the intent of the question. However, many students who do not visibly demonstrate their boredom may equally need the challenge. So, the screening committee always considers the recommender's response to the question without rating it. Conversely, not every student who is bored is ready for a mentorship; he may be a passive learner.

To evaluate recommendations, the screener tabulates the points a student receives on a recommendation and the percentage of the total calculated. Finally, the recommendations are awarded one to four points on the screening sheet based upon the percentage of total points received. If the recommender chooses not to respond to a trait, it is not tabulated into the results so the student will not be penalized.

Ability to learn

While grades and class rank are not the only indicators of ability or achievement, good grades and a high class rank indicate consistency in performance. In addition, good grades and high class rank can reflect a desire to achieve and learn. Consistent high performance and the desire to learn and achieve are import to successful learning in a mentoring experience as well as the classroom.

Often, however, grades cannot reveal exactly what the student has retained. Also, students may have high potential in one subject area and less in other areas. Therefore, *Mentor Program* applicants are rated only for grades received in the student's field of interest, and screeners always look for other indicators of ability besides class rank such as the Preliminary Scholastic Aptitude Tests (PSATs), other standardized test scores, or unusual accomplishments in the student's area of interest.

PSATs are not always available when students apply to the *Mentor Program.* This happens either because students have not reached the age or time of year when PSATs are administered or because students opt not to take them at all. Because they are not always available, existing PSAT scores are always reviewed, but optionally rated on the screening form. These can complement grades and class rank by indicating intellectual abilities that may not surface in a high school transcript. For example, one young man had a C− average, but PSATs in the top three percentile of the nation. The PSAT scores caused the screening committee to pay closer attention to his application and to ask him about the discrepancy between his grades and test scores during the interviews. The interview revealed his strong desire and ability in the interest area, but impatience with classroom instruction. Another young woman received all A's in math and D's and F's in subjects which required a lot of reading and writing. As one might expect, she scored very poorly in the verbal area of the PSATs and in the top five percentile in the nonverbal. She was contending, both academically and emotionally, with a learning disability. Because mentoring programs are highly individualized, we were able to tailor her study within the program to meet her learning needs.

Attendance

School attendance provides one indicator of the student's reliability. A student who does not consistently appear as scheduled at a mentor site will create major problems! If a student is qualified and motivated but has a poor attendance record, an attendance contract can be established for *Mentor Seminar* and, perhaps, other school classes. If the students do not fulfill the requirements to which they agree, they are not placed with mentors. However, we have observed some dramatic turnarounds when students are strongly motivated to find mentors!

Attendance patterns can also alert instructors to possible health problems. This allows the student and instructor to plan appropriate options and to alert a potential mentor.

Interviewing Student Candidates

All students who apply to the *Mentor Program* participate in an interview. A written application and a personal interview offer students opportunities to express themselves in their preferred forms of communication while enabling screeners to become better acquainted with each candidate. The screening committee has generally interviewed students in groups of four or more. Occasionally a screening committee has opted for individual interviews.

In the group interviews, candidates meet with others who share as similar interests as possible. Depending on the applicants, the group could consist of four students all interested in veterinary medicine or five students with a general interest in science and technology. Students appreciate getting to know a few potential classmates in advance of the first day of class and not being put on the spot all alone. The group situation also prevents repetition of explanations and details, such as the purpose of the interview or the date candidates will be notified about the outcome of the interview.

Individual interviews allow the screening committee to pay personal attention to each applicant and to focus on his or her abilities, accomplishments, expectations, and needs. A group interview takes about forty-five minutes to an hour; the individual meetings generally take fifteen minutes.

Interview agenda

The interview agenda generally remains the same whether candidates are interviewed individually or in a group. For the purpose of this discussion, a group setting is assumed.

At the beginning of the interview, screeners and students introduce themselves. Students are asked to share their names, grades, and high schools (if the interview sessions consists of students from different schools), and their specific area of study. (5 minutes)

Next, the screeners summarize the purpose of the interview, stressing the belief that this is also a time for students to assess whether the mentorship course will offer them what they want and need. Screeners continue with a program summary to be sure that each candidate has adequate information. (10 minutes)

The main section of the interview probes in as much detail as possible how each student became interested in the field they wish to study; what they have done to pursue their interests and develop their knowledge of the field; and the next steps they foresee in their learning.

The interviewers and students brainstorm new ideas and identify additional resources for each participant so they can pursue their studies over the summer. That way, the interview will have as much value for the students as possible whether they actually enroll in the *Mentor Program* or not. (30 minutes) (If they are accepted, students will be asked to report on their progress just prior to the beginning of the course.)

In the closing section of the interview, screeners allow a few minutes for questions about the program or program logistics, especially if it appears that some students have not been thoroughly briefed on scheduling or the basic curriculum and mechanics of the course. A guidance counselor can provide helpful advice during this section of the interview. (10 minutes)

Finally, screeners ask students if they remain willing to participate in the course if accepted. Then they tell students the date by which they will be notified of acceptance and thank them for their time and attention. (5 minutes)

Final Selection of Candidates

During the interviews, screeners keep summary notes to be used for future reference (see Figure 2-13). After the interviews the screeners review and discuss the abilities, attitudes, and ideas that emerged from discussion with each student. Next they tally the total number of points received on the screening sheet and rank the students by total number of points. Between the information gleaned from written material and the interview, a profile of "readiness" to take advantage of mentorship emerges.

It may be surprising that the *Mentor Program* must refuse very few applicants. Through this screening process, students seem to recognize whether or not their needs "fit" with the *Mentor Seminar* and *Field Experience*. For example, the first time it was offered, a high school announced this course option to all of their 1,100 students in the appropriate grades. The size of the first *Seminar* group was targeted at twenty students.

Including those recommended by their teachers, approximately 110 students obtained applications. Forty-eight students attended an informational meeting. Twenty-nine students initiated applications,

Fig. 2-13

MENTOR PROGRAM INTERVIEW SCREENING FORM

STUDENT NAME	STRENGTHS	WEAKNESSES	POSSIBILITIES

Notes for debriefing discussion:

and twenty-four completed the entire process. Of the twenty-four, all but one student met the basic criteria established for acceptance.

This twenty-fourth student thought he wanted to be a psychologist. However, during the interview he could not define what a psychologist does in basic terms, and his reason for seeking mentorship was to find out the difference between a psychologist and a psychiatrist. The student's academic record was below average, and the commitment did not seem present. He appeared anxious speaking in front of the other students.

After all the interviews, a counselor and I asked to meet with the student. We intended to suggest that he learn more about the fields, then reactivate his application for the following year if he remained interested.

As we began the discussion, we asked if the student was uncomfortable during interviews. He said he was so the counselor asked how his discomfort would affect his plans. The student sighed with relief. He said he would like to withdraw his application if this wouldn't disappoint us. We assured him that if he chose to withdraw, it would be fine. Then we told him that if in the future he wanted to reapply, he could. We strongly recommended more background work to help him be more comfortable and better prepared. He never reapplied.

So it goes. Like the student just described, most students can determine if this option is appropriate. However, some require a little help either in addressing their needs or in determining if their choice was well thought out and realistic.

The *Mentor Program* steering team recognizes that students may apply if they are seeking any option different from traditional classroom instruction. They may have an unusual learning style, be a divergent thinker, or have need for a one-on-one relationship. If the mentoring classes seem inappropriate, students are always referred back to a guidance counselor to explore other options. Everyone involved wants applicants to receive support in meeting their needs and in learning of other options available to them. These can include college courses, independent study, private lessons, or even an alternative program.

When students are notified of their acceptance into the course, they are asked to make a firm commitment to participate in the course (Figure 2-14). They must also confirm availability of transportation to a mentor site with their parents and see a guidance counselor to appropriately arrange their schedules. After student, parent, and counselor "sign-off" on the acceptance form (Figure 2-15), it is returned to the program instructor. When the new term begins, students and staff are ready to begin the *Mentor Seminar.*

The Rewards

To answer the question posed at the beginning of the chapter, Dave was accepted into the program, albeit hesitantly. Despite Dave's questionable academic performance, he was motivated, responsible, and informed. However, no one could confirm his ability in the area of clay animation. Ultimately, Dave's proven motivation, responsible behavior, and informed conversation suggested that he might need a mentoring program to further his development.

In the first weeks of *Seminar,* I scheduled an informational meeting for Dave with a local animation firm to continue his learning. They not only showed him their work, but several artists took the time to view Dave's animation films. The artists responded with comments like, "Yeah, that's just what I was doing at your age!" or "You've got a start, keep working." I'm not sure who was more excited, Dave or me. This might have been an excellent screening activity, if I had thought of it then and if time allowed.

In *Mentor Seminar,* I tried to get Dave to read a book about Walt Disney's animation. His parents wanted him to study about the more practical, business components of creating clay animation. He flatly refused all of us—Disney didn't work with clay and he didn't care about business, he said.

Seeking a proverbial carrot, I called the animation firm we had visited to inquire about a field experience, but they felt they could not spare time to work with Dave on a regular basis. Furthermore, Dave wanted to work with clay, and they produced mostly drawn animation. The office manager empathized with our situation so she gave me the

Fig. 2-14

MENTOR PROGRAM ACCEPTANCE NOTICE

Dear [Student Name],

We are pleased to tell you that you have been accepted for the Mentor Program beginning [_____ Trimester/ Semester]. We enjoyed meeting with you and learning about your interests. I very much look forward to being your teacher in the next school year.

Please be certain to arrange your schedule for this program. Also, check to be sure you will have transportation readily available for your mentorship and to and from class. Then, please return the enclosed response form by [Date] so I can officially register you.

So you can make the most of this opportunity, please continue to explore your area of interest during the coming months. You may pursue some of the activities suggested at your interview or any others that seem appropriate to you. Remember, I am only expecting about 8-10 hours of work all summer. If you have any questions or need suggestions, you may call me during the summer months at [Phone Number].

First/Second trimester and first semester students will hear from me again sometime in August with first day details and to inquire about your progress. Second semester students will hear from me in the fall. Until that time, please feel free to call me during the summer. Honestly, I'll be happy to help you!

I would like to invite you to attend this year's Annual Open House (invitation enclosed). During this time you will be able to meet Mentor Program students from the entire metropolitan area and observe the work they have done this year. I hope you can attend!

Once again, welcome. I look forward to hearing from you soon.

Sincerely,

Instructor/Coordinator
Mentor Program

Fig. 2-15

MENTOR PROGRAM RESPONSE FORM

NAME

SCHOOL

Please indicate whether or not you plan to be in the Mentor Program during the [19   ] school year.

___ **Yes** – I plan to take the Mentor Program

___ **No** – I have decided that the Mentor Program is not for me at this time

TO BE FILLED OUT BY COUNSELOR

I have reviewed _____'s registration for _____. He/She has been scheduled to attend the Mentor Program during _____ trimester/semester.

Counselor's Signature   Student's Signature

Please mail this form by [Date] to:

[Name]
[Address]

If you have any questions, don't hesitate to call [Name] at [Phone Number]. We look forward to your response!

• • •

63

name of one of the two firms in our region which produced clay anima-tion. Those men agreed to become Dave's mentors.

Suddenly, at the suggestion of his prospective mentors, Dave was reading the same book I had offered him earlier. He designed a project covering the entire process of making a clay-animated film. Dave agreed to plan the budget, write the script, build the sets and charac-ters, film the action, and log his hours of work—because it was good business!

Dave revealed more of his potential when he took the *Seminar* research skills test. He received the second highest grade in a class where 90 percent of the students were in the top 20 percent of their classes. Throughout *Seminar* and his *Field Experience,* Dave maintained an A average on all phases of his work.

At the time of this writing, Dave was attending college where he studied business and the skills relevant to producing clay animation and special effects. His mother proudly told me that for two years Dave has received all A's and B's in college work. He was also working regu-larly for his mentors. Dave achieved more than his high school record ever indicated was possible. Through a one-to-one mentorship, Dave's learning needs were better met. Dave later explained why he was so suc-cessful: "It's [Mentoring is] a good learning experience for me. They work with you more on the topic about which you want to learn."

Dave's potential developed, and both he and the *Mentor Program* staff more fully realized his capabilities. Dave's story provides an exam-ple of the importance of utilizing each of the criteria suggested in this chapter to help reach screening decisions and, perhaps, a dose of open-minded intuition.

In order to begin a mentoring program, staff must build awareness of the opportunity within their schools. Once students understand the program, they apply and screening becomes necessary to assist both the students' and the mentors' in establishing successful relationships. The three essential traits for success in a mentoring program are strong motivation, above-average ability in the student's field of interest, and well-developed self-management skills. The *Mentor Program* screening process strives to identify these traits in prospective students through their written applications and interviews with them. When students have confirmed their enrollment, they finalize their preparation through *Mentor Seminar.* This is the topic of Chapter 3.

References

Apple Valley High School. (1990). *Student registration guide.* Rosemount, MN: Independent District 196.

Beard, E. M., & Densem, P. A. (1986). News around the world. *Mentoring International,* 3(4), 111-115.

Burger, C. R., & Schnur, J. O. (1981). The mentor approach: Something for everyone, especially the gifted. *Roeper Review,* 4, 29-31.

Feldhusen, J. (1989, March). Synthesis of research on gifted youth. *Educational Leadership,* 6-11.

Gardner, H. W. (1983). *Frames of mind: Theories of multiple intelligences.* NY: Basic Publishers.

Glenn, C. (Director), & Pullen, J., (Producer). (1987). *The Mentor Connection* [video]. White Bear Lake, MN: Intermediate District 916. Available from:

> The Peg Schaefer Memorial Fund for Mentor Connection, Metro ECSU, 3499 Lexington Avenue North. St. Paul, MN 55126

Marland, S. P., Jr. (1971). *Education of the gifted and talented: Vol. 1. Report to the Congress of the United States by the U.S. Commissioner of Education.* Washington, DC: U.S. Government Printing Office.

Parke, B. N. (1989). Educating the gifted and talented: An agenda for the future. *Educational Leadership,* 4-5.

Reilly, J. M, & Schaefer, M. (1989). *Real life. Real people.* (Student brochure for *Mentor Program.* St. Paul, MN: Metro ECSU.

Renzulli, J. S. (1977). *The enrichment triad model.* Mansfield Center, CT: Creative Learning Press.

Renzulli, J. S. (1978). What we don't know about programming for the gifted and talented. *Phi Delta Kappan,* 60, 180-184, 261.

Renzulli, J. S. (1986). The three-ring conception of giftedness: A developmental model for creative productivity. In R. J. Sternberg & J. E. Davidson (Eds.), *Conceptions of Giftedness* (pp. 53-92). New York: Cambridge University Press.

Sternberg, R. J. (1984). *Beyond I.Q.* NY: Cambridge University Press.

Sternberg, R. J. (1986). *Intelligence applied.* NY: Cambridge University Press.

CHAPTER 3

Mentor Seminar: Preparing Students and Polishing Their Skills

Whatever you can or dream you can, begin it;

Boldness has genius, power, and magic in it!

— Goethe

Don, his parents, and his resource teacher had identified and used the resources suggested in Chapter 1. Don had successfully completed computer classes offered to students in his junior high school. He had created a medieval war game with help from the computer specialist at the high school and had even taken a course in the computer language, BASIC, from the local science museum. Don also had read books and magazines on creating computerized games available from the public library.

In eleventh grade, Don's knowledge and skills in computer programming generally matched those of the computer specialist at his high school. Still, Don craved more learning on the subject. He applied for and was accepted to the *Mentor Program.* Surely he was ready to work with a professional mentor. Perhaps—but the answers to several questions will provide the complete picture:

1. Was Don aware of his own preferred ways to learn, his learning style? Understanding his learning style would help Don determine the right situation when his instructor and he look for a mentor.

2. Did Don understand the ways he preferred to relate to people and how his interpersonal style might affect his interactions with others at the mentor site?

3. Did Don have adequate information to decide what more he would like to accomplish within his interest area? Did he know the difference between a programmer and an engineer? Did he realize that people program more than games? Was he aware of computer languages beyond BASIC? If so, with the help of a professional would he able to assess the "next steps" in his development? If Don could not answer these questions, how would he and his instructor determine the skills his prospective mentor would need?

4. Were there resources Don had not yet tapped which he could utilize independently?

5. How sophisticated were Don's social skills? How comfortable was Don around adults? Did he know how to meet and greet them? Was he comfortable formulating and asking questions? Could he sustain a conversation? If a problem arose with a mentor, did Don have the skills to address it? If Don's mentor came from a cultural background different than his own, did Don have the skills to respond sensitively?

If his instructor and Don could respond affirmatively to these questions, they might have raised one final question as they assessed his readiness for mentorship:

• • •

6. What might a prospective mentor appreciate knowing
   about Don's individual learning needs in order to decide
   if she wished to mentor him? In what form should Don
   and his instructor present this information?

In working with Don, I could see he certainly was a computer whiz!
The programs he'd written revealed exceptional capability for a person
of his age. However, when I discussed Don's work with him, it was like
"pulling teeth." I never worked so hard to get a simple "Uh-huh" or
"No"! Wondering about Don's comfort and ability to communicate with
others, I contacted his computer instructor who advised me that Don
"is a man of few words." If Don had difficulty expressing his learning
needs or even maintaining a conversation with his mentor, would a
mentorship succeed?

After "pulling teeth," I discovered that Don had almost no concept
of what computer programmers did besides create games. When I mentioned the range of possible programs that could be created for a multi-
tude of different fields, Don was surprised. When we discussed the
differences between programming and engineering, the information
really stretched his knowledge-base. Don began to rethink which skills
he would like to acquire.

When Don completed an informational meeting with a professional, he was shocked to learn that the programmers generally divided
their work into sections and worked as a team to create the whole. That
meant communicating closely with one another and only some of their
time spent in prolonged retreat to the computers. Don also discovered
that the programmers must negotiate for time on the mainframe!
These necessary interactions were not a part of his normal skill repertoire, personal nature, or learning style. At this point even Don began
to wonder if he was ready for a mentorship.

Reprise: When Is a Student Ready for a Mentorship?

In their preliminary search for information, students need some
self-awareness and interpersonal and research skills to most effectively
utilize the resources offered by organizations and individuals. As the

students' research progresses and the need for mentors becomes imminent, students must narrow, or focus, their areas for study into manageable topics which can be pursued in-depth during a limited period of time. For example, a student certainly cannot study medicine in a semester, but can learn a great deal about eye diseases over that period of time. That student can gain even greater depth in his learning if he narrows the topic to glaucoma. Focusing demands that students learn enough about the field to allow them to select a topic that genuinely interests them. Don found that despite years of preparation, his self-awareness and interpersonal skills still needed strengthening. He also needed to focus more in order to target the appropriate mentoring situation.

Without an understanding of their own learning needs, the ability to communicate effectively with adults, or the ability to research independently, the students and their mentors are at a disadvantage. The students cannot communicate their needs or function effectively in an adult environment. The mentoring program is instrumental in helping students to find answers to their questions and in preparing them for a mentorship. Of course, a mentoring program also has a commitment to the professionals. Empowering students with these skills also helps mentors to better determine and respond to the needs of their mentees and to establish a more comfortable relationship with them.

This chapter discusses the curriculum found to be most beneficial in preparing high school students for a mentorship. This curriculum can also help adolescents with other issues they may face in their daily lives such as relating to others, finding a suitable learning situation, college and career planning, and applying skills for lifelong learning.

Increased Readiness through Mentor Seminar

The goal of *Mentor Seminar* is to prepare tenth-, eleventh-, or twelfth-graders with the background knowledge and skills necessary for a successful mentorship. *Mentor Seminar* is the prerequisite course for the *Mentor Field Experience*. It is a complete or "crash" course which requires roughly sixty instructional hours. It is offered for a grade and one credit. Currently, the course is offered in two forms: two-hour

Working World Survival for the Well-Traveled Student.

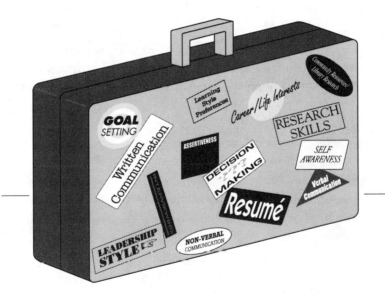

Learn these skills and feel better about
yourself and others. Become more confident in your
abilities; feel comfortable in any situation!
The Mentor Program is your ticket.

blocks daily for six weeks which lead directly into placement with a mentor for the remainder of the semester, or a separate one-credit course offered one class period daily for one trimester (twelve weeks). Students are placed with mentors in another trimester during high school. The form depends on the high school's scheduling structure.

The *Mentor Seminar* curriculum has evolved over years of observation of students' needs and experiences and has been adapted for use with an entire class, thereby satisfying students' needs in a more cost- and time-effective fashion. While offered to high school students, much of what is taught could also be easily integrated into the curriculum throughout junior high as well. Some of the curriculum has even been introduced at the elementary-school level.

The syllabus

After students introduce themselves to their classmates, the instructor explains the course syllabus. The syllabus provides a written overview of *Mentor Seminar* including purpose, philosophy, expectations, grading, and major assignments. A sample syllabus is shown in Figure 3-1.

Mentor Seminar is divided into three separate areas of study: self-awareness, advanced research, and interpersonal communication skills. When students better understand their personal learning needs, they begin to determine how to best meet these needs and to better focus on their topic for study. Thus, *Seminar* begins with a unit on self-awareness

Self-Awareness

The *MBTI* and *LSI*. Instruction begins by raising students' awareness of their individual personality traits. The *Myers-Briggs Type Indicator* (MBTI) (Myers & Briggs, 1962) helps students think about how they relate to people, ideas, and learning situations. It also helps them consider their needs for structure. Based on the work of Carl Jung, the indicator results suggest an individual's preferences in these areas.

When students have responded to the *MBTI*, the instructor explains the four pairs of preferences suggested by the indicator. Students assess

Fig. 3-1

MENTOR PROGRAM MENTOR SEMINAR SAMPLE SYLLABUS

Purpose
Students will gain background knowledge and skills necessary to advance their learning in a selected field of interest.

Community as Classroom: An Important Seminar Philosophy
This course considers the community as our classroom and as a resource. As a result, guest speakers will frequently visit our class. We will also take two field trips to allow students easier access to resources. Students are expected to apply learning within the classroom to experiences in the community as a means of reinforcing learning and demonstrating that they have satisfactorily met the course objectives.

Expectations of Students
Student responsibility and reliability are essential for a successful experience in Mentor Seminar.
  • The student's ability to study and work independently
    is vital throughout the course.
  • Students will focus on a specific topic for study, conduct
    research, and develop their knowledge of the topic.
  • Students are expected to report to class punctually
    and regularly.
  • It is the student's responsibility to make up missed
    classwork and to notify the instructor about reasons
    for absence.
  • All assignments are expected to be turned in on time.
    If that becomes immpossible, it is the student's
    responsibility to discuss the problem with the
    instructor before the assignment due date or as soon
    as possible after the emergency.

Study Topics
  • The student's individual field of interest
  • The student's individual approach to people and learning.
  • Career and educational background in student's field of
    interest
  • Advanced-level research skills
  • Interpersonal communications and relations in the
    workplace, including verbal, nonverbal, and written
    communications; assertiveness and conflict resolution;
    interviewing skills; and valuing cultural diversity.

Course Texts
  • Mentor Program Notebook: Materials will be distributed
    in class and kept in a three-ring binder which the student
    will provide. Students will be given binder indexes which
    they should insert and label in the binder as follows:

    Blue Tab: Introductory
    Yellow Tab: Self-Awareness
    Red Tab: Research Skills
    Clear Tab: Interpersonal Communications
    Green Tab: Project and Journal

  • *College Comes Sooner Than You Think* Worksheet Booklet:
    Students will periodically hand in excercises, but may
    keep booklets at the end of the course.

• • •
73

Fig. 3-1, cont'd.

Supplies

- One three-hole punched spiral notebook with at least three section markers.
- One three-ring binder
- Pen
- Supplies needed to complete project at the end of the course.

Grading

Students will receive points for each class assignment. At the end of the course grades will be awarded on the total percentage of points earned:

90-100%	A
80-89%	B
70-79%	C
60-69%	D
Below 60%	F

If assignments are turned in late, the maximum grade a student may receive is 89% on the late assignment. Students must earn a minimum of an 84% average to be eligible for the Mentor Field Experience.

Assignment Highlights

Project

Each student will complete a project that demonstrates advanced-level learning in a field of interest. Each student will share his or her results in writing and orally. The project will count for 30% of the student's grade. May be shown to prospective mentors. Due: [Date].

Journal

The journals are assigned to increase personal communications between student and instructor. Students will be responsible for a minimum of two journal entries weekly. Journals will be kept in a three-hole punched spiral notebook so they can be clipped into the course notebook. Journals will be collected each Monday. Some entries will be assigned, but students should always include a paragraph about what they have encountered through the course each week--learning difficulties, areas to explore further, words of wisdom, project ideas, resources to explore, reactions to events or assignments. Due: [Date].

A Personal Resumé

Each student will prepare an in-depth resumé which meets professional standards. Resumés will be presented to prospective mentors and may be used for many other purposes. Due: [Date].

Library Research Assignment

To help you learn about important tools for researching your field of interest and completing your project. Due: [Date].

Fig. 3-1 cont'd.

Informational Meeting

Each student will conduct an informational meeting with a professional working within the student's field of interest. While students may choose whom they want to interview, the instructor will gladly assist in identifying an appropriate person. Students will hand in a list of questions they prepare to ask at the interview as well as the professional's reponses. Written report of informational meeting due with Journal.

Faculty Contact Meetings

To provide students with the support of a faculty member who has expertise in the student's field of interest. (This will be explained further in class.) Two meetings are required.

Reference Sheet

Students will maintain a list of all references they have used to explore their areas of interest (minimum of 7). The reference sheet must be completed in American Psychological Association (APA) style. Will be given to prospective mentors. Due: [Date].

Project Abstract

Students will write a paragraph-long abstract or summary of their projects. Will be given to prospective mentors. Due: [Date].

Tests

Self-awareness and research skills: [Date].
Communication Skills: [Date].
Final exam will be a project exhibit for parents and contacts on [Date].

which preferences describe themselves *before* they see results from the *MBTI*. After the results have been distributed, students gain a deeper understanding of type through classroom activities and one of several fine videos on the *MBTI*. They also receive written explanation of the sixteen different *MBTI* types and are invited to borrow audio tapes on the subject.

Because research has indicated that type does not stabilize until adulthood (Myers-Briggs, 1962), the main purpose of utilizing the *MBTI* in *Seminar* is to nudge students to think about their own personal preferences. Even if students only can identify a few definite personality traits, their progress is satisfactory. This may be the first time they have been given to simply think about themselves.

Once students become comfortable with identifying their own traits, they learn about and discuss differences between themselves and people who react differently to their environments. Of course, under-standing how and why others might differ from us is essential to good human relationships and, therefore, mentorships.

Next, the students explore their individual learning styles thorough the *Learning Style Inventory (LSI)* (Kolb, 1976). Students discover that each person has his or her own preferred way to learn, and they identi-fy their own learning styles. With teacher support, students apply this information to possible independent or mentorship situations and strive to determine the individual situation most suitable for them-selves. Students also begin to recognize, and tolerate, differences in teaching and learning styles and learn how to adjust to various ways of delivering instruction. They become empowered to request the infor-mation or assistance they need while remaining respectful of others' differences.

Career exploration

As they enter *Seminar,* students wonder how to best use their many gifts and talents. They are unsure how to direct their diverse interests into viable careers. Students also wonder how to select a career which will allow them to lead the life-styles they envision and will be a good "return" on their educational investments. Like Don, most students begin *Seminar* with no concept of the realities of a profession. Obviously, in-depth career exploration becomes a must!

While advanced learning is the primary objective, *Seminar* students need to research the various occupations related to their fields of interest. They should learn, for example, not only what a mathematician's professional duties are, but also about other careers which rely heavily on excellent math skills. Students should discover what a person *actually does* on a day-to-day basis in each position and the life-style each position demands. Reading helps; a brief, informational meeting with a professional promotes an even clearer picture.

These needs were well illustrated by two exceptionally talented guitarists, Jason and Todd, who were in the same *Seminar* and *Field Experience* classes. Both hoped to become professional musicians. Jason was "into" fingerstyle acoustic guitar performance and composition, but could not sight-read well or transpose the music he composed into sheet-music form. Jason had no interest in developing either of those skills. He wanted to improve his composing and performing skills. During the career exploration section of *Seminar,* Jason discovered that those "boring" sight-reading and transposing skills might be necessary to achieve his personal goals.

Similarly, Todd was the finest jazz guitarist in a high school known for the arts. However, he had already decided that he would not pursue performance as a career because he wanted to have time for "relationships and a normal family life." He thought he would learn to be a sound engineer. As Todd explored sound engineering, he learned about the irregular hours and alternative life-style sound engineering demands. Despite the new information they obtained about the career situations in their chosen fields of interest, both Jason and Todd chose to pursue a mentorship in them.

When Jason and Todd responded to the *Mentor Program* they were asked what gain they felt was most valuable to them during the program. Todd replied: "Realization that I wished to be financially stable (nothing to do with music). *Very valuable.*" Todd entered college with a physics major. His decision to make music a serious hobby instead of a career was based on the proven conflict between his personal values and the life-style musicians and sound engineers must lead.

Jason, on the other hand, found "sight reading, performing and interaction with my mentor" most valuable. He discovered that the "boring" skills were necessary and rewarding in his goal to perform and compose. Jason plans to earn a doctorate in music. Both young men learned in depth and had excellent grades in the course, but they felt their most significant benefit from the course was career insight.

Values

Becoming self-aware, making decisions, and pursuing mentorships, as in Todd's and Jason's case, require that students grapple with their values. So, students are encouraged to think about individual values through "The Value Pac Exercise" found in *College Comes Sooner Than You Think!* (Featherstone & Reilly, 1990, pp. 55-58). Instructors also can ask students how their values are consistent with their choices for mentorship. Being asked, "Do you live by your values?" is even more difficult for students to assess.

One young woman, Anna, provided an example of how values may conflict in a mentorship situation. Anna wanted a genetic engineering mentorship. She had an outstanding science background including advanced-placement biology and chemistry classes. In addition, she had completed a college-level honors program in genetics. Her initial mentorship meeting was with a genetics professor. He was working with a foreign government to generate more food by genetically increasing the flesh on a species of fish.

When Anna heard about the project, she was adamant. She felt strongly that it was immoral to alter the genetics of living animals in order to slaughter them for food. She would not participate. While others may disagree with her stance, only Anna could make that decision. In a time when our nation seeks the moral education of its young, Anna needed support in upholding her values—even if the consequences cost her an outstanding opportunity. Fortunately it didn't. The professor arranged for Anna to work with a member of his staff who was studying the genetic structure of a virus associated with AIDS.

Compiling a resumé

If students are to "greet and meet" new adults and if they and their instructors ask a professional for assistance, they need a written summary of their education, interests, and accomplishments. Resumés that high school students design help introduce them to prospective mentors and establish common ground with an adult. Designing resumés increases their self-awareness by prodding them to understand what they offer others.

After the concept of a resumé is introduced, students list the personal traits and skills they would most want prospective mentors to know about them. Sometimes even after several days work on self-awareness students remain reluctant to respond to this task. To elicit a response, the instructor can suggest that if students can't pinpoint their own strengths, a complete stranger certainly may have difficulty in identifying them. If they need more feedback, students can ask their parents, teachers, and friends about what each sees as the student's unique personal traits and skills.

If the task seems particularly difficult for a class, students can be grouped in fours, then asked to write the traits and skills they observe in each of the others in the group. This not only provides the necessary feedback, but also boosts morale—and class teamwork!

When everyone has developed a list, volunteers can share their responses. If Richard responds, "I am intelligent and hard working," ask his classmates how he might demonstrate these traits on his resumé. They might answer, "List a grade point average or class rank or show how many honors classes you have taken," as proof of intelligence. Grade point average, class rank, and honors classes might also demonstrate hard work, as would a list of difficult extracurriculars or ongoing volunteer or paid employment. Listing strengths helps students to prepare resumés that show their skills to best advantage, and they become more confident in the process.

Of course, compiling the resumé and preparing it in a neat and orderly format requires instruction and effort. Students create a draft, then work in pairs to provide feedback on all aspects of the resumé including completeness of entries, form, spelling, and grammar; they also look to see that the resumé projects a positive and accurate image both in its content and how it is arranged on the page. With a word processor, corrections are easy. Without one, they are still necessary. Of course, resumés must be typed in order to be taken seriously in the "real world."

Finally, resumé instruction might include an explanation of the differences between a curriculum vita and a resumé. A curriculum vita more extensively lists a person's life work including publications and professional presentations than a resumé would. We always ask that mentors allow us to share their resumés or curriculum vitae with students and interested school personnel. The response from mentors has been positive, and their resumés are a true lesson in life for students— plus an excellent public relations tool for staff.

Careers and colleges

After students have reflected on their personal and learning traits, they are assigned to link the information and insights they gained about themselves to the career fields they wish to study. They need to see if the job realities fit with their own needs. Another significant distinction which students do not usually consider on their own is the difference between what a person does when they practice a career and the knowledge and skills required to practice.

Jason, for example, saw himself performing his guitar compositions on stage. At the career exploration stage, he wanted to know how one becomes a performer, the life performers lead, the salaries earned, and how rehearsals are scheduled. Jason never once considered what skills he would need to survive as a performer, such as the ability to transpose his compositions into sheet music so a publisher could consider them, or to sight read so he could quickly and accurately learn new pieces for a concert.

Career exploration asks "What do you do?" while college-planning is partially based on "What information will I need to know to do it?" or what I call *content information*. When students understand what they want to do, at least for purposes of the course, they become motivated to learn even more about the information and skills required to function in a career. After enhancing their awareness of self and understanding of potential careers, students are better prepared to make good choices regarding their education.

They begin thinking about the topic by imagining an ideal college situation. Then they prepare an ideal "College Shopping List" [found in the text, *College Comes Sooner Than You Think!* (Featherstone & Reilly, 1990, pp. 90-93)] which includes information gained about education required for entry into selected careers, personal learning styles and needs, and personal preferences in college environment.

When everyone has considered their "ideal situations," the class takes a field trip to a local college campus. Students are assigned to individually evaluate the college according to the college-planning priorities they set. When calling the college to request a campus visit, I ask for a student-guided tour, a brief meeting with an admissions officer, information on honors programs, and to tour and use the library.

When students see what a college campus looks like and how it functions, they are often amazed! High school students don't realize the variety of options available in college courses and activities nor do they grasp the independence with accompanying responsibilities, the increased educational resources, or even what a dormitory room looks like until they see it firsthand. As one student responded to the visit, "I didn't understand the need to visit colleges before this. I also didn't know what to expect. Now, I understand better how to achieve my goals!"

Advanced Research Skills

The brief college library visit provides a transition between the self-awareness and advanced research skills units. More sophisticated research skills empower students to continue in-depth study of their fields of interest. By the time they apply to a mentoring program, many students express frustration with their inability to locate new and challenging information about their areas of interest.

While on tour of the college library, students discover that college libraries have resources which cannot be found in public libraries. Students may never have seen an on-line card catalog system or collaborative data bases which list resources from a group of libraries. These data bases allow a search for materials on highly specific, rarely requested topics such as creating clay-animation characters or the international laws regarding borrowing works of art for an exhibit.

Colleges also offer indexes geared more for the professional than is the *Readers' Guide to Periodic Literature.* These might include an art index or a science and technology index which may not be part of the collection at a local library. Students also may not be aware that local and nationally known newspapers are indexed and could potentially offer valuable information. For example, a student interested in the stock market or investment planning should begin to read the *Wall Street Journal* regularly. In the index for the *Wall Street Journal,* that student might also find articles that provide in-depth information about specific businesses and their stock or other investments. The *Washington Post* offers thorough coverage of national politics for the student interested in government. *Corporate Report Minnesota* provides an invaluable resource when a Minnesota student wants more information about a local company. Other regions or states produce similar references which deal with their own locale.

Once students have had the opportunity to see the resources at a college library and attempt to use them, their interest is ignited. When they return to the classroom, students receive more detailed explanations and practice on how to use the resources available through college and professional libraries. In addition to the resources suggested above, students learn how to use *Ulrich's International Periodicals in Print* (Bowker International Serials Database, Annual) which lists titles of periodicals from around the world that are currently in print. One student who had raised—and loved—poultry for most of his life was amazed to discover a few English-language periodicals which were devoted solely to veterinary and management concerns about raising poultry!

As students identify periodicals specializing in their areas of interest, they also become acquainted with Union Listings. Union Listings pinpoint the libraries in which specific periodicals may be available. The parts of a research article are also explained, and pointers given about which portions of the article are most likely to be comprehensible to them.

Students research the names of dictionaries specific to their fields and where they can find them. Then when they encounter unfamiliar technical terms, they have an immediate resource. They also learn about the cataloging system at university libraries. Finally, students role-play situations in which they request assistance. They all say they are perfectly able to ask for help. However, when they try to form the words, many of them find it much more difficult than anticipated.

When students have completed advanced research instruction, they take a field trip to a university library system to apply newly acquired information and practice new skills. University libraries are generally vast systems with several huge libraries and some smaller, more specialized ones. This provides an even greater challenge than the smaller college library the class visited earlier in the course.

In addition to a sheet stating their assignment, each student receives a university map upon which the instructor highlights the library containing the collection he or she needs. Students are asked to observe where they are when they get off the bus, so they can return for pick-up at the appointed time. Most students have never been on their own at a university campus, and their faces reflect their awe.

Students spend several hours researching in whichever library has the most appropriate resources for their topic. An instructor circulates throughout the libraries while they work. When students return to the bus stop, their faces now reflect a glow of confidence. Not one student has ever been lost, nor has anyone been more than five minutes late for pick-up.

The Seminar project

By the time the students complete their university library field trip, they should have begun to focus on a project topic. For the remaining weeks of *Seminar* (slightly less than half the instructional hours), students are assigned a project to further enhance their backgrounds in areas of interest and to demonstrate to prospective mentors their current level of expertise. These projects are completed primarily outside of class. However, five class hours are allotted for independent research.

Depending upon how the *Seminar* course is structured—whether it meets for two hours each day for six weeks or one hour daily for twelve weeks—will make a difference in the project requirements. The more condensed version allows less time to complete out-of-class research and other assignments than the twelve-week model. The projects can be as simple as reading and summarizing five current articles which stretch the student's expertise or as elaborate as conducting anesthesia experiments on fruitflies to prepare for a mentorship in anesthesiology.

Regardless of the scope of their projects, students maintain a reading list in standard bibliographic form. I prefer APA style. The reading lists can be invaluable when students want to retrieve information. Potential mentors also receive these lists. Some of the best introductory conversations begin when the mentor notes a book from the mentee's reading list that both have read.

Faculty contacts

To help with these preliminary projects prior to being assigned to a mentor, students select a faculty member with background in their chosen topic. Students refer to these people as their "faculty contacts." Serving as a faculty contact is voluntary. Each faculty contact can share resources and exchange ideas with a high-ability student who shares a strong interest in their specialty area.

Students receive instruction, guidance, and evaluation from the *Mentor Seminar* instructor. However, because the class instructor does not have expertise within each specialty area, the faculty contact provides additional support and more specific background knowledge.

Students arrange a meeting with the faculty member they have selected to discuss becoming a faculty contact. Students are also responsible for setting future appointments. A faculty contact has the following three objectives:

To exchange information:	Ask questions about the student's interests and background.
To challenge:	Suggest resources and methods to help the student develop new skills.

• • •

To encourage:	Support the student's efforts by listening, suggesting, and sharing experiences and expertise.

During *Mentor Seminar* students arrange two meetings (and sometimes more) with their faculty contacts. The purpose of these meetings is to exchange information and share ideas about the student's learning needs and how best to meet them. During the first meeting, faculty contacts listen and respond to students' ideas for projects. They recommend resources, discuss key concepts, and suggest further reading and projects. During the second meeting, the faculty contacts review the final projects and suggest finishing touches.

Faculty contacts are not obligated to continue in this role beyond the *Mentor Seminar* unless they wish to participate during the *Mentor Field Experience.* (For continued discussion of the faculty contact's role during *Field Experience,* see Chapter 4.) Initially, some faculty contacts expressed concern about the additional time they would have to spend. However, by the end of the first *Seminar* everyone had only good things to say. The biggest attraction seemed to be working with bright, enthusiastic students on an individual basis.

Some projects seemed to intrigue the faculty contacts as well as the students. One student studied the mating behavior of exotic birds; surprisingly, the biology department chair had completed his master's degree thesis on this topic. Two students interested in wildlife management completed a twice-daily survey of a wooded portion of the school property. As rumor had it, several science teachers became curious about their findings and were seen outside monitoring the results. They even received portions of the morel mushrooms the students found. As an additional benefit, the district committee awarded clock hours toward re-licensure to teachers who participated as faculty contacts.

Two bonuses students derived from the independent research instruction are best described by Erica, a prospective small-animal veterinarian who wrote in her **MPG Survey** after her freshman year of college. She gained:

Self-confidence: I know I can understand tough, foreign material if I work at it. This keeps me going when I don't understand.

Enthusiasm: I really want to go into vet medicine and thinking about mentor experiences is the only thing that keeps me in chemistry, because it's really tough!

Interpersonal Skills

After students have expanded their repertoire of research skills, and they become involved with their projects outside of class, they begin the unit on interpersonal skills. They find interpersonal skills such as meeting people or asking quality questions very helpful when their projects demand an informational contact with professionals. Students must also be able to courteously and effectively state their needs and expectations when they request a mentorship. The final phase of instruction in the *Seminar* addresses the interpersonal skills students need to comfortably and effectively learn with professionals in the workplace.

Poised and proper

The interpersonal skills unit was developed in response to questions such as: What is appropriate etiquette for young adults in business situations? How do I formulate good questions? How can I help sustain conversations with an adult? How do I politely and effectively request information or assistance? How can I assert myself and get my needs met in a bustling adult business environment, yet still be perceived as courteous? How can I improve my skills in working with people from diverse backgrounds? How do I prepare for and conduct an informational or mentorship interview?

Students, especially gifted ones, may answer these questions well on an informational level but many are unable to apply the techniques until they have practiced. They may know that a firm handshake and eye contact replaces "Yo dude!" in business situations, but ask them to apply the more formal greeting with one another or with an adult and there's instant discomfort. While teaching how to greet people or to ask

●●●

quality questions may appear to be "remedial" education, a little practice really does go a long way.

Letitia Baldrige's Complete Guide to Executive Manners (1985) provides guidelines on a broad range of issues including introductions, telephone etiquette, business communications, protocol, and dress. One caution: students need help to interpret Baldrige's guidelines to a level acceptable for an adolescent. For example, in some business situations a man must wear a dress shirt, jacket, and tie, but a sixteen-year-old in the same situation would be dressed appropriately in less formal attire. In fact, many sixteen-year-olds don't own a jacket. If teachers are unsure of the appropriate attire or etiquette for an adolescent in a particular setting, they can always ask at the business or tell the student to check, depending on the situation.

Addressing mentors

Students also need to be encouraged to ask their mentors how they would like to be addressed. Of course, "Mr.," "Ms." or "Dr." is always safe. It would be unthinkable, for example, for a Persian expert on the Shiite sect of Islam to be addressed by his first name by the young woman who is his mentee. More often, however, mentors prefer to have students call them by their first names. Mentors, like some students, may be reticent to suggest using their first names because they think schools require a more formal title. In *Field Experience* class, students may call instructors by their first names to help them become comfortable with a more adult style prior to meeting their mentors. Some students have commented that calling instructors by their first names enabled them to feel worthy of a "more adult relationship," although a few students never wished to use their instructor's first name.

Quality questions

Learning how to ask good questions also demands practice. Students start by formulating questions they want answered. They also observe an interview and the question-asking strategies, then practice sustaining conversation through active listening and question formulation. Reading a thought-provoking editorial, then responding with questions about it also stimulates students' question-asking skills. The questions can be geared to obtain further background, new information, or to refute or support the author's point-of-view.

Telephoning for information

When they have formulated questions about their topics, students must find ways to get them answered. Calling by telephone, particularly to request information, offers another avenue to get answers besides library research. Students may want to find out about a relevant lecture or exhibit, inquire about which resources an organization offers the community, or gain more general background about businesses with which they hope to gain mentorships. Knowing which products a business markets, current issues or developments a business faces, or the demographics of the population which the business serves all have proven helpful to students seeking mentorships with their "dream" companies.

Letitia Baldrige's Guide provides complete information on telephone skills and etiquette. It lists key points in effective telephone use and what students should mention when they request information, such as their name, and field of interest, and reason for calling. It also reminds them to thank the person who responds. Students actually make a telephone call to request further information on their topics. They receive a checksheet listing calling techniques and are required to have someone in the room, but not on the telephone line, listen to their call and provide feedback on their performance.

To prepare, we role-play in class. Again, it really is necessary. Students think they know what to say, but frequently when they role-play, they miss critical information or points of etiquette. Once, I tried asking a confident and skilled young woman to actually place a call from our classroom so other less-confident students could listen. Since Mary shared my husband's field of interest, I obtained a speaker phone and asked my husband to respond to the call at an appointed time. He agreed that my class could listen. Unfortunately, my husband told one of his co-workers about the call. Mary was prepared and polished, but my husband's co-worker made distractingly silly faces and gestures throughout the conversation and my husband's performance barely passed. Now I have students role-play with one another.

• • •

Nonverbal communications count!

Subtleties truly are important in communications. Even sophisticated students may lack awareness of how nonverbal communications impact upon the message listeners receive, so we invite a guest speaker with theatrical skills to demonstrate. In one especially effective activity, students observe a monologue presented with two entirely different sets of nonverbals, but the same words. Then they examine awareness of their own bodies and the messages they communicate nonverbally through expressions, nonverbal intonations, using space with their bodies, facial expressions, and gestures.

A video entitled *Body Business* (Cooper, 1983), teaches students how to apply nonverbal communications to a business setting. They also read about nonverbal communications. One article that students have enjoyed stresses regional differences and compares Minnesota nonverbals to those of New Yorkers. Once students understand the impact of nonverbal communications, they can better consider good listening skills. After practicing good listening skills, students are ready to practice being heard.

Assertiveness

Next students discuss how they, as mentees, can express their needs effectively and courteously to their more senior mentors. While teachers plan a course of group study prior to student contact, mentors frequently rely heavily on the individual student's expressed learning needs and desires. Students often feel too intimidated to express their needs to adults. If students are reluctant to express their wants and needs, mentors quickly become uncomfortable about what they offer to the student. They don't know if they are giving the students what they require. If an unexpressed gap remains between each person's perceptions of the situation, a real crisis can develop. Of course, assertiveness skills apply to many important life situations besides mentorships.

Students begin their study of assertiveness skills by examining the differences between assertive, passive, and aggressive behavior. A particularly helpful resource for teaching teen assertiveness training is the chapter on "Being Assertive" found in the book, *Fighting Invisible Tigers* (Hipp, 1985). Following Hipp's "assert" formula, students can role-play a response to a plausible mentoring situation . One realistic case for practice in *Mentor Seminar* might be:

> *It is Wednesday afternoon in the chemistry lab of your mentor's work place. You are struggling with a crystallization procedure she assigned you to complete. You have attempted the procedure ten times without getting the results you were instructed to expect, and you need help in order to continue your work. Your mentor has had an extremely hectic week filled with meetings and deadlines, so she has not been available to you for any length of time. You don't know if she is aware of the difficulties you are having or when she plans to meet with you next. How will you address this situation? (Reilly, 1991).*

Conflict resolution

When students feel comfortable formulating assertive responses to situations, they touch on conflict resolution skills. Before instruction students almost always perceive conflict as negative. David T. Kearns, Chairman and CEO of Xerox Corporation says (1990), "To a business leader, a 'problem' has only one function: to open the door to a solution." Indeed, as Irving Kristol (quoted in Drew, 1987) has observed, "If there's no solution, there's no problem" (p. 18). Attitude is one essential component here; conflict signals the potential for change which can be very positive.

Students can find it helpful to begin their study of conflict resolution by brainstorming a list of conflicts that have arisen in nature, in history, in music, etc. Then they consider what happened as a result of resolving those conflicts. The students realize that the effect of resolving conflicts can be positive. One good resource for this topic, although geared toward elementary-school children, is *Learning the Skills of Peacemaking* (Drew, 1987). While Drew's approach is more global than required for a mentoring program, she does provide some interesting activities and a complete resource list.

Cultural diversity

Another segment of the interpersonal skills unit addresses valuing cultural diversity. Students in high school and adults in the business world live in two largely different cultures. The differences in age and experience generate the need to value and understand diversity as do differences in ethnic origins, race, gender, and socioeconomic status. Students will encounter such diversity as we strive to place them with appropriate mentors so they must develop awareness and sensitivity to it.

Janet Jackson's "Rhythm Nation" (Jam & Lewis, 1989) or other works of music, art, or literature which address differences in cultural background can provide an interesting introduction to the topic. As students consider a work's meaning, they also try to determine why the author created it. Surprisingly, while students may grasp the meaning of the song or painting, they often cannot determine why an artist chose to create it. Discussion about the issues raised in the piece or its creation may clarify reasons for thinking about cultural diversity in our society.

Next, the students read and learn about the changes in the American workforce. When they realize that the Caucasian male may soon be in the minority in the workforce, students better perceive the need to consider differences.

The video, *Valuing Cultural Diversity, Part III*, addresses barriers to communication between cultures and how to eliminate them. *The Handbook of Nonsexist Writing* (Miller & Swift, 1988) stresses the importance of nonsexist communications and provides a complete guide to nonsexist writing. National and local newspapers address diversity regularly, providing additional items for discussion.

A speaker addressing cultural diversity adds power and credibility to class discussion. Several major corporations within a community generally can provide speakers through their personnel departments. In the *Mentor Program,* a speaker shared his personal and professional experiences as a native-born midwestern Hispanic; an African American from New York shared her experiences with different cultures—not only between Blacks and Whites, but also between Easterners and Midwesterners. A panel discussion has also proven effective. Since this course bridges education and the workplace, corporate representatives seem most appropriate. However, local universities and agencies committed to advancing acceptance of diversity might provide this resource as well.

Interviewing: Seminar synthesis

As they prepare to conduct an informational interview with a professional in their field of interest, students mount a new and concluding challenge. An informational interview draws on many of the interpersonal skills that the class studies, such as telephoning to make an appointment, assertiveness, meeting and greeting people, asking quality questions, and other verbal and nonverbal skills. An informational meeting with a professional also requires that students draw on most of what they learned in their research. Often, this meeting is the highlight of the *Seminar* course. For example, Marissa expressed a strong desire to learn about the work of an art museum curator. Through her instructor, she arranged to meet with a curator, Mrs. Johnson, who was mounting an exhibit of Korean furniture. Along with Marissa's faculty contact, Mrs. Johnson provided information and encouragement throughout Marissa's project, which combined a study of Korean furniture with planning and arranging an art exhibit. When Marissa presented her completed project to our class, Mrs. Johnson travelled across the metropolitan area to observe.

To prepare for interviewing, a professional seasoned in the process shares research and tips on effective interviewing. He or she covers topics such as the importance of impressions made in the initial minutes of an interview, the sequence and content of questions that may be asked, poised verbal and nonverbal responses to questions, and appropriate attire. Then the class practices.

Each student must respond to one "hardball" question. The question must provoke thought, yet be one the student can handle. For example, a student interested in dolphin behavior was asked her opinion about the morality of confining dolphins in zoos, and the prospective pilot was asked her opinion about whether pilots should submit to tests for substance use.

After this warm-up activity, a local personnel administrator volunteers to conduct a brief, videotaped interview with each student. Students are likely to be anxious about this experience, so sometimes they are allowed to "gang-up" and interview the instructor either before we begin or as a reward at the end.

After the interviews, the students watch the results. If the group remains highly uncomfortable, popcorn helps ease the tension. The serious task is for students to note the strengths of each individual. Each "interviewee" also must identify one skill to continue to develop. Depending on the group, the individuals find their own area for growth or other students and the instructor might suggest one. Classmates can be an excellent source of critique if they respond sensitively. After the videotaped interviews, students should have the poise and skill to comfortably conduct real interviews with professionals in their fields of interest.

Concluding Activities

In place of a final *Seminar* examination, students write a brief project summary and present their projects to the class. Parents and faculty contacts can be invited to hear the students' presentation or to attend a project exhibit. As was the case with Marissa's Ms. Johnson, an occasional professional also asks to attend. The presentations provide an excellent opportunity for students to rethink what they have learned through public speaking. It also allows classmates to exchange information, to ask questions, and to experience a sense of accomplishment!

As a closing activity, the *Mentor Seminar Course Evaluation* can help students reflect on their experiences and provide instructors with valuable feedback (see Chapter 7 for a copy of this form).

When instructor and students breathe a sigh of relief at the end of *Mentor Seminar,* everyone will discover that the students have learned a great deal, gained critical social skills, and are well-prepared to begin a mentorship. Through the students' course work, the teacher will have a resumé, an up-to-date reading list, and a written project summary to send to each potential mentor.

Finally, in case you are wondering about Don, the young man introduced in the beginning of this chapter, he wrote to me recently. It has been more than four years since he completed his mentorship. Don's project was to help author a computer program for accounting. The program ultimately was marketed by his mentor's software firm. When Don graduated from high school one year after he completed his mentorship, the software firm awarded Don a scholarship in appreciation of his efforts there.

He told me, "[Currently] I have moved up from computer programming or operations [to computer engineering] because I felt I wanted more of a challenge than programming could provide." He graduated in 1991 from a fine midwestern school with a degree in computer science and engineering.

References

American Psychological Association. (1983). *Publication manual of the American Psychological Association* (3rd ed.). Washington, DC: American Psychological Association.

Bowker Internationals Serials Database. (1989-90). *Ulrich's international periodicals directory* (28th ed.). NY: R. Robert Bowker.

Colangelo, N., & Zaffrann, R. T. (1979). *New voices in counseling the gifted*. Dubuque, IA: Kendall/Hunt Publishing Company.

Cooper, K. (1982). *Body business: Nonverbal communication* [Video]. Santa Monica, CA: Salenger Films.

Copeland-Griggs Production. (1989). *Communicating across cultures, Part III* [Video]. San Francisco, CA: Copeland-Griggs Production.

Corporate Report Minnesota available from:
> Corporate Reports, Inc.
> A subsidiary of MCP, Inc.
> 5500 Wayzata Boulevard
> Minneapolis, MN 55416]
> Mark William Hopp, CEO

Drew, N. (1987). *Learning the skills of peacemaking: An activity guide for elementary- aged children on communicating, cooperating, and resolving conflict*. Rolling Hills Estates, CA: Jalmar Press.

Erikson, E. (1963). *Childhood and society* (2d ed.). NY: W. W. Norton.

Featherstone, B. F. & Reilly, J. R. (1990). *College comes sooner than you think! The essential planning guide for high school students and their parents*. (2d ed.). Dayton, OH: Ohio Psychology Press.

Fredrickson, R. H. (1979). Career development and the gifted. In N. Colangelo & R.T. Zaffrann (Eds.), *New Voices in Counseling the Gifted* (pp. 264-276). Dubuque, IA: Kendall/Hunt Publishing.

Gelles-Cole, S. (Ed.) (1985). *Letitia Baldrige's complete guide to executive manners*. NY: Rawson Associates.

Herr, E. L, & Watanabe, A. (1979). Counseling the gifted about career development. In N. Colangelo & R. T. Zaffrann (Eds.), *New Voices in Counseling the Gifted* (pp. 251-263). Dubuque, IA: Kendall/Hunt Publishing.

Hipp, E. (1985). *Fighting invisible tigers*. Minneapolis: Free Spirit Publishing.

Jam, J., & Lewis, T. (Producers). (1989). *Janet Jackson's Rhythm Nation* [Compact disc recording.] Hollywood: A & M Records.

Kearns, D. T. (1990). Let the free market reign. *School Administrator,* pp. 17-18.

Kolb, D.A. (1976). *The learning style inventory: Technical manual.* Boston: McBer and Company.

Miller, C., & Swift, K. (1988). *The handbook of nonsexist writing* (2d ed.). NY: Harper & Rowe, Publishers.

Myers-Briggs, I. (1962). *The Myers-Briggs Type Indicator manual.* New Jersey: Educational Testing Service.

Pleasantville Media. (1988). *Self image and your career* [video]. Pleasantville, New York: Pleasantville Media.

Reader's Guide to Periodic Literature available from:
>H. W. Wilson Company
>950 University Avenue
>Bronx, New York 10452

CHAPTER 4

Finding Mentors and Developing Mentorships

Children must be raised by the community of adults—all adults.

— William Bennett
former U.S. Secretary of Education

Katie ranked fifth in a high school class of 750. She had successfully completed every advanced class in her high school and loved each one. As a senior Katie had good people skills, was an active musician, involved in her church, and captain of the cheerleaders in her school. With so many skills and interests, she wondered what career field to enter. She wanted most of all "to be successful."

Early in her senior year, she asked for assistance in selecting a college. Her counselor responded with surprise, "Katie, you're so good at everything. You don't need help; you'll be a success wherever you go."

Katie described her feelings at that time as "confused"; she felt pressured. She knew everyone at home and in school expected her to be successful in a career. As a result, Katie felt she should attend one of America's most prestigious universities. How could she best use her diverse talents and interests?

She persevered and asked teachers, two friends of her parents, and finally a college planning consultant for help in sorting out her options. She recounted that her English teacher said she would be a wonderful writer; her chemistry teacher encouraged her to pursue a career in chemical engineering, stressing the outstanding options open to women; and her church youth worker reminded Katie that she was "wonderful with kids."

When the college-planner asked her what she enjoyed most about school, Katie recounted the excitement she experienced in chemistry class when the class observed the reactions that occur when making peanut brittle. However, Katie also told the planner that when she mentioned chemical engineering to her parents, they wondered if she would be too isolated in an engineering profession. Katie also wondered about the life-style she would lead as a chemist or chemical engineer. Would she have enough "people contact?" In addition, Katie's mom had devoted her energies to creating a cozy home life, and Katie wanted that along with a career. She expressed concern about her career interfering with the family life she envisioned. How could she accomplish it all?

Katie entered *Mentor Seminar* with these questions in mind. After preliminary reading and discussion, I arranged for Katie to have lunch with a small group of classmates and engineers at the international headquarters of a prestigious company. Three of the four engineers were women.

During the luncheon Katie learned more about balancing the roles of professional with wife and mother. One woman noted that she needed a nanny-housekeeper to maintain a personal and professional life at the same time. Another described the woes—and joys—of daycare. Katie also met Dr. Marie Huston, who had earned her doctorate in polymer engineering.

Katie heard more about balancing talents from Dr. Huston. She, like Katie, had excellent people skills and needed people contact. She told Katie:

> *Most people who enter engineering have the scientific skills they need to be successful. However, those who have people/communications*

skills advance more rapidly. So, your skills will be valuable to you even if they aren't the central focus of your work [personal communication, January 1985].

Dr. Huston explained that to exercise her other talents she had expanded her interactions with people, speaking to school children about her role as a scientist. In her leisure time, she had also taken clown training. Dr. Huston expressed great satisfaction from the enjoyment she brought people in hospitals, community events, and parades.

When Katie had received the support she needed, she decided to tackle a field experience in chemical engineering. We contacted Dr. Huston to tell her that Katie had decided she wanted to further pursue this field. Dr. Huston was delighted and assumed a "leave-it-to-me" attitude. She arranged a mentorship in a chemical engineering lab at the company where she worked. Given her own office and lab space, Katie stretched her skills in chemistry and gained a better understanding of her place within the field. She calibrated equipment and conducted tests for producing a new, lightweight material for setting broken limbs. She also observed the roles of researchers and managers, males and females, within the field.

When Katie completed the mentorship, her researcher-mentor, her mentor's manager, and Dr. Huston all attended the program banquet and open house to celebrate Katie's accomplishments. Katie's mentor became a member of the *Mentor Program* steering team for two years. Katie later reflected about her mentorship:

The most obvious thing that Mentor Seminar *taught me was interviewing and how to use resources to get information. In* Field Experience *I learned that there were women who were happy in the field. My overall impression was that women did enjoy their work, and they were happy in the field. I also saw the application of the science. This told me that this was the focus of my college career.*

Katie continued her chemical engineering education at a leading university. Today she works as a chemical engineer for a Fortune 500 company.

This chapter examines the process of finding mentors and supporting them in their efforts to work effectively with students. In a sense this chapter also provides a training manual for mentors and for those who seek them. It includes information about establishing contact with prospective mentors and training them about the basics of the program. The traits of good potential mentees have been outlined, and considerable attention has been devoted to the role of a mentor.

Questions are offered which may help in deciding whether to become a mentor or whether to accept them on behalf of students. The chapter also contains suggestions for mentors on how to screen mentees and for businesses on how to effectively engage in business and school partnerships like the *Mentor Program*. All of the information here helps mentors and program instructors come together on behalf of students.

Often, the biggest concern of a high school staff when they consider starting a mentoring program is "Where will we get the mentors?" However, finding a professional who fits the student's focus area, learning needs, and often complicated daily schedule can be easier than people think. I found that the generosity and genuine concern of the business and professional community far exceeded my expectations. Like Dr. Huston, professionals often make the task of developing mentorships a joyful—and surprisingly easy—one.

Why Mentors Are Willing

Instructors express concern about "bothering" professionals when they request assistance in the form of a mentorship—or even just a single informational interview. One teacher commented that she would "gird her loins" whenever she contacted anyone in her community for assistance. The discomfort instructors feel in approaching a new person with a request is real. I can only suggest focusing on the goal: Providing a talented young person with an opportunity of a lifetime to learn and grow.

Prospective mentor's schedules *are* busy, and their first priority at work probably will not be educating an interested teen. However, most of the people I have contacted have been gracious, and many have been enthusiastic about the idea of contributing both to the development of a capable, interested student and to the quality of people who enter their profession.

It becomes easier for *Mentor Program* instructors to approach prospective mentors if they understand why professionals in a broad range of fields *want* to mentor a high school student. This section explores the reasons prospective mentors give for their willing participation in the *Mentor Program*. I've arranged the reasons in order of the frequency in which they are heard.

"I wish I had had this opportunity."

The single most frequent response potential mentors offer when introduced to the mentoring program concept is: "I wish I had had the opportunity when I was that age!" They sometimes will expound on the interests they had and the loneliness they felt when no one shared their interests. Other times the prospective mentors will exclaim about the opportunity to explore an area in more depth and to test their interests and themselves. If prospective mentors know what a mentorship would have meant to them, helping someone else to have that chance feels wonderful—and not like an imposition.

Sharing responsibilities

Another very important factor for mentor participation revolves around an effective school-based program. A program that shares responsibility for supporting and monitoring the student's progress with the mentor adds credibility and insurance to the option. The mentors, known experts in their fields, may offer tremendous resources for students' cognitive development. These resources fulfill a primary goal of the program. However, businesspeople and professionals appreciate the intense preparation that the students complete, and regard the resumés, project summaries and reading lists developed in *Mentor Seminar* as concrete evidence of the student's readiness for advanced work with them.

Furthermore, mentors who work outside of schools generally feel less comfortable with needs that arise from a formal educational setting such as developing a learning plan, dealing with attendance, and evaluating students. They also express concern about their ability to meet adolescents' intellectual, social, and emotional needs, and they may be unprepared to deal with these psychosocial factors that impact the relationship for which instructors have been trained (Fox, 1979). In addition, reporting on his work with The Mentor Academy Program, Runions observed (1980):

> *One of the greatest threats to mentoring is to make mentors into surrogate teachers, required to evaluate, report, and record rather than maintaining their roles as scientists, lawyers, academics, retired photographers, or students (p. 155).*

So, *Mentor Program* instructors assume responsibility for teaching, evaluating, and reporting. They also provide essential support, not only to students, but to mentors. Instructors schedule and attend an initial meeting with the mentor to introduce them to the *Mentor Program* and to familiarize them with its structure. They also meet with mentors to follow up on the students' experiences. In addition to written and telephone contact, mentor, student, and instructor have a minimum of one face-to-face meeting between the placement and the time students complete their field experiences. Providing such support makes it much easier for professionals to agree to a long-term volunteer commitment. This "double mentoring" approach (Clasen & Hanson, 1987) assures mentors that the school, especially the *Mentor Program* instructors, will provide resources in these unfamiliar, and perhaps difficult, areas .

New perspectives

School personnel concerned about approaching the business and professional community also ask, "What initially motivates potential mentors to accept the challenge?" Generally, potential mentors respond most favorably to motivated, academically capable teens with an interest in their own field of expertise. People enjoy sharing interests to which they are committed, and top-level executives and professionals are no exception. High school students can bring a spark, enthusiasm, and a new perspective to an adult's work. In a discussion of benefits to mentors and business, a fashion designer commented on this direct benefit to her, "Looking at my work through the student's eyes made me see it in a fresh, new light. Explaining why I do things helped me reevaluate my approach to some tasks."

A research chemist in the field of endocrinology admitted:

Since I don't have much contact with high school–aged people, I was willing to believe the worst about them all. Being a mentor proved me wrong and reaffirmed my hope for young people and their future in this country (Dimond, 1990).

In a different way, through his enthusiasm, intelligence, and perspective, the young mentee reignited a concern about education in his mentor, the son of a teacher. This man became the first mentor on our steering team and has continued to provide steadfast and studied guidance ever since.

Developing new talent within the profession

Mentors express strong feelings about contributing to talent development within their own professions—and they do contribute. The *Mentor Program Graduate Survey* questioned students who had completed the course one to five years prior to the date of the survey. Eighty-six percent of all students responded. Of the respondents, eighty-nine percent had continued on the same or similar career path they began with their mentorship. One hundred percent indicated that their mentorships had been instrumental in their career decisions (Reilly, 1990).

Two other independent studies of the *Mentor Program* confirmed that mentors influence the professional development of their mentees. Beck (1989) found that mentors had a significant effect on the personal, academic, and career choices of their protegees. Bathke's (1990) results suggest that the program may reinforce the values of seeking job satisfaction and opportunities for creativity within the students' careers. That mentors want the chance to share their profession is reflected in the comments of a distinguished veterinarian when asked what he valued most about his experience as a mentor:

One is given the opportunity to introduce their chosen profession to a bright, interested and eager person. The students in the Mentor Program *are special; they are motivated to learn and are appreciative of the opportunity to gain new information (Dimond, 1990).*

Returning the favor

Mentoring a high school student also offers professionals the opportunity to "return the favor" of the mentoring they received which helped them to achieve their own aspirations. Former mentoring program students also have become mentors themselves. One mentor explained the rise in her career as a network news anchor this way:

When I was trying to get into this field I had mentors I looked up to—I couldn't have made it without them. That is why I am involved in the Mentor Program, to try to help give a gifted student a chance.

Early in her career, a mentor had decided that this woman was gifted enough to merit opening doors to a highly competitive field. The news anchor would not have "made it" without this opportunity. She now was in a position to select another gifted person for whom she would open professional gates. She also felt that she was returning the favor her mentor had offered her.

Finding Mentors: People and Places

Once they are convinced that the people with whom they have formed contacts may want to serve as a mentor, establishing a network of people to assist in finding mentors can save instructors even more time, energy, and stress. Some instructors had a very limited network of their own when they began to work in a *Mentor Program*, but they rapidly learned to establish a variety of contacts. In turn these contacts have their own networks of additional contacts. The following two sections suggest workable ways to identify prospective mentors.

Co-workers

The first resource to explore can be interested co-workers. Distribute a "Mentors Wanted" list to people on staff or make an announcement through a staff bulletin and follow up with an informal call or visit if an individual has contacts within a particular field.

Steering team

When a steering team is established, the members can provide considerable assistance. Team members can receive a list of the mentors needed as soon as students are selected for the following year. If the school has a site council, a school board, or other steering teams or advisory boards for different programs each can help. Familiarizing these groups with a mentoring program can also pave the way for future assistance.

Parents: Past and present

Parents whose children are entering a mentorship program frequently provide the names of those who might assist their own children. However, they are often reluctant to participate as mentors themselves or to recruit their own contacts. A tactful reminder at a parents' meeting held at the beginning of *Mentor Seminar* can help: If they wish these services for their children, parents can really help by assisting students interested in their own fields. They can help locate a person willing to provide an informational interview, a mentorship, or even become mentors themselves. Each parent can receive the current "Mentors Wanted" list and several subsequent lists by mail as well (for a sample form to send parents and other prospective mentors, see Figure 4-1). It is encouraging to note that after their children have received valuable attention from others, parents are more eager to return the favor.

School volunteer programs

If a school is fortunate enough to have a volunteer program, a mentoring program can dovetail efforts with them. For example, if the school volunteer program surveys their volunteers about possible ways in which they could assist the school, a brief explanation of mentor-

Fig. 4-1

MENTOR PROGRAM PROGRAM INTEREST FORM

The Mentor Program is an exciting course option for juniors and seniors in metro-area high schools. The course includes university, business, or community mentorship placement for each student.

Individuals who are willing to provide one informational meeting (30-60 minutes) or who wish to consider mentoring a bright, motivated, and creative young person are encouraged to complete this form and return it to the Mentor Program instructors [Names] at [School District/Address/Phone]. Prospective participants will be contacted by the Mentor Program instructors before they have become involved with the program to answer any questions you have. The student, prospective mentor, and instructor also participate in a preliminary interview prior to finalizing the mentor/ student agreement and schedule. If you might be interested in assisting the Mentor Program, please complete and return this form.

Fields for which the program needs immediate expertise are listed on the back of this form.

....
NAME   PHONE
....
WORKPLACE
....
ADDRESS
....
CITY   STATE   ZIP
....
TITLE

PLEASE INDICATE YOUR WORK AREAS AND PROJECTS.
....

....

Thank you for your interest and response. Please mail to:

[Instructor(s)]
[Title(s)]
[Address]
[Telephone]

Receipt of this information will be acknowledged by a phone call or letter from staff with further program information.

ships might be added to the form. The volunteer coordinator also can
be an excellent resource for identifying specialists in a particular field
who have already spoken to classes within the district.

Community education programs

Like a school volunteer program, community education programs
can be an excellent in-district resource for a mentoring program. Community education has the mission of developing life-long learners and
continuing the education of its constituents, so these programs offer
classes in a broad range of topics. Community education programs
often establish in-depth files or data bases on resources available within
the community. Through community education the *Mentor Program* has
obtained the services of a recording engineer, a stock broker, and a
computer programmer.

Community education or relations personnel might also become
involved in the actual placements of mentees with mentors. The Blue
Valley School District in Overland Park, Kansas reported that they use
this approach to finding mentors [personal communication, Septem-
ber, 1990]. This relieves the instructor of a substantial task.

Chambers of Commerce

Local Chambers of Commerce and individual businesses provide
another excellent resource. Chambers of Commerce often will survey
their memberships and compile a data base of those businesses and/or
employees who are willing to serve the community in many ways,
including as mentors. The Chamber staffs also know their membership
well enough to provide excellent suggestions. This can be a very
efficient way to identify appropriate businesses and locate willing
mentors.

Individual businesses

After you identify a company that serves a student's interest area,
locating the correct person with whom to speak can be a challenge.
Most companies have not designated someone within their organization to be a contact for schools. This makes it difficult for school staff to
initiate communications with them. The most important step for a

• • •

mentoring program instructor to take in finding a mentor through a business is to firmly establish someone as a contact.

An instructor can start with any number of people. The community relations or personnel manager often serves as a liaison with the community and generally knows the company's structure and individual's roles. A knowledgeable switchboard operator can be a tremendous help. Frequently the manager's secretary, whether in personnel or the specific department within which you seek a mentorship, can pave the way for an appropriate contact or even a mentorship.

Once the instructor establishes appropriate contacts, these people frequently help to establish credibility and support for the program among employees throughout the company just as Dr. Huston has continued to do over the years since she met Katie. The contacts have conversations with prospective mentors and mention the program at appropriate meetings such as staff, departmental or special interest group meetings, or technical forums. Some business liaisons to the *Mentor Program* also have been instrumental in obtaining official company approval for participation. When this happens all employees who wish to become mentors receive company support.

If the mentoring program staff drafts articles which provide a summary of the course and specific mentor needs, many companies will print them in their own in-house publications. Sometimes the businesses prefer their own staff to write the articles themselves, but even then providing a fact sheet with necessary information about the mentoring program will not only save time, but assure accuracy. It's important to check publication deadlines to allow adequate time for the company to respond before a student must be placed. These deadlines typically run a month or two before publication, so you need to plan ahead.

The program instructor or team may find help with publicity from students. Composing these corporate newsletter articles can make an interesting mini-project for mentor students interested in public relations or journalism.

Postsecondary educational institutions

College professors have the additional advantage of being teachers as well as experts in their field of inquiry, and they have been some of the *Mentor Program's* most outstanding mentors. So, don't overlook higher education institutions as a resource.

Identifying a professor with an interest similar to a student's presents little difficulty. Most higher education institutions publish a staff and department directory. Two further issues can be somewhat more challenging to answer: How to find a professor with a strong interest in a student's more narrow focus area and how to enter the system through the correct chain of command. Two examples will help clarify.

James wanted to study extremist political parties in his state. His community had several colleges and universities, all of which offered political science majors. However, his instructor experienced difficulty in identifying an expert who would have enough interest in this somewhat unconventional aspect of political science to assist with a project.

One approach might be a call to the political science department secretary or chairperson. Many of the colleges or universities working with the *Mentor Program* prefer school-based educators to receive approval from college administration prior to responding to any request. Some colleges even require that administration arrange all mentor contacts. In this way they can gauge the amount of faculty time given to the community outside of the college or university. This may be *the only* correct approach for some schools.

Another way to find the appropriate mentor is to scan the undergraduate research opportunities bulletin which emphasizes specialized or research interests of some faculty. This accomplishes the work of finding a person who shares a unique focus with a student. Several *Mentor Program* instructors have been referred to a senior faculty member who "really knows" the department. In James's case, he asked a friend at one of the community's more liberal colleges about who she thought would be a good mentor for him. She had one or two ideas, so she asked the professors about their interests and willingness. James's friend, in essence, began the relationship. His paper is now in progress, and I hear it's very good! Sensitive and beautifully done.

A problem may arise when some college professors express concern about allotting time to "their own" students; however, the majority welcome the opportunity to advance the learning of an eager high schooler. Another difficulty can occur when arranging a *Field Experience* for a hands-on learner at a college or university. There can be a lack of real-world application if the student wants to understand how the information is applied in a career outside of the university. This issue can be averted by understanding students' interests and learning styles prior to placement, so prospective mentors can hear about the student's learning needs and suggest ways to meet them. The program instructor also may suggest additional activities to add real-world applications or the possibility of splitting the mentorship between two professionals.

Dual mentorships work well where the situation requires two different kinds of expertise or experience or when a mentor's time won't allow for him or her to assume complete responsibility for the mentorship. For example, a student wanted to compare Buddhism with Islam in a scholarly fashion, and she wanted to observe each faith in daily practice. She worked with a university professor for the in-depth analysis and also received practical experience under the guidance of a religious leader in each of the faiths.

Service organizations and clubs

As programs expand and more students seek mentorship opportunities, community organizations can generate program awareness and, possibly, a commitment to help. Clubs formed to gather people with a common interest such as a horticultural club or an amateur radio operators' club readily welcome a young person with a similar interest and provide a wealth of expertise. Organizations with a civic or human service bent, such as assisting burn victims, sponsoring youth development, or recognizing people's accomplishments, also have contacts and expertise within their interest areas.

The young woman pictured on page 111 found her mentor through this kind of resource. She wanted to learn about airplane mechanics, history, and all about flight. A school administrator suggested an organization which restores World War II aircraft as a resource. The group welcomed her to visit their hangar, and there she found a cadre of experienced airplane mechanics and pilots with an historical past. Along with her own special mentor, the entire group took an interest in her, and they still do. As she studied at a college of aeronau-

tics, the entire club took an almost parental pride in her accomplishments.

If an instructor, steering team member, or student speak to the general memberships of a group, the organization's comfort level rises as does their willingness to work with students. With the support of the instructor, students can be the best emissaries at a service organization or club meeting. I have never seen a group more interested in what a teacher says than when the students contribute.

In the *Field Experience* course, students are required to speak publicly about their experiences at least once during the quarter. While they concentrate on teaching what they have learned to other students, speaking to a community group along with an instructor can be another, equally gratifying means of stretching the students' communication skills. This also gives students an opportunity to return to the community what has so graciously been given to them through their mentorships.

Over the years, a few service groups have made the *Mentor Program* a priority. As a result they have provided some outstanding mentors to students within their communities. Service organizations may designate a "contact" to help mentoring program instructors access the mentors they need. When mentors volunteer through the commitment of a service organization or club, mentors, students, and the organization report a strong sense of community unity and pride—a wonderful, added bonus!

Voluntary Action Centers

Voluntary Action Centers (VACs) act as brokers to fulfill the volunteer needs of a broad range of community agencies. Their policies about assisting schools or school programs may vary from community to community. Many metropolitan and local newspapers offer a "volunteer want ads" service to these Centers.

While the *Mentor Program* has never requested this kind of help, the Voluntary Action Centers have provided excellent information about and access to various human services mentorships. For example, one student wanted to learn more about crisis counseling. The VAC helped place her with the director of a teen crisis telephone line where she trained and became an active telephone volunteer as a portion of her mentorship. Voluntary Action Centers can provide some excellent resources which are unavailable elsewhere.

Finding Mentors: Additional Resources

When asked how I find mentors, I usually respond, "By being a little bit of a Sherlock Holmes." When all the above suggestions fail to yield results or the obvious person-to-person contact does not surface immediately, more creative detective work may be required. Never fear. "Going it alone" requires some sleuthing, but doesn't demand much more than a desire to look for mentors and a few, rather obvious resources. This section suggests some additional resources for a mentor search.

Directories

Your city's *Yellow Pages* provides the broadest information available and may reveal an entry or two—or more—on almost any topic. For example, Denise wanted to learn more about how to program a robotic arm. Not knowing anyone in the robotics field, I looked under "robots" or "robotics" in the *Yellow Pages*. Two companies were listed: one an internationally known conglomerate and the other a smaller firm of which I had not heard. Because there is less sorting through departments and people in a smaller company, I contacted them first. This company provided sales representation for several robot manufacturers. The representative who spoke with me knew the names of several people in our area who purchased robotic arms, a few of whom worked at designing programs. The representative happily shared names and telephone numbers with me.

Following this lead, I located a person at the same conglomerate listed in the *Yellow Pages* who agreed to meet with Denise. After an informational meeting, Mr. Wilkins told us that his company was phasing out their robotics department. In his assessment, Denise's need for experience with robotics was greater than the amount of work his company was doing. He suggested that I contact David Black, a department head at another corporation with a large defense contract to develop robotic systems. David Black became Denise's mentor.

Another excellent way to identify prospective mentors is the *Job Bank Series* (Toropov, 1987) which lists primary employers and government jobs. This directory cross-indexes each entry by industry and is published for several different metropolitan areas. The listings include the name of the company, address, telephone number, the company's basic products or services, and, for most listings, the contact person for professional positions. Other employer almanacs, internship directories, or listings of particular types of businesses also can provide leads.

Local newspapers and magazines

Mentor Program instructors frequently scan local newspapers and periodicals for references to prominent people working in fields for which they frequently or currently seek mentors. The business section of the newspaper refers to business community members daily, and the arts and entertainment section describes people employed in such diverse fields as fashion design, writing, the fine arts, and sound engineering. City magazines also feature articles on prominent citizens, interesting role-models, or unique jobs in each issue.

Building resource file

A list of interesting people and their places of employment becomes a treasure when students are focusing or exploring possibilities as well as when they are ready to be placed with a mentor. A clippings file of the articles that attract your attention becomes an even more detailed resource. Students love to read articles about people "making it" in their fields of interest! Students sometimes clip articles about local people whom they admire and with whom they would like to meet. With encouragement, they can surprise you with their resourcefulness and with the information they obtain. Even if a formal mentoring program remains in the distant future, starting a clippings file now can provide a headstart. When the program begins, be sure to keep a record of each interview or mentor candidate contacted for future use. The resource file is the best tool for identifying the people you seek.

Initiating a Mentorship

Arranging a mentorship does take time and perseverance. At least equally important, finding mentors takes skill in researching possibilities without the aid of a textbook or curriculum, and a willingness to depend on the assistance of others. This approach is fundamentally different from planning and executing a lesson taught in class. But as witnessed by the responses of the Mentor Connection teachers, this approach provides its rewards just as classroom teaching does.

Mentor Connection Instructor/Coordinator, Dorothy Welch, a teacher for over three decades and a doctoral candidate, describes her Mentor Connection experience as, "the most exciting job I've ever had as an educator. It ties together many facets of education to meet students' needs in a meaningful way" [personal communication, February 7, 1991]. *Mentor Program* instructor, Elizabeth Jenner, a former Spanish teacher and guidance counselor says:

> *It is the thrill of my heart to connect highly motivated students with top level professionals. What is inspiring to me is the student, desirous to learn, in face-to-face communication with the mentor, so willing to teach. You can sense the rapport developing almost immediately. Students are so enlivened by being recognized and appreciated by the expert [personal communication, March 20, 1991].*

All of the instructors involved with the Mentor Connection echo Welsh's and Jenner's sense of excitement and rejuvenation in their personal conversations and in more formal situations.

However, as mentioned earlier, most people find it difficult to approach someone new with a request. I find it the most difficult part of my job. For this reason, I believe, people frequently ask how to approach an initial contact with a prospective mentor.

The initial call

Usually the first contact is by telephone. Obviously, the person contacted needs to know who is calling, his or her name and position. When giving the reason for the call, four points seem most important:

1. A high potential student has an interest in the professional's field.

2. The student has exhausted the resources at the high school.

3. The school has an established mentoring program to help meet the student's needs for advanced learning.

4. The mentoring program is searching for a person who can help this student continue his or her learning in the field.

If the contact indicates an interest to continue the conversation, the instructor can continue with an outline the nature of the program, specific logistics such as what time students are released from school, what is required of mentors and students, and the mentoring program's role in the endeavor. Prospective mentors seem much more comfortable with a course offered through a school for grades and credit than with student inquiries about assistance.

Written information

After a positive initial response to a telephone conversation, professionals appreciate written information which includes a program description, the reasons mentors are needed, mentor responsibilities, time commitment, and benefits for mentors. The *Mentor Program* has developed an introductory brochure for all adults interested in the program, and a mentor handbook which provides more in-depth information for initiating a mentorship. The article which appears at the end of this chapter, "Mentor May Have Learned More Than Student in the Program" [see Figure 4-3 (Suzukamo, 1987)] is included in the prospective mentors' informational packet because it is brief, humorous, and reflects a mentor's point of view. If the mentoring program has access to a fax machine, mentors appreciate receiving materials while the original conversation is still fresh in their minds.

As prospective mentors become acquainted with the program, their formal training as a mentor has begun. They have received an overview of the program, its goals and objectives, and their possible role within the program. The next step is to make a preliminary assessment of the mentor and mentee match.

Assessing a Prospective Mentor: Traits To Consider

Of course, the first step in arranging a mentorship is to identify people who might have the appropriate expertise. But there are other considerations as well. Mentors do not always have sufficient time in their schedules to help students carry out a learning project of any length or significance or they may not be patient enough to work with young people. Student safety is sometimes an issue, and it is the instructor's responsibility to make sure the mentorship doesn't place mentees at risk. The following list examines these and other concerns.

Technical expertise

By the time an instructor initiates a mentorship, the student should have a clearly focused topic and preliminary goals for the mentorship. After the instructor has identified an individual who appears to have the skill and telephoned to ascertain interest, it's important to verify that the individual offers the skills the student needs. This information can be obtained simply by asking about the prospective mentor's business, his or her position, and education or training. If any doubts remain about his or her qualifications, schedule a personal meeting before pursuing a placement for a student.

Time

Prospective mentors need a careful explanation of the time required of them. Students are required to spend a minimum of eight hours per week on their learning, and mentors should allow approximately two hours per week of their own time. Likewise, mentoring program instructors need to feel comfortable that the mentor and/or his staff will make adequate time to spend with the student. While the mentor's time is a tricky variable to assess, it's worth explaining to mentors and asking if they believe they can do it. Nothing is more frustrating to mentees than mentors who cannot give the time to keep them learning. The students begin to feel lost in a strange place. They either feel they are wasting their time or that they are not worth the time.

Communication skills

The next question to consider is whether the professional has the personal and instructional skills—and the patience—to communicate information to the student. If the instructor experiences difficulty in assessing these skills over the telephone, a face-to-face meeting may be necessary. Sometimes even an initial meeting will not reveal this information.

One enthusiastic and personable prospective mentor sincerely wanted a mentee yet he tended to overcommit his time and energies. He was late to his first meeting with the mentee and appeared stressed throughout the time they spent together. He cancelled the next meeting and, by the third one, the mentee grew frustrated with the lack of attention and the mentor's inability to make time for her. Ultimately the mentee and I tactfully suggested that the situation was an additional pressure for him at that time, but that perhaps he could mentor another student in the future. He quickly agreed although he never initiated communication about his needs. Ending the mentorship was clearly a relief.

Student safety

Determining whether the mentor will provide a safe atmosphere for learning is another very important criteria. Instructors need to know if the work involves any unusual risks to the student. This requires considerable thought. For example, a student who goes on location with a news reporter might be at risk at a crime scene or if he is required to knock on doors to check facts. In the laboratory, chemicals, fumes, or power sources are potential dangers. At a veterinarian's office, there is the risk of animal bites. In situations with a risk factor, the most important questions to ask potential mentors are if the student will receive safety training and whether adequate supervision will be provided.

Additional considerations

The literature offers lists of positive traits for mentors in several situations which differ from the *Mentor Program*. Haeger and Feldhusen suggest "what to look for in a mentor" who will work with gifted children and adolescents (1986) and so does Boston (1976). Flaxman, Asher, and Harrington (1988) consider traits needed to mentor tenacious youth, and Gray (1988) draws on studies of spontaneous mentoring to suggest traits to ensure successful planned mentoring programs in businesses. While the priorities just discussed remain foremost, other traits to consider include:

- Is the prospective mentor flexible?

- Does she have good people skills; is she people-oriented? Enthusiastic?

- Is he comfortable with teenagers?

- Is she sensitive to student's needs and in setting expectations for him?

- Can the mentor generate new questions or research for the student to pursue?

- Is he willing and able to help identify potential problems and find solutions for them?

- Can she provide constructive evaluation and feedback to nurture the student's growth?

- Does he perceive possible benefits to the student, business, community, and most important, for himself?

Finally, Boston (1976) suggests that the mentor's teaching styles match the student's learning style. While all *Mentor Program* students assess their personal learning styles, it would be very difficult and time-consuming to assess a mentor's teaching style. However, if both student and/or instructor can clearly explain the student's particular learning needs to a prospective mentor, the mentor will have the opportunity to respond to those needs. Then the instructor can assess the match. The mentor's response to the mentee's learning needs may reveal all that is necessary to determine whether the match has potential.

For example, some students need to learn in a logical, sequential order and others require active participation or variety. If Gina wants to actually design a prom gown, and the mentor feels that she should only learn design theory, the match may not be appropriate. However, do not overlook the possibility of negotiation: Perhaps the best way for Gina to create her prom gown is to learn the design theory, then apply it to her gown. She can sketch a garment which brings theory into practice. In this way, Gina can learn experientially and still gain the theoretical knowledge necessary to design a gown.

The initial mentor meeting

When the instructor has completed the initial telephone and written exchanges, he or she may choose to schedule a meeting with a potential mentor to further assess the situation or to provide more detailed information. If preliminary questions seem well-addressed and the mentor seems agreeable to meeting the student along with the instructor, the instructor may choose to include the student in an initial face-to-face meeting. Before final placement, however, students should always have the opportunity to meet with prospective mentors. Each of the three parties involved, instructor, student, and prospective mentor, should retain the right to veto pursuing the relationship any further until after the three parties have met and agreed to the terms of the mentorship.

Allowing students an equal say in establishing a mentorship fits with Richardson's (1987) observation of a shift toward greater mentee control in the mentor/mentee selection process. Richardson reports that those involved with youth mentoring believe greater mentee control establishes a relationship more like a spontaneous mentorship. However, no hard data has been derived to determine whether this method is better than matches made solely by program staff.

Zey (1985) also suggests that despite the additional effort, it may be advantageous to give participants in a mentor/mentee relationship as much control as possible in the selection process. Boston (1976) concurs, stating that mentor and mentee should "select each other in the context of a commitment [to the profession] which is being shaped (in the case of the pupil) or is already formed (in the case of the mentor)" (p. 33).

For Mentors: Your Expectations of Prospective Mentees

So far, this chapter has focused on selecting an appropriate mentor. Mentors may also wonder what they should look for in a prospective high-school-age mentee. *Mentor Program* staff can assist by suggesting criteria for selecting mentees to professionals. Certainly, if the student has been carefully screened and has completed a preparatory course like *Mentor Seminar*, the school has given considerable effort and expertise to the screening process. Most mentors really appreciate that. Yet, they should have the opportunity to assess students for themselves. They may also insist that their prospective mentees meet their own additional criteria, and rightfully so. The following section presents suggestions for mentors on selecting a mentee.

The first question a mentor might ask is: "Does this student really need a mentor?" The chart, "Identifying and Using Resources," Figure 1-1, suggests a broad range of ways for students to grow in their knowledge and skills in a particular field. Keeping in mind that not all of these resources are available to every student, mentors might consider whether the student has made an intensive effort to utilize available resources before requesting a mentorship.

Other questions to flesh out the answer to this question include: Has the student reached a level of expertise where her questions cannot readily be answered by school curriculum or basic library research? (The *Mentor Program* instructor can help answer this question.) Is he able to clearly articulate those questions? Does she have a strong vocabulary in the field? What products does he have to demonstrate previous work? (This might include a resumé of experiences, a reading list, a portfolio, written papers, project summaries like "I wrote a 30,000 word novel when I was fourteen," or " I conducted breeding experiments with waterfowl starting at age twelve.") Be sure to ask the student to explain the products to you in more depth to determine what he actually accomplished.

Other mentee traits to consider are based less on students' academic prowess, but on their personalities and interpersonal skills:

- Does the student communicate well with you, not only posing clear questions, but by listening carefully and responding thoughtfully to your conversation?

- Is the student committed to the opportunity? Has he left adequate time to meet your scheduling demands? Is he willing to meet your requirements as mentor and "go the extra mile?"

- After you have described what you have to offer the student, does she appear receptive to the opportunities and methodology you suggest? If the answer is no, this may require a bit more discussion with the student to determine why. Together you may be able to adapt and modify a plan.

- Does the student show signs of creativity, approaching problems in new ways?

Boston (1976) demands that prospective mentees have courage even if they "lack full competence" (p. 33). Courage, or the ability to take risks, is necessary for a student to attempt the transition into the adult world. However, students who pursue a nontraditional course like *Mentor Field Experience* and have completed the rigorous *Seminar* instruction are by definition risk-takers. Simply leaving the high school environment for instruction requires courage.

How a Business Decides To Participate in a Mentoring Program

Not only must prospective mentors be satisfied with their roles in a mentoring program, but their businesses must approve as well. Naturally, the *Mentor Program* staff wants satisfied businesses, too. While the benefits of participating in a mentoring program will be discussed in depth in Chapter 8, even understanding those benefits doesn't provide enough information for business managers to decide whether to become involved, nor does a strong sense of goodwill toward the community within a company. It's important to consider several additional issues to ensure a company's satisfaction with a mentoring program. A satisfied company helps ensure a successful educational experience for students, too.

The following section poses questions that businesses may want to resolve internally before deciding to participate in any business/school partnership. This demands communicating clearly and devoting company time and employee effort. If the commitment is there, the following points may help to ensure a successful experience for all. The key issues addressed throughout this section are summarized for easier use in Figure 4-2.

"What's in it for us?"

Several years ago I approached a large international corporation as a potential mentorship site for Carrie, an exceptionally capable young woman interested in chemical engineering. The company had an outstanding reputation for community service. Yet, as an outsider, I was intimidated by the vast corporate structure. The company's corporate campus resembles a major university with top-quality security measures. Fortunately, I established contact with a knowledgeable, well-respected employee who guided me through the company's infrastructure.

When I finally met with the research manager, Mr. Engle, he had already consulted with his superior, a vice president. When he began our meeting with the question, "What's in it for us?" I was taken aback. This corporation held high respect for its altruism and interest in the education and welfare of the community. Certainly, Mr. Engle and his

Fig. 4-2

Considering Business School Partnerships

For Businesses

1. Why are we willing to be involved as a partner?

2. What educational needs do we have as a business, and what needs must be met within our community's schools? What is the company's stake in education and the community?

3. What are we willing to offer in the partnership?

4. Who within our business will be a direct participant? In what capacity?

5. What do we expect in return for our contributions? Be as specific as possible.

6. How will we know if the partnership has met our expectations?

For Individuals

Review the above questions, seeking answers on a personal basis.

superiors must recognize the value of a mentoring experience for high school students.

In response to the question, I recited the litany of benefits for mentors and businesses presented in Chapter 8. I ended by saying that the best mentorships included a project where students not only advanced their learning, but also provided some service to mentors. Bingo!

Because neither mentors nor mentees receive pay for their services, the corporate research management had decided that in exchange for the learning, the student must contribute to the company in some way. They felt the best possible experience would be one which met the mentee's learning needs and simultaneously contributed to the company. Mr. Engle and his superior decided to train Carrie as a lab technician first, then allow her to conduct research under the direction of Mr. Lyons, a highly skilled chemist. In order to meet both sets of goals, Carrie would need to spend an additional four hours at the lab beyond the eight hours required by the program, plus travel time. In return the facilities and reputedly brilliant staff were at her disposal.

From this experience I learned that it's critical for businesses to ask themselves why they're willing to enter into this partnership. Whatever the answer may be, the decision to participate and the satisfaction of everyone involved results from a clear response to this question. By the time Carrie completed her experience under her mentor's direction, she had completed lab work on a chemical compound with new properties. The company applied for a patent including her mentor's name *and* Carrie's.

Other related questions business managers can ask are: What educational needs do we have as a business? What needs must be met within our community's schools? What is the company's stake in education and the community? The answers to these questions help to determine how much the company is willing to invest in a business and education partnership.

Assuming that the company's stake in the partnership is sufficient to proceed, the company must decide what it can contribute to the partnership. Possible issues might include:

- Can staff time be allocated?

- Can the company offer access to its facilities and specialized equipment?

- Is security or confidentiality an issue?

- Is office space available if needed to house the mentee?

- Will the company absorb certain expenses? In a mentoring program expenses beyond staff time are generally minimal; the cost of time on a mainframe computer, lab supplies, a smock or surgical garment might be examples. On occasion, mentors have offered to take students in the field or to a conference with them. The costs of any supplies needed to complete projects and of those outings have been negotiable in the *Mentor Program.* Most often, the companies absorb these costs, but sometimes students and their parents pay.

Another important question is: At the mentee's current level of expertise, what might he be able to learn from us? A resumé, portfolio, or interview with the prospective mentee may help to answer this question.

Not all businesses are as savvy as the chemical research corporation cited earlier in this chapter. When I asked a bank president, "What do you expect in return for your contributions to our program?" he became indignant. He thought the question was insulting, because I implied that businesses always expect a monetary payoff. At the time I was simply thinking about what support the business would need from the *Mentor Program* such as helping the student get a university library card, taking care of grading, or resolving any problems that might arise with the student's behavior. However, after the encounter with Mr. Engle, I believed businesses were entitled to a payoff—monetary or social.

While these are good examples of the communications pitfalls that arise between business people and educators, the bank president's interpretation certainly was not what I intended. The question, however, may be one of the most important ones for businesses to ask themselves. The success of the end result can only be determined by defining goals and expectations at the beginning of an endeavor.

Altruistic motives can indeed be realized if a business enters into a partnership with an educational program. Those motives must be clearly articulated so the business will be able to evaluate the outcomes. Among its altruistic motives, is the business looking for: increased feelings of satisfaction for its employees? a corporate opportunity to advance education or to become an active contributor to the community? to develop better citizens? an opportunity to reward the most skilled or dedicated workers? or all of the above? Whatever the goal, it will determine the company's approach to a mentorship.

For example, if the motive is to reward skilled or dedicated workers, then only those identified by the company as being deserving of the reward will be allowed to become mentors. If the company's goal was to increase employee satisfaction, their means of sanctioning mentorships would be very different. Likewise, a company would approach mentoring differently if its main goal was to help develop better citizens than if it were to reward employees or increase their job satisfaction.

Mentoring programs have been shown to influence career choice. By allowing interested students access to the workplace, they not only test their career preferences, they gain entry-level skills and sometimes beyond. This may be another reason for businesses to support mentoring. By allowing mentees access to a business and helping them build skills, business can develop a good recruitment process for mentees who show promise.

Business sense dictates that other payoffs are important, too. What business wouldn't want to generate goodwill in the community it serves? The publicity always helps, not only with goodwill, but in developing product awareness and a positive company image. There can also be tax incentives for partnering with education.

Besides projected goals, other company expectations should be considered. For example, if a business commits to mentoring, they agree to meet certain requirements defined by the high school. Fair play dictates that businesses should have expectations of the school and the student. The business might ask the school to prepare the student for the experience and be ready for it in general or more specific ways. The school may be asked to set these criteria or the business may assume that role. The business might inquire about the supervision the school will provide for the student to support the mentor's role. The business should also set the standards by which mentees must function within the organization such as punctuality, dress, work responsibilities, and interactions with people. Knowing what is expected never diminishes good intentions; it clarifies them and helps everyone be successful in their roles.

The individual mentor

Once the business approves participation and recruits prospective mentors, many of the issues the company discussed must also be considered on an individual level:

- What can you as a prospective mentor offer a young person interested in the field?

- Why do you want to participate? To guide a young person? To contribute to the profession? To improve the education of a young person? Because the responsibility was assigned?

- How might you accomplish your goal?

- What do you expect from the young person in return? This may be the most important question for prospective mentors in laying the foundations for a successful relationship.

One more suggestion. If the company intends to remain open to partnerships in education, it helps to designate one or two people as "education liaisons." Then, when questions arise internally, as well as externally, employees can access someone within the company as well as the mentor program instructor.

Establishing Mentorships that Work!

The instructor has approved the prospective mentor and the mentor has approved the prospective mentee. The match is in place. Two more factors must be addressed: The logistics of when and where the pair will meet and how they will proceed. This section explores those issues and offers advice on the role mentors can assume in aiding their mentees.

Planning logistics

With the broad variations in personality and style come a broad range of logistical possibilities for students: When will they meet? Where? How often? For how long? Perhaps the best way to approach meeting arrangements is to allow mentor and student to negotiate it themselves—being certain, of course, that students have allowed ample time in *their* schedules to be able to accommodate the mentors' needs.

For example, Carrie wanted to learn about chemical research and she had the opportunity for a mentorship with a research chemist employed by a corporation investigating nonlinear optics. Mr. Lyons, her prospective mentor, said that Carrie must spend large blocks of time (four hours minimum) three times weekly in order for her to have sufficient time to master the technical lab skills necessary for research and to be able to observe any chemical reactions.

Carrie was involved with many activites at her school and hesitated to commit that much time—and that much driving—but Mr. Lyon's demand was non-negotiable. She agreed to a regular Tuesday, Thursday, and Friday schedule. In a similar situation, another student opted for three afternoons to be decided each week to allow flexibility in his schedule. Another student asked to be released from school for one full day each week to learn with Mr. Lyons in his second *Mentor Program* experience.

Some mentorships demand far less time at the mentor's workplace: A student-writer needed much more time alone to write her play, and only one meeting a week to review and critique the writing with her mentor. They met each Friday at the mentor's home office or at a restaurant.

Allowing for the mentor's perspective

Mentors, of course, view things quite differently than either the course instructor or student. They want to know the time commitment they and other mentors must make to the student. They wonder about how the commitment will impact their work schedules. We have found that mentors do not want to be involved with disciplinary measures—students who do not report as scheduled, who consistently arrive late, or who do not clean up after themselves. Also, although they willingly write evaluations of students' skills, communications, and work habits, most mentors do not want to determine a letter grade (see Chapter 7).

Furthermore, mentors, like instructors and students, come in all shapes, sizes, personalities, and teaching styles. Some mentors may want an instructor to actively participate in designing a week-by-week learning plan for the student, or they may wish to devise their own structured plan independent of the instructor. Other mentors insist that they "go with the flow" of daily events and instruct students as the opportunity arises, not as planned. Therefore, while it is important to establish goals, guidelines, and a "blueprint" or plan for the mentorship (see Chapter 5), instructors must also allow mentors flexibility in each individual situation. However, instructors can share several key ideas about mentors' roles with their mentees.

The mentor's role

The mentor and pupil are *"servants of tradition,"* Boston (1976) has observed. They "share commitment to the truth of the tradition being communicated" (p. 16). Whether it be the literary tradition, the scientific realm of superconductivity, or the heritage of the field of human psychology, both mentor and mentee make a moral commitment to the tradition. That commitment is enhanced by the privileged relationship between them. Each relationship will be unique and will require special circumstances suitable to the two parties.

First and foremost, because of their greater experience, mentors *shape the circumstances* of the learning and the relationship for their mentees. Mentors provide their mentees with the opportunity to learn and time for instruction to take place.

The environment in which the student learns is also very important. Mentors can *shape the environment,* both physical and emotional, to meet the student's need. Mentors set the emotional tone of the relationship through, for example, their willingness to share information or include mentees. Emotional tone is also conveyed nonverbally through eye contact, tone of voice, and body language, as well as through conversation.

In the physical world, mentors offer mentees access to facilities and equipment that will help their pupils develop. Examples might include a modest work space, an electron microscope, lab equipment, or a priceless collection of original manuscripts and illustrations. Mentors teach from their world to that of the student.

Mentors *encourage dialogue.* Boston (1976) notes that mentors recapitulate the mentees' experiences. They "focus on the *appropriate* details of feelings and perceptions [of a situation]. What counts is what happened and what the mentor, because of his greater experience and knowledge, knows to be significant." (p. 16). Mentor and mentee exchange ideas about how to most accurately depict a character in a computer game, the appropriate supplies to create a work of art or to frame it, or how to remove a deeply imbedded brain tumor with minimum damage to the surrounding tissue.

Sometimes these challenges also allow the mentor to structure situations that *generate problems* for the mentee to ponder and suggest original solutions. One helpful process students can use to generate fresh answers is called creative problem solving (Nash & Treffinger, 1986; Feldhusen & Treffinger, 1985). In her book, *Mentoring: A Voiced Scarf,* Noller (1982) described how mentor and mentee can use creative problem solving as they work together.

Mentors provide *regular feedback* to their mentees on all aspects of the mentorship. They clarify the student's questions and their responses. Selecting the appropriate moment for feedback can result in greater strides for the mentee, "the teachable moment." For example, if the mentee is struggling to perfect the design of a pattern for a prom gown, the wise mentor will help her find a way to solve the problem before calling her to work on something different. The moment is right to give feedback on the pattern design. Mentors also find ways to regularly evaluate the students progress.

Through their examples, mentors *provide role modeling* for their mentees in situations such as courtroom etiquette, buying and selling stocks, restoring an airplane engine, or "sweet-talking" an upset chimpanzee. When mentors share their educational and work backgrounds, they model a path for an eager mentee to pursue.

Mentors can also role model personal traits such as a positive attitude, a sound work ethic, steadfast commitment, empathy, risk taking, flexibility, and communications skills. They can show mentees how to be aware of what is happening around them and to take advantage of their opportunities. Mentors can also actively encourage and instruct their mentees in developing these traits.

Mentors *establish connections between other professionals and their mentees.* This results in an invaluable resource to the mentees. It might include simply introducing the mentee to other staff, accompanying a mentee to a professional conference, allowing him to observe a meeting with clients, or requesting an appointment with a colleague who might further develop the mentee's knowledge of an area of mutual interest.

Mentors *advocate for their mentees,* give advice, and guide them in their learning. As a mentee noted of her mentor: "She makes me think about things, but never tries to force me . . . She treats me with a lot of respect, and I think she realizes the amount of respect I have for her."

Chauvin says (1988) that the role of a mentor can be "a powerful force in leadership development" for youth. On a lighter note, Noller (1982) summarizes the mentor's role through the adage "a guide by the side, not a sage on the stage" (p. 1).

Training mentors

Mentor Program staff have repeatedly asked mentors if they would like a formal training session, and they have collectively responded with a firm "no." The reasons most often cited are that a formal training session would take additional time away from the workplace and that the process described in this chapter serves as adequate training. Of course, instructors are always available to answer new questions as they arise.

At the end of our course, mentors complete a program (and student) evaluation form; responses confirm that training can be adequately completed through the process just described. In the Mentor Connection First Year Progress Report (Hess, 1984), for example, 90 percent of the mentors responded that the course structure and expectations of them were explained satisfactorily through contacts with the instructor and written material. This percentage has remained consistent ever since.

Given the individual nature of each mentor and student, and the unique circumstances of each mentorship, the *Mentor Program* staff considers this statistic ample evidence that a formal training session is unnecessary. In any case, the diversity of mentoring situations makes it difficult to be highly specific about what must occur within each placement. Furthermore, it takes time for student and mentor to understand the other's needs and situations. The instructor also generally enters a first meeting with limited knowledge of the field, the business, and the mentor.

Periodically, a mentor will suggest meetings to share experiences with other mentors. This seems to indicate a need for additional training or at least support. In response, the *Mentor Program* offered a voluntary mentor meeting about halfway through the course during two different school years. Approximately 25 percent of the mentors attended the first meeting and just one came to the second. Yet, more than 75 percent of the mentors have always attended the recognition or other events where students were involved. This seems to indicate that mentors will prioritize time for supporting their mentees, but do not feel they are able—or possibly need— to make time for meetings to support their mentoring. Since mentors work across an entire metropolitan area, travel time and, perhaps, winter weather may be factors.

Much of the training must occur as the instructor introduces the program and the mentorship is established. Again, clear communications count. If instructor, mentor, and student exchange ideas and goals, listen carefully and question, and maintain regular contact, training can be accomplished whether in formal sessions or through an evolving process.

One Mentor's Experience

Now that the mentor's decision to participate in the program has been discussed, it may be helpful to examine the experiences of one mentor. The following piece was written by Les Suzukamo, a mentor in the field of journalism. The article appeared in Suzukamo's column in the *St. Paul Pioneer Press Dispatch* in 1987. It is reprinted in its entirety with permission of the author and publisher.

Fig. 4-3

Mentor may have learned more than student in program

By Les Suzukamo

The call from Jill Reilly at the Dakota County Vocational Technical Institute was as bad as I feared.

Here's the pertinent information, she said:

The student's name is Holly Hillestad, age 17...a Hastings High School senior...Interested in journalism...Wants to be a foreign correspondent...

So happy to have you on board as her mentor this semester, Reilly added cheerfully before hanging up.

"Foreign correspondent," I thought to myself. "Lovely."

I had volunteered to be a "mentor" in the Vo-Tech's Mentor Connection program. The program pairs Dakota County high school students with professionals and business folk, and we, the professionals, are supposed to show the kids the ropes.

This was supposed to be fun but I was grumpy. It seems as though every high school kid interested in journalism wants to be a foreign correspondent. Have trench coat, will travel.

But what could I tell a kid about becoming a foreign correspondent?

I cover Dakota County and it's not as if I need a passport to go to Hastings.

I've been to France, but strictly as a tourist. (My wife promised dire things would happen to me if I took notes on vacation.) And I once hitchhiked to Canada when I was 19, but you can't exactly call the Great White North foreign territory.

But the first meeting with Holly wasn't so bad.

She and Reilly, the program's coordinator, came to the newsroom and we sat and chatted for awhile.

Holly impressed me. She was bright and showed initiative. Her resumé said she was in honors English and social studies classes and taking her fourth year of French.

It also said she had written a 30,000 word novel at age 14, written and directed skits, worked at an orphanage in Mexico and "read a lot of good books."

She was quick too. So quick that she ended up finishing several of my sentences for me. I guess senility slows you down at 30.

But boy, was she an awful speller. I counted several errors on her resumé and in her writing samples.

I set up a study program for Holly.

First of all, every week she would talk with a different reporter or editor about his or her job. I tried to choose a wide range of people to give Holly a flavor for the variety of a newspaper.

I concentrated, however, on loading her schedule with people with overseas experience. I was in luck at this paper.

We had Jacqui Banaszynski, one of our top reporters and a finalist for the Pulitzer Prize in international reporting for her powerful section in 1985 on the famine in Ethiopia and Sudan.

We also had Mitchell Pearlstein, an editorial writer. He visited the Soviet

Fig. 4-3 con't.

Union in 1986 and wrote a series of columns about his experiences, particularly his efforts to talk to "refusniks" – Soviet Jews who have been denied permission to emigrate to Israel.

The second part of the mentorship would consist of reading assignments, stories and exercises. The fun stuff.

Holly didn't always think so, however.

"I...got my two-and-a-half page critique," she wrote Jill Reilly in one of her regular progress reports. "He wasn't thrilled with it and I got my first taste of what it feels like to get a story back from an editor all hacked up. It's not a wonderful feeling."

Well, I had fun anyway.

The weeks did not always run smoothly. Things sometimes fell apart at the last minute. Once, I had three reporters in a row bow out of appointments to talk with Holly.

Ah, well, I told Holly. This is what sometimes happens at a real newspaper. Chaos. Confusion. The best laid plans of mice, men and journalists gone astray.

Secretly, though, I worried. Am I giving this kid what she really needs?

Sometimes the communication broke down, too.

Once, while discussing journalism ethics, I pulled out a golden oldie from my childhood in Los Angeles. It involved a 1969 story involving an allegation that Mayor Tom Bradley, then only a city council member and candidate for mayor, had won the support of the Black Panthers, the black radical group that reached its zenith in the late '60s.

Holly just stared at me, polite but without a clue as to what I was talking about. "What are the Black Panthers?" she finally asked.

I fumbled for words. "Uh, well, you

know. The Black Panthers!" Blank look. "The radical group?" More blank looks. "1969? Don't you remember?"

There was a long pause. "I was born in 1969," she said.

The Generation Gap lives.

I dredge all this up because the semester is over and we recently had a graduation ceremony of sorts at the Vo-Tech in Rosemount.

The participants presented their mentors with certificates of recognition and as each pair was introduced, Reilly told about different projects in which the mentor and student engaged for the semester.

Now that it's over, I occasionally wonder whether I gave Holly enough guidance. Too much? The right kind?

Beats me. I did the best I could, and now it's up to her. Which is as it should be.

As my final act as mentor, I was mailed a form by Jill Reilly asking me to evaluate Holly and the program. I did so, but I am writing now in the hopes that other adults out there will read it and maybe consider volunteering to be a mentor too.

I can remember teachers I admired and tried to emulate, and writers and reporters whose work I pored over, hoping to absorb their wisdom. Or at least a flashy *bon mot* or two.

I say this because I remember another high school kid, bright, gawky, but unlike Holly, a bit more of a smart aleck. He too wanted to be a foreign correspondent.

He too didn't know what the job required, except maybe speaking a foreign language.

He nearly flunked all his college French classes but somehow turned out OK.

He still is a horrendous speller.

Yeah. Me.

References

Bathke, J. L. (1990). *Mentor Connection: Students' perspectives.* Unpublished master's thesis, College of St. Thomas, St. Paul, MN.

Beck, L. (1989). Mentorships: Benefits and effect in career development. *Gifted Child Quarterly, 33*(1), 22-28.

Boston, B. O. (1976). *The sorcerer's apprentice: A case study in the role of the mentor.* Reston, VA: The Council for Exceptional Children.

Chauvin, J. C. (1988). Mentoring: A powerful force in leadership development. *G/C/T,* 24-25.

Clasen, D. R., & Hanson, M. (1987). Double mentoring: A process for facilitating mentorships for gifted students. *Roeper Review,* 10(2), 107-110.

Dimond, D. (Ed.). (1990). *Mentor Brochure.* (Rosemount, MN: Dakota County Mentor Program).

Feldhusen, J. F., & Treffinger, D.J. (1985). *Creative thinking and problem solving in gifted education.* Dubuque, IA: Kendall/Hunt.

Flaxman, I., Asher, C., & Harrington, C. (1988). *Youth mentoring: Programs and practices.* NY: Eric Clearinghouse on Urban Education.

Fox, L. H. (1979). Programs for the gifted and talented. In A. H. Passow (Ed.), in *The Gifted and Talented: Their Education and Development.* Chicago: University of Chicago Press.

Gray, W. A. (1988). Developing a planned mentoring program to facilitate career development. *Career Planning and Adult Development Journal,* 4(2), 9-16.

Haeger, W. W., & Feldhusen, J. W. (1989). *Developing a mentor program.* East Aurora, NY: D.O.K. Publishers.

Hess, K.M. (1984). *Mentor Connection first year evaluation report.* Minneapolis: The Educational Cooperative Service Unit of the Twin Cities Area.

Nash, D., & Treffinger, D. (1986). *The mentor.* East Aurora, NY: D.O.K. Publishers.

Noller, R. B. (1982). *Mentoring: A voiced scarf.* Buffalo, NY: Bearly Limited.

Reilly, J. M. (1990). [Fifth-year survey of Mentor Connection graduates]. Unpublished raw data.

Richardson, H. P. (1987). Student mentoring: A collaborative approach to the school dropout problem. In W.A. Gray & M.M. Gray (Eds.). *Mentoring: Aid to Excellence in Education, the Family, and the Community.* Proceedings of the First International Conference on Mentoring (Vol. I). Vancouver, BC: International Association for Mentoring.

Runions, T. (1980). The Mentor Academy Program: Educating the gifted/talented for the 80's. *Gifted Child Quarterly,* 24(4), 152-157.

Suzukamo, L. (1987). Mentor may have learned more than student in program. *St. Paul Pioneer Press Dispatch,* 1B.

Toropov, B. (Ed.). (1987). *The Minneapolis job bank.* Boston, MA: Bob Adams Inc.

Zey, M. G. (1985). Mentor programs: Making the right moves. *Personnel Journal,* 64(2), 53-57.

CHAPTER 5

Monitoring Students' Progress and Guiding Their Experiences

Because children are gifted does not mean that they will discover,

on their own, the opportunities available to them, nor the

multidimensional potential of their abilities . . . The potential

contribution of such a population to society is staggering and every

effort must be made to help gifted students make informed career

choices that will be comfortable for them and productive for society.

— Robert Simpson and Felice Kaufman
"Career Education for the Gifted"
Journal of Career Education

Has any teacher ever escaped the eternal question, "Why do I have to learn this? I'll never use it outside of school." An eleventh-grader's weekly progress report illustrates the impact of making real-life connections through a mentorship. The connections between learning and life in a mentorship increase students' motivation and their sense of direction. However, the learning is most powerful when nurtured by both partners in "double mentoring," the mentor and the *Field Experience* instructor. Kara's story provides one example.

Kara had always been identified as gifted, but she was not achieving in high school as one might expect. She described herself as being "burned out with school." Searching for new resources, Kara applied to the *Mentor Program.*

Kara's family had a history of concern for wildlife, and she was an active young woman. Kara wanted to combine those interests in her *Field Experience.* After extensive research, she was placed with a field biologist specializing in raptors, or birds of prey, at a nationally renowned rehabilitation center. Her mission was to learn to help return eagles to the wild after they had been found injured then rehabilitated. Kara and her mentor also followed the eagles' nesting patterns after their return to the wild.

The experience described here took place in January 1990. Kara had just observed veterinarians reconstructing a tail for a peregrine falcon and technicians working on hematology in the laboratory. She wrote in a weekly progress report to her instructor:

> *The whole day I did understand what was going on, but I don't have enough background classes to understand the things there the way I want to know them. I want to learn the specific, detailed hard stuff like anatomy or the parts of a cell. I think realizing this has motivated me to try harder and learn more in my regular classes. I know I can't learn this in my mentorship, but I can define what I want to learn outside of it. I almost died when I saw my advanced algebra trigonometry in a procedure report for sexing an eagle!*

Unlike other animals, the gender of an eagle cannot be determined simply by looking: An eagle's gender can be determined either by algebraic calculations or by surgically opening the eagle to observe *internal* organs. For Kara and other students like her, connections rapidly occurred when she realized the value of "book knowledge" in a professional setting. Her desire to learn became reignited, and she received considerable support from her *Mentor Program* instructor in "getting her act together."

Together they worked on organizing her calendar and her work. The instructor helped her find background readings to help her make even more sense of what she observed. Her school grades began to rise, and the following fall she reported, "I did get an A in advanced algebra trig that semester and my grades went up overall."

With proper guidance and support, many students experience dramatic learning surges both in a particular topic or field and in their own self-awareness. This chapter includes strategies for reinforcing and advancing the skills students develop in preparation for the mentorship and for clear and efficient communications with students and mentors. It also describes the teacher's role in effectively monitoring the individual student's progress and guiding the class as a unit.

Time Commitment for Field Experience

Becoming involved

By the time students enter *Mentor Field Experience,* they have been screened for the program and have done extensive background work not only on their fields of study, but also on the interpersonal skills required to function in the workplace. Students should have a clear focus within the field (not medicine, but research on liver glycogen metabolism) as placement with appropriate mentors is under way.

Students enroll for the *Field Experience* course during the last two class periods every day. They are expected to spend a minimum of eight hours of class time (two class periods x four days weekly = eight hours) learning directly about their fields of interest under the direction of their mentors. Students are released from school after fifth period each day, so they can pursue appropriate meetings and activities. Commuting time is not included in accounting for hours of work.

The last periods of the day allow the greatest flexibility for students to schedule time with their mentors. For example, students whose mentors' workplaces are within the community may spend four afternoons within the sixth and seventh periods at their mentor sites. Others may choose to spend from one o'clock to five o'clock two days a week to meet the eight-hour minimum requirement, or some even choose to spend all day Saturday. Hospitals and weather services are among the mentoring sites that regularly offer this option.

Mentor students reserve one two-class-period session weekly to meet with their instructor and other *Field Experience* students. The weekly *Field Experience* class meetings provide students with a nucleus of expectations and support for their mentorships. The functions of the class include communicating about the mentorship, completing related assignments including the project, sharing learning with the class, solving any problems that arise, and supporting each mentee.

Attendance

Keeping attendance records in a uniquely structured class like *Mentor Field Experience* challenges the system, particularly if the system demands that teachers rigorously monitor students' presence. However, the *Mentor Program* staff have devised an attendance system that works well. The system reinforces three of the traits critical to successful mentorships: responsibility, reliability, and student initiative. The policy is stated in Figure 5-1. After the policy is explained to students and they have the opportunity to ask questions, they sign one copy and return it to the instructor. Students receive a copy of the attendance policy to keep with the course syllabus (see Figure 5-1 and Figure 5-2).

Monitoring Mentorships through Weekly Class Sessions

Class discussion

If the school grants credits and grades equivalent to two courses for *Field Experience* and the mentors do not wish to grade the experience, the instructor's primary task will be to monitor and validate students' experiences. The instructor accomplishes this in two ways: through conversations with students in class and with assigned written weekly reports.

Many students like to share their experiences verbally with an audience. In classroom conversations, most students will discuss readily the positive events of their mentorships. Through sharing and respectful responses to what is shared, a climate of trust develops between the

Fig. 5-1

MENTOR PROGRAM FIELD EXPERIENCE ATTENDANCE POLICY

1. One attendance day equals two hours of time in class or with mentor.

2. Because class is more difficult to make up, students will be allowed three absences from class from the start of school until the end of the trimester. You must telephone your instructor when absent from class. A notice will be sent to parents and attendance office after second absence from class. Upon the fourth absence, the student will fail. Students must request make-up assignments from the instructor the first day they return from an absence.

3. If you are going to miss time with your mentor or be late to a meeting, you must telephone him or her immediately. Regardless of the reason for missing any time required outside of our classroom, you will have two weeks to make up the work. If you miss more than eight hours of time for work on your mentorship, you must present your instructor with a written proposal explaining how the work will be made up at the class meeting following the eighth hour missed. The instructor will approve the plan. You will have two weeks from the date of your return to class to make up the work. A notice will be sent informing parents and attendance office of the absences and the make-up work the student must complete. (Make-up work will be based on the student's individual topic of study.) If the make-up work is not completed within two weeks, the highest grade the student will be able to receive for the course is a B.

   If you fall 16 hours behind in work, you will have two weeks from the date of the last absence to submit an amended make-up proposal and complete all make-up work. The instructor will approve the plan. At the time of the 16th hour of missed work, a failing notice will be sent to parents and attendance office. If the work is not made up within two weeks, the student will fail the course.

   I have read this policy and understand what is expected of me.

   _____   _____
   Date   Signature

Fig. 5-2

Class Meets:
Tuesdays sixth and seventh hour in room [   ]. In addition, you are
required to work a minimum of eight hours per week with your mentors or on
tasks relating to the mentorship. Mentors and students determine which hours
they will work.

The Mentor Field Experience Course
For students who have successfully completed Mentor Seminar and who wish to
continue their studies with a professional in the field. Students will be
placed as promptly as possible with a mentor. Together with their mentors and
the instructor, students will develop an individualized learning plan and a
project in their individual fields of study.

Student Expectations
Learning
• Students will study and work independently throughout the course.
• Students will focus on a specific topic about which to learn at an
  advanced level.
• Students will demonstrate advanced-level learning about an individual
  field of interest through a final project and oral presentation.
• Students will write in-depth reports of their learning experiences each
  week to meet standards set on weekly evaluation sheet attached.
Interpersonal relationship
• Students will sustain a successful working relationship
  with their mentors.
Responsiblity & Reliability
• Students are expected to report for mentorship and class
  punctually and regularly.
• You are required to telephone the mentor if you must be late or miss a
  meeting, and to contact the instructor if you will miss class.
• It is the student's responsibility to make up missed mentorship
  and classwork.
• All assignments are expected to be turned in on time. If that becomes
  impossible, it is the student's responsibility to discuss the problem
  with the instructor before the assignment due date or as soon as possible
  after that time.

Course texts
• Mentor Connection Notebook received during Seminar.
• Seminar Journal & Notebook: 3-hole punched spiral notebook with at least
  three section markers begun during Seminar.

Supplies
Supplies needed to complete project.

Transportation
Transportation to and from mentor site including gasoline and parking fees
is the responsibility of the students and their parents.

Grading
Students will receive points for each class assignment. At the end of the
course grades will be awarded on the total percentage of points earned:
   90-100%   - A
   80-89%   - B
   70-79%   - C
   60-69%   - D
   below 60%   - F

Continuation of Field Experience
Students must earn a minimum of an 85% grade average to be eligible for the
Mentor Field experience. If you wish to continue Field Experience beyond
one trimester, you must submit a written proposal for learning and a
project two weeks prior to the end of this quarter. The learning and
project must be at a more advanced level than the previous timester and
must continue to challenge you to achieve your best. Of course your mentor
and your instructor must approve continuing at your current mentor site,
and your instructor must approve a new placement.

Project
Each student will complete a project that demonstrates advanced-level
learning in a field of interest. Students will exhibit their projects at
the Annual Dinner and Open House, tentatively scheduled for [   ].

Faculty Contacts
Faculty contacts will receive written weekly report of the student's
progress while working with a mentor in the student's interest area.
Students are required to meet twice during the trimester with their
faculty contacts: During the first meeting (by   ), you should discuss
and review your mentor placement and student blueprint (individualized
learning plan). A second, follow-up meeting with your faculty contact
should take place toward the end of field experience (by   ) to review
your project as you come close to completing it. Reports on these meetings
will be included in the weekly letter due the Tuesday following the
meeting. Faculty contacts are invited to participate in a on-site visit
with the mentor and will be invited to attend the Dinner and Open House
when the student completes the field experience.

instructor and the students. Each class session can add to the overall atmosphere. Once trust becomes established, the instructor can learn a lot about what happens on a day-to-day basis in the mentorship and offer support at the same time. In addition, students learn from hearing the similarities and differences between mentorships and from helping others resolve their difficulties.

Regular questions of the day help establish a more thoughtful approach to the mentorship. Some helpful questions include: What was the most exciting part of your week (or your mentorship to date)? What was the most challenging part of your mentorship this week? What did you learn about this week? What does your mentor like best about his job? What does she like least? Can you see yourself continuing in this role? In what situations have you observed your mentor using any of the skills (or a single one like assertiveness) we discussed in *Seminar*? How is the company organized? What is the chain of command? How does your mentor make decisions? When you observe your mentors making a decision, ask them to share how they arrived at it. Describe your mentor site in five sentences.

These questions stimulate discussion on issues ranging from how to handle working with a dying child to a mentee's sense that he is not learning enough within the placement. They also reinforce interpersonal skills introduced during *Mentor Seminar*. With a particularly thought-provoking question, asking the students to quickly write their responses before sharing can enhance the depth and quality of their comments.

Class discussions work well because everyone can hear all the comments; small groups allow more time for each person to speak. In small groups, students seem better able to support each other. With a particularly important topic, an instructor might choose to start discussion in small groups, then have students share the most salient points with the entire class. Students really appreciate and enjoy each other in any of these situations. As one student recently told me, "I've made a whole new set of friends in mentor class." Others said that they rarely had the opportunity to develop rapport with a class as a group before, and this is important to them.

Integrating past lessons

During class discussion many of the topics introduced during the *Seminar* class resurface. While students applied the skills they learned at that time, the topics gain even more relevance with a real-life backdrop, the mentorship. Kubota and Olstad (in press) found that students need several related experiences for concepts to be learned well, and the mentorship provides exactly that for ongoing *Mentor Program* students. Harte (1989) noted that "activities must regularly stimulate mental connections between experiences and abstractions as effectively as Spielberg movies stimulate the senses" (p. 98). When a student very much wants to be included in an activity with his mentor but feels he cannot ask, for example, the moment has arrived to link the concept of assertiveness to practice.

Wagner (1983) noted another task of a *Field Experience* instructor is to create an "educationally productive tension between the classroom instruction and the off-campus experience" (p. 8). Students are forced to probe their initial observations and responses to their mentorships and the skills demanded of them. They rethink the underlying concepts relevant to their experiences and arrive at a new depth of understanding. Kubota and Olstad (in press) found that connecting this kind of higher order thinking—analyzing, synthesizing, evaluating—to students' experiences ensures that they will achieve their personal bests.

Periodically, students experience new situations and need information which can be supplied through the classroom. For example, a student told the instructor that her mentor called her gifted, and she wonders what that really means. The class shares their understandings of giftedness with the perplexed student. Next week, the teacher or a guest expert on giftedness might follow up on the original class discussion. Another example involves the inevitable moment when students declare they are "stressed out." A class session on stress management would be appropriate.

In another situation, a mentor invited his mentee to a business luncheon. The student wondered about etiquette for the affair. The next class session, the teacher provided information and resources about etiquette. Another approach to this situation might be to ask for student volunteers to research business etiquette during the week and to present what they learned.

Examples like these arise frequently and can be incorporated into the *Field Experience* class curriculum. The real power of a mentoring experience is the opportunity for students to think about their personal experiences and integrate their realizations into their daily lives just as Kara did at the beginning of this chapter. These moments of inquiry are treasures which the wise instructor will nurture into meaningful personal growth. When students ask, it's time to teach them.

Weekly reports

To be sure that each student's experience is carefully and regularly reviewed, everyone submits a weekly report. In a business-letter format addressed to the instructor, students account for the total numbers of hours they spent working each week, detail the various activities in which they were engaged, and account for the number of hours spent on each activity. The key to the report lies in a thorough explanation of what the student learned during the week. This leads students to rethink the week's events and to recapitulate their learning in layman's terms. Since instructors want to know how students feel about their work, students are also asked to describe their reactions.

In closing students outline their plans for the next week. This helps them form the habit of planning ahead and of asking their mentors to provide a preview of the coming week. Also, when mentor and mentee plan for the following week, mentors begin to consider the tasks ahead a little more in advance. Mentees know what to expect and the days to meet; and if the mentor plans to be gone, the mentee can ask for suggestions about what to do in his or her absence. Mentees are always responsible for having backup tasks in case the mentor is not available. They may have reading to do, tasks to complete for their projects, other staff or professionals within the field with whom to confer, or an exhibit to visit. The backup activities can be any form of independent study which meets the mentor's approval. The concept of students assuming responsibility for independent learning is important because mentors will be absent and the student's time should be used as wisely as possible.

Students also complete a Weekly Evaluation sheet which is handed in with the letter. The evaluation prods the students to think about how well they accomplished what was expected of them (see Figure 5-3). It would be easier for students to let the instructor worry about evaluating their work, but self-evaluation holds them more accountable. Besides, in the workplace the individual is responsible for his or her performance.

After receiving the letters and evaluations, the instructor may grade the week's work and provide feedback to the students. The instructor keeps the letters, but returns the Weekly Evaluation sheets to the students with comments. Students are urged to keep copies of the letters for their own reference.

On the Weekly Evaluation form, students are asked to account for their personal reading or reference list in standard APA style. They also keep a contact list—a directory of all people with whom they have made a connection—including titles, companies, addresses, and telephone numbers. Students often wonder about the value of these assignments, but in months and years to come most are pleased to be able to locate again an article they read or to contact someone with skills or information they need.

After receiving the letters each week, the instructor mails a copy to the appropriate mentor. This is why instructors demand that students write their reports in correct business-letter format and pay attention to usage, spelling, and the appearance of the letter. The students want to represent themselves well to a significant individual and also to demonstrate the standards of written communications expected within their schools.

Generally, the instructor will also enclose a note to each mentor along with the letter. The note might include observations, comments, questions or suggestions such as "I've watched Dave come alive since he met you! He can't wait to show us what he's done each week." "Thank you for the special opportunity you gave Angie when you took her to the marine life convention." "Do you think Katie can complete the project she has planned in the time available?" or "Please let me know if Sandy misses another meeting or arrives late."

Fig. 5-3

MENTOR PROGRAM WEEKLY PROGRESS REPORT EVALUATION

DATE .... **STUDENT NAME** ....

STUDENT'S EVAL.	TEACHER'S EVAL.	POINT TO EVALUATE (MAXIMUM)
____	____	How well did you complete 8 hours of work outside class? (15)
____	____	Rate the quality of this week's work. (20)
____	____	How much improvement did you make this week in the areas on which you are working? (5)
____	____	How accurately did you detail activities and the time spent on each? (10)
____	____	How well did you explain what you learned this week? (20)
____	____	How honestly did you describe your reaction to this week's work? (5)
____	____	How well did you describe your plans for next week? (5)
____	____	Rate the form and content of your reference list. Is it up to date? (5)
____	____	Rate the form and content of your contact list. Is it up to date? (5)
____	____	Rate how thoroughly your letter reflects acceptable business format. Include neatness, appropriate paper, procedure, spelling, and grammar. (10)
____	____	TOTALS (100)
____	____	Subtract 10 points for each week this letter is late.

• • •

149

The weekly reports allow instructors to keep abreast and minimize the time mentors must spend reporting. Mentors regularly say that they find the letters the most valuable assistance they receive from the program. They enjoy the weekly reports and appreciate them. Students, on the other hand, find the letters less enjoyable to prepare although they recognize their value.

Individual meetings with students

In addition to group meetings and activities with their *Field Experience* class, students also have individual appointments with the instructor during the two-hour class period of the term. This provides each student and the instructor with an opportunity to communicate about all aspects of the *Field Experience* including class time, the student's relationship with a mentor, and aspects of the learning that are particularly rewarding or troublesome.

Instructors pay particular attention to how the learning is progressing: Does the student seem to make gains each week? Does the relationship between mentor and mentee appear conducive to learning? Is the project progressing on schedule? Instructors also simply want to chat with students to see if new information surfaces regarding the mentorship. Individual meetings are good times to build rapport with students.

Establishing a Blueprint for Learning

Mapping overall goals and how to attain them.

Perhaps the most difficult part of the entire mentorship comes when students are asked to write a plan. This written plan is called a blueprint for the mentorship. The planning process requires students to set priorities for their learning, then discuss those goals with their mentors. This process decides the course of the mentorship. When planning, mentor and mentee should consider not only what the mentee wants to learn, but what she can realistically accomplish during the weeks allotted. The blueprint should list as specifically as possible each of the skills the mentee must acquire to achieve his goal. It generally takes mentor and mentee two to four weeks to get to know each other and the situation, and, therefore, to plan and write the blueprint.

It is the student's responsibility to schedule time with the mentor to plan the blueprint; the student then writes up the blueprint.

Sometimes students know immediately what their goals are in general terms, but don't know how to break each goal into manageable steps. The mentor's technical expertise helps here. For example, consider Paul's goal: "I want to learn to teach a lesson to an entire elementary class." Paul had tutored extensively and taught religion to a small group. He had concerns about managing a large group, but did not know what he would need to learn in order to teach a lesson well. After careful thought, discussion, and evaluation, Paul and his mentor, Mr. Arnold, a fifth grade teacher, decided that Paul would need to expand his repertoire of classroom management skills before he could successfully conduct a lesson which included the whole class. In addition, he would need to learn the basics of lesson design.

From reading his letters and hearing his comments in class, I began to understand how Paul's planning had progressed. Because his goal centered around gaining instructional expertise, I suggested that he take a two-day "Elements of Instruction" workshop given to new teachers in our district. Paul agreed, and his high school allowed him the two days away from his other classes as a field trip.

Paul's blueprint outlined his plans to continue to tutor one-on-one to gain more experience in instructional technique. Paul also would begin to assist Mr. Arnold with small portions of classroom lessons and their grading and evaluation. Paul agreed to read a book on assertive discipline and another on lesson design. As his knowledge of classroom management developed, Paul helped more with teaching the class. When he felt ready, he had the opportunity to plan lessons and to teach them. Mr. Arnold's feedback and coaching provided the catalyst for putting the theory Paul learned into practice. Paul's blueprint allowed him to progress in his development as a teacher and to achieve his ultimate goal of teaching the class lessons.

Secondary goals

As students write their blueprints, naturally they focus on their personal preferences for learning. In selecting to learn about what they love, students may disregard other options for personal growth that might be equally beneficial and easily incorporated into their blueprints for the mentoring experience. Consider Don's plan for mentorship as a case in point.

In Chapter 4 Don, the computer programmer and "man of few words," was introduced. Don wanted to write programs for accounting systems. The learning goals written into his blueprint focused on learning the appropriate computer language, operating a mainframe, and obtaining the accounting background necessary to write a portion of the company's current programming project. Don was happy; his learning needs were being met—or at least that's what he thought.

As a result of *Mentor Seminar* Don had shown considerable growth in his verbal communications and use of body language. He understood the basic concepts of interpersonal communications, and he greeted people with a firm handshake, eye contact, and an occasional smile. He even grasped the importance of his nonverbal messages; but these skills do not develop overnight nor does practice with a teacher and classmates constitute "the real thing." Don, his parents, and I all knew he needed to continue to develop those skills, but they were not as much fun or easy for him to acquire as programming expertise. Communications skills never entered into his thinking when he planned his mentorship.

Acting as "the second mentor," I asked Don and his mentor if Don would have any responsibilities for collaborating with or reporting to other staff. Don's mentor told me that a team of employees created all of their programs, and they definitely would include Don as a team member. Without really raising the issue of Don's needs, Don and his mentor agreed that clear communications with the team should be added to Don's blueprint as a secondary goal. This would keep Don more formally aware of developing those skills.

Depending on the student's individual needs, a vast range of skills may be incorporated as secondary goals. Other skills that may become secondary goals of mentorships are organizational, time management, or written communication skills.

Project

Because learning takes place outside of the school and away from the instructor, students must further validate and document their experiences in a clearly observable fashion. This is accomplished through a project in addition to weekly progress reports and other class assignments. In recent years, educators have begun to demand much more of this outcome-based learning. In addition, students have said that they gain real satisfaction from creating a tangible product.

What the project entails is as unique as each set of individuals who participate as mentor and mentee. Certainly, the best projects are ones which assist mentors with their work in some way. Projects also should stretch and challenge the students' learning. However, the projects should not constrain students so much that they are unable to participate in other activities or experiences.

Some projects do become the entire focus of the mentorship. All of Don's learning—including oral communications—centered around his project, that of designing a portion of an accounting program. The final product, which was sold as part of a software package, did not directly reflect the gains Don made in communicating with others. The project reflected most of what he learned, but not everything.

Another student researched the migration, mating, and breeding habits of waterfowl on a local lake. His mentor worked with a state department of natural resources, and the question they sought to answer was whether that particular lake should be maintained in its natural state to preserve the waterfowl or if it could be developed for housing. Again, everything this student learned was focused toward completing his project.

A third student created the first edition of his own comic book series. Through this project, he learned the cartooning techniques he so wanted and needed. His project actually entailed much more than his learning goals. In addition to improving his drawing techniques, he had to work on dialogue, profile characters, block space for each drawing, find new and better materials for his work, and design a business card.

In other cases, the project reflects only a few components of the entire experience. Paul designed lessons to teach "his" fifth graders when an aquarium was installed in their classroom. He also launched a clean-desk project to help students better organize their belongings and to prepare for lockers in middle school. While he accomplished this at a professional level, Paul's projects hardly demonstrated the scope of all he planned to learn in his blueprint. He had assisted in every afternoon activity of that class four days a week for twelve weeks, tutored, assisted with teaching in most subjects, designed original curriculum, taught his own lessons, graded papers, planned bulletin boards and was generally "in the trenches," as he put it. He demonstrated this learning to his mentor. His *Field Experience* instructor visited the class twice to observe, in addition to reading his weekly reports.

Completing the blueprint

Students and mentors need to know the instructor's expectations, but learning and project guidelines should not be too confining. Some mentors would truly prefer to have the instructor outline and structure the entire learning experience for them and their mentees. Unfortunately, instructors know far too little about many of the fields to help much beyond asking relevant questions and listening carefully.

For example, one mentor expressed concern about how to plan a blueprint for his mentee in aviation. I knew nothing about the field. All I could do was explain the basic program structure, hours the mentee would be available, and that while the mentee would have loved to have ground or flight training, he could get that at a flight school or college. The *Mentor Program* does not include lessons which are readily available from other sources. Given the guidelines, I asked the mentor what he thought would be most important for his mentee to learn. Immediately he listed several topics. Then we chatted for a while about how much time each of those topics would take to teach and how they would fit into the time frame of the course. Ultimately, the mentor and his mentee developed a clear, structured plan that allowed for investigation of flight planning, airplane mechanics, understanding the instruments in the cockpit, and piloting for private business versus commercial piloting.

Another mentor told me that he understood why the project was a valid requirement. However, doing the project well consumed time he felt could have been used for more valuable activities such as taking his mentee into the field to see architectural designs being built and coming to life. He also asked that he be allowed to leave the experience unstructured so he and his mentee could capitalize on opportunities as they arose.

Many other mentors have felt this way, too. Some like to instruct their mentees according to the flow of business, like the mentor in public relations who provided a substantial and diverse learning experience while conducting business as usual. However unstructured the learning plan, the student must write the overall goals of the mentorship and develop a project which demonstrates that at least a portion of the learning goals was accomplished. I also ask that mentor and mentee establish a timeline for the project. This allows mentees to gauge their progress regularly.

The pilot and the architect have very different needs when it comes to establishing a plan for the mentorship and different approaches to a project (and so do their mentees). This challenges the instructor to remain flexible while providing guidance in creating an educationally meaningful experience. Sometimes, mentor and mentee will find that their blueprint doesn't fit with a new interest or problem which emerges. Again, the instructor needs to remain open to a change, yet insist upon clear communication between mentee, mentor, and instructor to renegotiate a blueprint plan.

Faculty Contacts

As seen in the example of the mentor in aviation, mentoring program instructors will not always grasp the technical subtleties of the fields their students explore nor will mentors always have the pedagogical expertise to generate the best learning strategies or project ideas. This leaves a gap for students as they plan their blueprint and projects. Sometimes they need a knowledgeable and interested person with whom to chat. Faculty contacts can fulfill this need.

As discussed in Chapter 4, during *Seminar* each student selected a faculty member with expertise in the student's own field of interest. The students met with their faculty contacts twice during *Seminar* for help with their projects. When *Field Experience* begins, the faculty contacts are generally abreast of students' progress and willing to continue to help.

Similarly, the instructor may need a second opinion or an interpretation on a particular person's activities. The instructor might need to ask: What does this technical term mean? Is the student taking on more than she can accomplish? How does this project stretch Tom beyond the school's science curriculum? The faculty contacts can provide needed support to the instructor as well as the student.

Reestablishing contact

Early in the *Field Experience,* students get in touch with the teacher who acted as a faculty contact during *Seminar.* Some students opt to change faculty contacts or ask for advice of another teacher they know outside of their high school. For example, once connected with his mentor, the cartoonist decided he no longer needed an art faculty contact as much as he needed an English teacher who would help him to edit the dialogue in his comic book. Students are again responsible for scheduling the meeting and requesting assistance.

As in the *Seminar* phase, faculty contacts commit to two meetings during the trimester. The first meeting allows contacts to review and discuss the mentor placement and blueprint for learning with the student. The second meeting is a follow-up visit at a time during the trimester when it seems most appropriate to the student. Generally, students like to show their projects to their faculty contacts when the projects are almost complete, but with enough time remaining to implement suggestions about improvements or "finishing touches." Faculty contacts may also want to receive copies of the students' written weekly progress reports to keep them informed.

Benefits

Of course, faculty contacts continue to receive benefits from the experience, too. Besides the satisfaction of supporting students to extend their learning outside of the classroom, faculty contacts are invited to attend a recognition event after students complete the *Field Experience.* Being a contact also gives teachers an opportunity to actively participate in a workplace partnership with education and to interface with other professionals in their specialty area by telephone or by on-site visit during the school day or after school. In addition, district relicensure committees have offered credit hours for assuming the role of a faculty contact.

Mentees Teach the Class: Reinforcing Learning

Mentees also receive support during the times when the entire *Field Experience* class meets each week. Some of the key functions of the weekly class are to monitor, reinforce, and support what the mentees are learning. Asking students to teach the rest of the group about their field of interest can best meet this goal.

The National Training Laboratory in Maine has compiled the following statistics on learning and retention:

We retain 10 percent of what we hear.

We retain 15 percent of what we see.

We retain 20 percent of what we see and hear.

We retain 40 percent of what we discuss.

We retain 80 percent of what we experience directly.

We retain 90 percent of what we teach.

According to these statistics, teaching seems the best way to maximize what students learn. The "teachers" are not the only ones to benefit. How often do any of us get to hear the latest from the fashion management of a major department store or cutting-edge neurosurgery techniques? These presentations open horizons for all who hear them.

So, at least once during the term, *Field Experience* students teach their class a brief lesson about their areas or study. After spending three to four weeks with their mentors, they have gained more than enough information and confidence to sustain a brief lesson. The class usually gasps when an instructor suggests that they teach a ten minute lesson. "Ten minutes seems so long," students say. "In speech class our final speech is only five minutes."

When they actually teach, most presentations run over twenty minutes; some students could continue for hours. After all, they have invested twenty-five or more hours in their mentorships at this point.

Because the mentorship consumes so much of their concentration, the *Mentor Program* instructors prefer to have the first teaching sessions remain informal. The instructor stresses a few key points that will most help the "teachers" organize their lesson and allow the audience to gain as much as they can from the presentation.

The first thing the students must consider is: When I have finished this presentation, what will my audience be able to do to *show* me what they have learned? After all, students give their presentations not only to crystallize their own learning, but to teach others about something of personal importance. They should be sure that others understand their points and leave with something worthwhile in mind.

The National Training Laboratory statistics which began this section show that in order to give their audiences the best chance of retaining the information presented, the audience must experience it or do it. How will the presenter know if the audience learned anything unless there is some way for them to show it? Examples of what to expect can help students decide their own goals for teaching. Will the class be able to label the anatomy of a bottlenose dolphin and state three different social behaviors of the species? Will they be able to label the main pattern pieces of the garment the student designed and will be constructing? Will they be able to create an advertisement for their own mentorship site? These are a few of the activities students have used in past teaching sessions.

Once students have decided what their audience will be able to do as a result of their own lesson, they list up to six key points they must explain in order for the audience to master their task. Then they plan how to share the information. Some possibilities include talking about the topic, using transparencies, maps, videos, or handouts like crossword puzzles, lists of terms, or fill in the blanks. In making these decisions, students must ask themselves which means of sharing information will most involve the audience and keep them interested. At this point, exchanging ideas with one or two other classmates can be very helpful.

Now the "teachers" are ready to devise an attention-getting opening. The best openings coax the audience to focus on what they already know about the topic. The opening should also summarize the main points covered in the talk. Similarly, the closing should recap those same points. Figure 5-4 shows a worksheet students may use to prepare for each aspect of teaching the class.

These original lessons presented by their fellow students interest the class greatly. When they are done informally, it is easier to use the lessons as experience in teaching or presenting clearly. I also ask the audience to write a short critique for each presenter commenting on strengths and one area to polish.

As a follow-up, *Mentor Program* staff try to arrange a more formal teaching session for each student to share with an elementary, junior high, or high school class or a community organization. This more serious engagement pushes the students to polish their presentations. It also offers students the opportunity to share with others the great experiences their mentors give them. In essence, these presentations expand the mentors' abilities to share their expertise with a larger audience.

In the Field: Coordinating Between Mentors and Mentees

The initial meeting between prospective mentor, mentee, and instructor sets the preliminary expectations and tone for the mentorship experience. The weekly reports provide a system of regular communications between the student, the instructor, and the mentor; the completed blueprint provides a draft for the mentorship. Much of the *Field Experience* is established through this channel of communication.

Telephone calls

Beyond the initial meeting and the weekly reports, mentor and instructor require minimum contact with each other. Instructors might telephone the mentor about three weeks after the *Field Experience* has begun to inquire about the mentor's perspective of the experience to date and to answer any questions that may have arisen. Most frequently,

Fig. 5-4

Purpose. What will the students listening be able to do when I have finished? Hint: This should relate to an **activity** the students will do. At the end of my talk the students will be able to:

Opening.

1. Gets attention.
2. Relates to what you are doing.
3. Helps students think about what they already know about the topic.
4. Summarizes your major points.

My opening:

Information I will share. Stick to no more than 6 main points. List them.

1.
2.
3.
4.
5.
6.

How will I share information? I will talk about what I know. I will give a handout. I will write on the board or overhead transparencies. I will ask the students. I will bring things to show (like maps, recordings, tools, examples, sheets you use, samples of your work, photographs). YOU SHOULD USE AT LEAST TWO DIFFERENT TECHNIQUES. List below how you will share this information.

Write up student activity. Be sure it suits your purpose as stated above.

Supplies you need to bring or the school should have on hand.
Examples: chalk, overhead projector, recorder, handouts, paper for students, pencils, rulers, magazine cutouts, things you want to show.

Closure. Summarize main points.

the mentors ask questions about the overall plan or the project. They also wonder about how to best deal with individual needs or quirks such as the student who expects to participate in activities that only true experts may tackle or the student who lacks confidence or ability to communicate what he needs or wants from the mentorship. Depending on the mentor's responses, instructors may call again within a month or sooner if some matter needs their attention.

Visits to the mentor site

After a telephone call or two, instructors schedule a visit to the mentor's work site at a time when the mentee can also be present. The visit may include three different phases: a mentee-guided tour of the site, a brief check-in with the mentor, and observation of the mentee at work.

During the tour, the mentees introduce the instructor to those with whom they are working and acquaint the instructor with the facilities at the mentor site. It is exciting to see young people become comfortable with their environment after the anxiousness of the initial meeting. Again, the mentees practice skills discussed in *Mentor Seminar* like the intricacies of introductions and their role as a junior member of the staff.

During this visit, the instructor and student listen to the mentor's report of the mentee's progress. Generally, this leaves mentees glowing. When face-to-face, new questions surface more readily from all three people. Instructors gain much greater insight into the dynamics of the mentor/mentee relationship at these meetings as well as greater understanding of the intricacies of the field they are studying. Both gains can be invaluable in deciphering weekly reports!

One final meeting between mentor, mentee, and instructor may take place as the course concludes. Instructors generally leave the exit meeting to the discretion of the mentor. Some mentors prefer to have an instructor present as they summarize and evaluate the experience with mentees. Others prefer to conduct this meeting privately with their mentees.

Phases of a Mentorship

Finally, let's look at how the actual relationship between mentor and mentee develops throughout the *Field Experience*. Understanding how this relationship grows allows those involved with a mentoring program to have a more complete grasp of the possibilities it offers.

The initial meeting

When young people meet a prospective mentor for the first time, they are generally excited about the possibilities ahead, yet very anxious about the impression they will make. They also wonder about their ability to interact on a more adult level with a mentor. Students tell me they usually play a subordinate role to the adults in their lives, so expressing *their* needs looms as a major challenge.

Yet, they also approach an initial meeting with excitement. They share a passion for the field with this unknown adult, and that person wants to help them learn in ways no one else has. Resources—books, equipment, people—await them and so does the "real world" about which teachers rhapsodize, but cannot show them.

The instructor can observe one sure sign of a good match between mentor and mentee if upon completing introductory pleasantries, an explosion of technical conversation (usually over the instructor's head) bursts forth. The student begins to satisfy a long-felt hunger; someone understands the world that fascinates her. She can converse about plasmids, depositions, coloratura, or whatever her heart's desire.

Some students may approach meeting a mentor with greater caution, evaluating the conversation, the person, and the facilities (so may the prospective mentor). This is the right of both parties. Although the instructor may experience initial disappointment that a wonderful rapport was not established the moment the pair were introduced, the mentor and mentee must also feel satisfied that their own needs will be met. As discussed previously, any one of the three parties may veto the mentorship after the initial interview— though few mentors, students, or instructors have.

During the initial meeting, instructors observe gruelling inquisition, albeit very courteous, from both student and mentor. Mentors want to know if students have a genuine interest and background in their field. Students wonder if mentors will provide exactly what they are seeking and if they will have enough time for the students. Most memorable of the mentor's inquiries was the magazine editor who quizzed her future mentee on the demographics of her magazine, the best articles the student had read in the magazine during the past year, and then asked for a sample of the student's writing. The student passed with flying colors! She was impressed with the mentor's dedication and professional approach to the mentorship.

Getting started

The first weeks of the mentorship are generally the most uncomfortable for mentee and mentor. The mentee feels awkward in this strange, new environment. He must learn the names of adults who have instantly become his co-workers, to navigate around the building, and, most important, to know his mentor. For even these basic needs and the learning beyond them, mentees cling tightly to their mentors.

Initially, students also hold fast to their idealized expectations. The young journalist does not realize how many edits a polished story may require. The promising fashion designer learns that she must be able to construct the garments sketched profusely on her drawing pad, so she can evaluate their wearability. Despite many warnings, Kara, the budding naturalist, couldn't quite fathom the cold and boredom of lying in wait to observe the bald eagle in its winter habitat. Students wonder why the situation is not like they imagined it and respond with a broad range of feelings.

Kara simply endured because she loved the other aspects of her work. Some students lose interest in the entire experience if they don't have the opportunity to discuss how they feel and consider modifications. So it is important for mentors and, especially instructors, to keep a watchful eye on week-to-week developments. If hints of discomfort or discontent surface, instructors will want to discuss them immediately and seek solutions if necessary.

For example, a young man excited by advertising envisioned himself developing and implementing marketing plans although he never directly communicated his dream. The mentor, a highly respected and knowledgeble advertising executive, spent hours sharing her expertise and assigning readings and exercises for the student. The student hated listening and and didn't perform the assignments—for the mentor or the class—with the same quality as he did at first. The instructor noticed the change and asked what the problem was. At first the student said he didn't know. When questioned, the mentor said things were going fine and that the student just needed to get into the experience a little more.

Assignments continued to be missed and the student also started missing class claiming illness. After about two more class sessions, the instructor called the parents as required in the program attendance policy. The student, parents, and instructor met to discuss the problem. The student finally, albeit reluctantly, shared his dream. Next the instructor and student met with the mentor to determine if the students' needs could be met. The mentor and student decided on a new plan of action, and the instructor agreed to find a second mentor whose duties entailed more of a marketing emphasis.

"The sparkle"

As the relationship develops, soon familiarity will aid in a transition. The mentee knows the "ropes" for names and places. Mentor and mentee spend time together learning and planning the blueprint. The mentee becomes part of the workplace and feels admiration and gratitude for the mentor's attention and teachings. Phillips (1977) aptly describes this phase as "the sparkle." *Mentor Program* instructors have regularly observed it shining on the faces of young mentees and in their vibrant descriptions of what takes place.

Increased independence and initiative

With time, the mentee learns the stark realities of working within a field and must cope with them. Don had to communicate with his computer programming team. The young wildlife specialist endured the cold and hours of waiting for the pleasure of sighting an eagle. The fashion designer struggled with pricked fingers and tangled threads while learning how to construct her garment, and the journalist revised and rewrote her articles. Reconciling oneself with reality prompts increased familiarity, confidence, and an openness to learn new skills.

With increased skill and awareness, mentees are better able to gauge what they need to do and what they are capable of doing to further their own learning, and to aid their mentors. The mentees become increasingly confident of their mentees' abilities to take initiative and to work independently. The relationship becomes increasingly reciprocal. Mentors spend less time supervising their charges, although they may spend more time directly instructing them. The mentees reciprocate the gift of instruction by assuming additional responsibility for their own learning. Depending on the situation, they may also complete tasks that directly assist their mentors.

Moving toward a collegial relationship

In a mentoring program, students may reach a stage of the mentor/mentee relationship where they are working with their mentors as junior and senior collaborators on a project. At this point, students not only have increased their knowledge and skills in the field extensively, but they have recognized that their mentors are people with talents and flaws just like themselves. To collaborate, mutual acceptance is essential.

When mentees reach this stage, they frequently obtain employment, or in some cases volunteer, with their mentors, and the relationship continues. Since students remain in the *Mentor Program* for a maximum of eight months, instructors can only follow the relationship beyond this time through student visits or calls and encounters with their mentors.

New Incentives

Kara's *Field Experience* provided her with new incentives to grow at a critical point in her high school years. However, more than two years later she continued to reap benefits. Immediately after she graduated high school, a raptor rehabilitation center in Alaska hired her although Kara told me they generally hire only college students or graduates from their own state. I received the following letter from her written on a card with a photograph of a single eagle flying over a glacier on the cover.

Dear Jill,

Alaska is wonderful! My job at the raptor center could not be better! I am an interpreter and take groups around the center and talk about eagles. I am shocked at how much "trivia" I learned just by hanging around my mentor and the university staff. I've had answers to enough off-the-wall questions I've been labeled one of the eagle experts at the center. I'm not really, but it's nice to have someone think you know what you're talking about! My public speaking skills have sharpened; talking to four groups of thirty tourists a day has practically eliminated any stage fright. Soon I'll be taking over the main stage position in front of 80-100 people when my boss goes out of town. I never saw myself doing this—but it is a lot of fun. Eagles swarm the island. They are everywhere—I see about five wild eagles a day. I wish you could see this place. Mountains are everywhere, and mountain climbing and hiking are great. Everything I've learned so far while I've been here has convinced me I made the right college choice. I'm enclosing a quotation I found on the bulletin board at the raptor center the day I got here. Leaving home was hard, but I'm sure glad I came.

Love, Kara

Kara will continue to develop her potential as a wildlife biology major at college, and her mentor still supports her in every way he can. He spent hours on the phone with Kara as she selected a college to attend and he brought her an elegant volume on raptors for her high school graduation. By the way, the quotation Kara mentions in the letter fits so well with the thoughts expressed in this book that it can be found as the start to Chapter 9.

Through experiences like Kara's, mentors and program instructors make a difference in students' lives. However, these experiences would not happen if not for the efforts of other school personnel, parents, and community members. These people also are essential for building a sound mentoring program. The next chapter explores their roles within the program.

References

Harte, P. V. (1989). Fine tuning the learning experience: An information age model for excellence. *NASSP Bulletin,* 73, 96-101.

Kubota, C. A., & Olstad, R. G. (in press). Effects of novelty-reducing preparation on exploratory behavior and cognitive learning in a science museum setting. *Journal of Research in Science Teaching.*

Phillips, L. L. (1977). *Mentors and protegees : A study of the career development of women managers and executives in business and industry.* Unpublished doctoral dissertation, University of California, Los Angeles.

Simpson, R., & Kaufman, F. (1981). Career education for the gifted. *Journal of Career Education,* 8(1), 38-45.

Wagner, J. (1983). Integrating the tradition of experiential learning in internship education. *Journal of Experiential Education,* 6(2), 7-14.

Involving School Personnel, Parents, and the Community: Building Your Program

The mentoring experience opened the school

for the community to come in as well as

for the students to go out.

— Cynthia Burger and James Schnur
"The Mentoring Approach"
Roeper Review

Jim Boesen, Principal of Apple Valley (MN) High School, first envisioned a mentoring program as the apex of a pyramid. The students begin high school with a basic background, then advance their learning with a broad array of courses. As they pursue their interests, students naturally become very skilled in the areas in which they've taken on the most coursework. As they reach the pinnacle of the "learning pyramid," students passionate in their interests eventually exhaust the high school's resources. At the learning apex, mentorship affords students the option to progress.

For example, in the visual arts program at Apple Valley High students begin with a general survey course. Next, they may enroll in two more specialized survey courses: the first develops and applies graphic and composition skills to two-dimensional art forms, and the other applies design to three-dimensional art.

After completing the prerequisite surveys, students may choose from more advanced courses in drawing, print-making, photography, painting, illustration, electronic design, ceramics, jewelry, and sculpture. If they wish even further study in a given area, students may enroll in independent study in any area for one trimester and continue with an advanced independent study in a second trimester. The portfolio class allows students to collect, prepare, and present a one-person exhibit and to apply for advanced-placement credit. Finally, as students seek something beyond independent study, they may apply for mentorship.

This high school principal envisioned mentorships at the top of a departmental learning pyramid. However, the actual progression of opportunities for artistic students was constructed by the art department chairperson, Roger McGaughey. McGaughey and his staff gave substance to the pyramid concept through their direct work with students and their design of the department's registration system.

The pyramid concept for a mentoring program began with the idea of advanced-level learning for students who have exhausted their school's resources. Reaching the apex, however, rests not only on the efforts of students, but on everyone who has bolstered them as they scale the learning pyramid. The efforts of staff members must be considered as a direct link to the apex, or students will never reach it. Furthermore, everyone supporting the climb must have a sense of direction and of the rewards at the top.

Another way to view the students' progress upward is through the paradigm of teamwork. A program that relies on the generosity and talents of so many shares ownership with those who make it possible. Besides the mentors, the most significant, albeit sometimes overlooked, co-owners of a mentoring program are school personnel, parents, and the community at large. This chapter suggests ways to involve these important program co-owners to build a stronger mentoring program.

• • •

170

Program Personnel

Like all teams, the educational team must synchronize their efforts. Just as it happened at Apple Valley High School, mentoring programs serve students best if they are built through the efforts of all those affected. A mentoring program advisory committee or steering team can be the nucleus for shared planning, adding ideas, support, and energy to the program. The team concept also allows for shared commitment to an innovative educational option for students.

The steering team's role in a mentoring program follows closely with the role of any advisory board or committee. They work toward a synchronized effort by lending each member's educational expertise to the program's development. While the exact duties and responsibilities of the team must be shaped by the circumstances of the individual program, a discussion follows about topics, issues, and organization that have been found most helpful to establishing steering teams in the *Mentor Program*.

As issues arise, the team thoroughly considers them and attempts to arrive at an agreeable solution. For example, start-up issues might include questions: How many credits should be awarded for successful completion of *Mentor Seminar* and *Mentor Field Experience?* Under which departments will the credits be issued? Will students gain elective or required credit for the courses? How will the course be noted on student transcripts? During which terms will the courses be offered? And then there are the questions about screening students: What is the profile of the student this program should serve? How will we know when we have found those students?

Different schools and different people find different solutions. The solutions to some of the questions raised may be delegated to an administrator, scheduler, counselor, or a subcommittee of the steering team. Others, however, must be resolved through the team in order to prevent the program basics from becoming divisive. For example, staff members may strongly feel that the material taught in *Mentor Seminar* conflicts with instruction that they give, or others may not want the credits for the *Mentor Program* to fall within their department because the program would compete with their courses and, therefore, their enrollments. Input from several perspectives may be needed to mediate these issues.

Forming the steering team

The steering team works well if each department including guidance and administration provides one representative. This way everyone's interests are represented and each department has an investment in the program. Of course, most departments will want to promote their fields to students, and involvement with a mentoring program offers just that opportunity. However, faculty do raise concerns about how a mentoring program will affect their department and their student enrollment. They wonder if a mentoring program will pull students away from some of their advanced courses. Faculty members will also raise questions about the role of faculty contacts (see Chapters 4 and 5). Generally faculty become interested and knowledgeable about all aspects of the program. Their educational expertise will prepare them to grasp any situation and make the best recommendation for the program.

In some places, a student representative, parent, and a mentor or two could be included to round the committee by offering greater perspective—what we call "a reality check"—on educational values and plans. Students can respond to whether planned assignments or activities seem valuable and how the *Field Experience* would fit into their time schedules and priorities. Student representatives also can present issues that arise among other students and lend their insights to help resolve those problems.

Parents have a different set of concerns and a different perspective. They want to know on which highways their children will be driving, how far away they will go, how often and how long they will be gone, and how much it will cost. They also want to know if their child will be required to drive in bad weather. They are concerned about the quality of the education their children will receive and how colleges will view a mentoring program. Parents worry about over-stressed kids and whether their children have all the advanced-placement credits they want along with a mentoring experience. They are less concerned with how the course is taught or lowering the enrollments of other courses.

Mentors, of course, view things with yet another perspective. Surely, they are also concerned about meeting the students' needs. However, mentors' individual needs go beyond receiving the benefits of helping the students; they must consider how mentoring a student can fit into their work schedules and still allow them time to fulfill other work priorities. As discussed in Chapter 3, mentors may be uncomfortable with issues that are commonplace to educators like students who do not report as scheduled, consistently arrive late, or do not clean up after themselves.

Mentors can provide invaluable insights about their vital role in the program. They can help all concerned understand what is valuable to them as mentors and how working with a student impacts their professional role. Because mentors are asked to write evaluations of student skills, communications, and work habits, they may have much to contribute in designing an evaluation. Through their role on the team, mentors can have a direct impact upon education and a forum for their beliefs on how education should occur. At the *Mentor Program* steering team meetings, there have been some stimulating exchanges about the needs of potential professionals, giftedness, elitism, the expectations schools place upon students, and many other topics.

There are vast structural and organizational differences between schools and corporations. On a steering team, mentor representatives can help "educate the educators," familiarizing them with corporate thought. They may also provide the program with additional contacts in their professional circles.

Finally, if organizations that advocate for the gifted exist in the vicinity, the steering team might invite them to appoint a representative to the steering team. The expertise and concern within these organizations can offer much to the program and yet another fresh perspective.

Getting started

Before the steering team is convened, those initiating a mentoring program may want to draft a proposal for how the program might operate. This proposal would include the basics: the who, what, when, where, how, and why. An initial goal of the steering team would be to review the proposal, then add details to the plan. Once the tasks ahead seem clear, a timeline for their completion can be devised.

The proposal presented at the first meeting might include some of the information presented within this book or the resources listed here, and the agenda might be similar to the one suggested for a student informational meeting in Chapter 2. Each member of the steering team needs to consider what the mentoring program proposes to accomplish and how it will fit into the overall educational picture at the high school.

The first meeting also allows the team to air pivotal concerns. For example, a few faculty members may be apprehensive about "losing" students whom they value or enjoy. If issues can be discussed and resolved within the team, then the group can develop a plan that increases the chances for success within the entire school. It may take several meetings to complete a basic plan, but the effort will be worthwhile. It will ensure a solid foundation for the rewards that lie ahead. The time between sessions can be used to share some specifics with departments, other prospective mentors, parents, and students and to obtain their feedback. Once again, new ideas result from the dialogue and program awareness also increases.

Defining the role of the faculty contact

The faculty contact option requires attention from the steering team early in the planning stages. The faculty contact system actively involves more staff in the mentoring program. The students benefit greatly from the support of someone who understands them, their fields, and the process of learning. Teachers, however, may be concerned about still another demand on their time. The steering team should review the faculty contact portion of the overall plan to assess the costs, benefits, and how the system may work in their program. If the team chooses to recommend that mentoring program students seek faculty contacts, the team will want to consider ways to minimize the faculty contacts' time commitment and maximize their benefits.

To conserve the faculty contact's time, two visits between contact and student per term can provide the support most students need. Students take the initiative to schedule appointments at their contacts' convenience. Besides the satisfaction of helping, other benefits might be offered to the contacts. Release time to visit mentorship sites allows faculty contacts to observe cutting-edge facilities and resources, share the technical expertise with mentors and, in some cases, garner new speakers for the classroom. Another "perk" for becoming a faculty contact could be to offer teacher licensure renewal credits for assuming this responsibility. This can be determined by the district's licensure renewal personnel. Still another reward can be to invite contacts to attend mentorship recognition events. These events can be scheduled after school hours or the team may request the principal's support in releasing contacts for a few hours to attend them.

Advising about curriculum and policy

As the steering team addresses the start-up issues of the program, they will provide advice about the curriculum and classroom policies of their mentoring program. The instructors gain invaluable support and a forum for important issues; the team can then resolve concerns with a well thought-out policy. In the early days of a mentoring program, the team will also want to establish a systematic approach to the program's development by setting goals and designing a means to assess how well the program meets those goals (see Chapter 7).

Assistance with recruitment and screening

When the time comes to accept applicants, the team also can plan how to best inform students. As mentioned in Chapter 2, we have found that recommendations from faculty members are the most effective means of informing and interesting students. This is particularly true during the early years of a mentoring program. The team members can channel information back to their departments so teachers can refer promising students to the program. The steering team may also form a screening committee to rate applications and interview students along with an instructor.

Identifying prospective mentors

Another important role the steering team may play is to assist in identifying possible mentors. After screening students or as they become more focused, the instructors may wish to circulate a list of possible interests to the team for suggestions about mentors. A community network becomes apparent through this progress.

Public relations

The team also can serve an invaluable public relations function. Members can provide a liaison to other interested groups within the school such as the various departments, a school-based management council, or the administrative team. In addition, team members might choose to publish relevant articles in the school's media including a principal's, counselors', or department newsletter, the school newspaper, or the district publications. The local media might provide publicity for program activities.

Three tips for cohesiveness

The *Mentor Program* has established three traditions for the steering team which everyone enjoys. The first is that every meeting begins with progress reports from at least one student who is currently participating in the program. The students describe where they are in their learning and how their needs are being met or how they could be better met. This tradition keeps everyone in touch with the roots of the program and serves to recognize the students' efforts. Periodically, the *Mentor Program* steering team even holds part of their one-and-a-half hour meeting right in a mentor classroom. The instructor provides an activity which engages the students and team members in small group conversation. The activity might be a question-and-answer time or a time for the team to review resumé drafts with the students.

The second tradition the *Mentor Program* steering team enjoys is an annual luncheon which takes place as students complete the first semester of the school year. The purpose of the luncheon is to recognize the efforts of students, mentors, and the steering team and to acquaint these special people with one another. The team meeting follows immediately after the luncheon (see Chapter 7).

The third tradition is to invite all active mentors to attend a steering team meeting to answer any questions that mentors may have and to learn of their suggestions to improve the program. We have found that mentors will make every effort to attend a luncheon with their mentees, but have more difficulty attending a steering team meeting even if it follows immediately after the luncheon. However, when mentors attend, they generally precipitate thoughtful conversation and valuable insights for everyone attending the team meeting.

Steering team guidelines

Establishing written guidelines for the steering team can clarify both the team's mission and roles for all concerned. The guidelines also smooth the team's operations through specified procedures of governance. Figure 6-1 provides a sample of steering team guidelines for a program model which serves more than one high school. The guidelines are intended to be simple, flexible, and not intensely formalized.

Parents: Contributors to Their Children's Learning

Parents have significant impact upon their children's overall learning, and their influence may be even stronger in a course that requires value judgments and provides options beyond the traditional classroom. When students consider career choices, their parents' wishes and experiences affect their decisions. How many people follow in their parent's chosen profession, or avoid it, because of their parent's experiences? In a *Mentor Program* which involves extra travel, monetary and time demands, parents must consent to their child's participation and will monitor their children more closely than if they had selected an in-school course.

Parents can influence their child's mentoring experience. Davis (1985) found that parents are stronger influences than best friends in determining the educational aspirations of adolescents. Noted educator and scholar Benjamin Bloom (1985) found that "where parents...in the individual's immediate environment devalue or scorn the qualities required to achieve well, they will rarely be well learned" (p. 545). Because parents' wishes and preferences will influence their children, it makes sense to include them in the work accomplished with and by their children in a mentoring program. That parents of students who enroll in a mentoring program wish to become involved is reflected in

Fig. 6-1

I. Purpose of the Mentor Program Steering Team

To provide input from schools, students, parents, mentors, community members, and advocates of the needs of high potential students on the Mentor Program and to offer students the best possible experience consistent with the following goals:

1. To provide students with an opportunity for advanced learning beyond the limits of the available curriculum.
2. To provide the students with access to a one-on-one learning experience with a professional leadership role model in the student's area of interest.
3. To provide students with access to resources and facilities not available within the high school.
4. To involve students in a meaningful research project.
5. To help students to develop the skills necessary to work effectively at a professional level.

II. Steering Team Membership

High school representatives. Representatives will be sought from each participating high school. Each high school will determine who their team representative will be. The Steering Team requests that appointed representatives remain on the team for a minimum of two years, but they may remain on the team as long as their job responsibilities include serving as a liaison to the Mentor Program.

Mentor representatives. Two mentor representatives will serve for one school year. One representative will be a person who has served as a mentor at least once. It would be desirable for the second mentor representative to be currently serving as a mentor. The instructors or any team member may recommend a mentor to the chair who will invite mentors to participate on the team.

Mentor Program students. Two student representatives will serve for one school year. It is desirable, but not necessary for one student to serve a second term as a past student representative. Team members may recommend a student to the instructor for this position. Because the instructor is most likely to know each student, the instructor will select student representatives.

Parent representatives. Two parent representatives will serve on the team: one for a two year term and a second for a one year term. Team members and the instructors may recommend parents for this position to the chair who will invite parent representatives to participate.

Advocates for high potential students. Organizations with a strong interest in high potential students may be invited to select a representative to serve on the Mentor Program Steering Team. The instructor or any team member may recommend to the chairperson that the organization be invited to send a delegate.

At the end of a term or at least every two years, the instructor and chair will send a letter of invitation to renew a member's service to the team.

III. Operating Guidelines

1. **Meeting times.** As a team, we will meet at least three times a year: November, January, and April.

2. **Meeting guidelines.** Team members may be asked to advise or make recommendations on curriculum content, student awareness and selection, student screening, mentor placement, student and program evaluations, fiscal budgeting, recruitment, staffing, and purchasing equipment.

3. **Chairperson.** A chairperson will be elected by the Steering Team for a one-year term. Nominations will be accepted at the winter meeting prior to the end of the chair's term of office, and elections held at the spring meeting. Term of office will begin at the close of the spring meeting.

4. **Secretary.** The secretary will be nominated and elected in the same progression as the chair. The secretary will take minutes of each meeting. The minutes will be typed and distributed to members of the Steering Team and the principal and mailed within three weeks of the meeting. Members are asked to retain the minutes and bring questions or corrections for the consideration of the team to the following meeting.

5. **Meeting agenda.** At the end of each meeting, the chair will ask members for agenda items for the following meeting. Agendas will be mailed to members at least one week prior to a meeting. Members are encouraged to contact the chair with any additions or suggestions for the agenda.

6. **Subcommittees.** As needed, the chair may establish a subcommittee to address any task relevant to the goals of the team.

IV. Member Responsibilities and Training

To adequately prepare to serve, team members commit to:

1. Prepare for meetings by reviewing any materials submitted prior to the meeting.

2. Regularly attend meetings.

3. Serve as liaison communicator about the Mentor Program to the high school, member organization, place of employment or community at large as appropriate.

4. Members are encouraged to attend at least one metro-wide Annual Dinner/ Open House event in May and to regularly attend the Annual Mentor/Student Recognition Luncheon in January.

5. Members are encouraged to complete a personal visit to the Mentor Program classroom or to conduct an on-site visit with a student and mentor. This visit may be scheduled through the instructor.

the fact that the *Mentor Program* has never held a parents' informational meeting where less than 85 percent of the parents attended.

Parents' meetings

To inform parents about the *Mentor Program* beyond what they may have heard from their offspring, instructors schedule a parents' informational meeting during the first two or three weeks of the *Mentor Seminar* course. This meeting affords time for instructors to inform parents about the program, and it can also allow parents to observe students' work and to learn with them. The wise instructor will also garner parents' insights about both the program and their child's particular needs in this community effort to educate youth.

Mentor Program instructors usually tell students about the upcoming meeting and send parents a letter of invitation and an agenda approximately ten days to two weeks ahead of the scheduled date (see Figure 6-2). The agenda for the meeting includes a history and overview of the *Seminar* course, a preview of the *Field Experience* to follow *Seminar*, and a discussion of issues central to most parents such as transportation, selection of mentors, student placement, and grading. See Figure 6-3 for a sample agenda.

If an actual mentor is willing, a talk about the mentor's role and expectations of students can be the highlight of the evening. A brief presentation by one or two students who are involved with or have completed *Field Experience* might also benefit parents and students. The mentor and student can also form a panel discussion.

Parents and students delight in hearing the experiences of mentors and other *Field Experience* participants. They want to know how the students arrived at a focus, about their mentors and their mentor sites, which experiences have been particularly rewarding or challenging, and what students have gained from their mentorships. Instructors should consider inviting both a male and a female to speak at a parents' meeting. This rounds out the perspectives offered. Don't be surprised if the audience directs all of the question-and-answer session to the mentor and student-speakers.

Depending on the needs of the individual program, parents may attend with or without the students. When students attend, instructors

Fig. 6-2

[Date]

To the Parents of:
[Name]
[Address]

Dear Parents:

Because the Mentor Program is such a unique program, I want to fully inform parents about what we hope to accomplish with students and what we expect of them.

You are cordially invited to an informational meeting on [Date, Time, Place]. Former Mentor Program students will also be present to share experiences and to answer your questions.

I have enclosed a meeting agenda, as well as a building floor plan to help you locate our classroom.

The class consists of interesting and capable students with diverse interests-- from [Topic] to [Topic]. I am delighted to work with these fine young adults and look forward to assisting them in their learning.

I hope you will be able to attend this meeting. I look forward to meeting with you personally.

Sincerely Yours,

Instructor/Coordinator
Mentor Program

•••

Fig. 6-3

MENTOR PROGRAM PARENT INFORMATIONAL MEETING AGENDA

[Date]

[TIme]

[Location]

Agenda

7:00 p.m.   Welcome and Introductions

7:15 p.m.   General Information about the
Mentor Program

- Video (Program History)
- Seminar Class Curriculum
- Selection of Mentors and
  Student Placement
- Transportation
- Required Student Research Project
- Grading

7:40 p.m.   Former Students Share Experiences

8:00 p.m.   Parents' Input and Roles

8:15 p.m.   Questions

can involve them in an interactive activity with their parents such as the "Who Am I" activity from *College Comes Sooner Than You Think!* (Featherstone & Reilly, 1990). This allows parents to play an active role in their child's instruction and to experience a real segment of the class. Because parent and student have shared this lesson, parents may also gain clearer feedback about the class from their students.

When students attend the meeting, however, parents often feel unable to discuss their concerns or ask their questions without embarrassing their children. The students in a mentoring program generally are very busy, so an evening commitment beyond class may seem like one commitment too much.

Regardless of who attends the parents' meeting, instructors need to clearly monitor parents' expectations of the program. Certainly, program staff will want to share their enthusiasm and the students' outstanding experiences with parents. On the other hand, parents must know that the responsibility for obtaining "the ideal" mentor does not rest solely upon the instructor. Particular businesses or mentors may not wish to participate for one reason or another. Instructors cannot control the amount of time a professional will take to return a phone call or to make the decision about whether or not to become involved.

The instructors should talk with parents about the degree of responsibility and independence demanded of high school students in the adult world. The *Seminar* course fosters many of the necessary "survival skills," but opinions may vary about what can be expected. One significant question to cover is "What are the students' responsibilities in identifying and contacting a prospective mentor?"

Because the demands of a mentoring program are quite different from those of a classroom situation, parents may feel uncomfortable with even slightly different approaches to commonplace events. For example, in the *Mentor Program* students may choose to address instructors by their first names or by the more standard "Ms." or "Mr." One parent asked if the instructors were trying to "be friends" with their students, which she felt was inappropriate. Many mentors prefer that their mentees address them by their first names just as their colleagues in the workplace do. Moving to a first-name basis with an adult is part of the transition into the adult world and establishes a more mature relationship. Calling instructors by their first names allows students to test their comfort level and bridges the transition. Even these small steps can boost a young person's confidence and help to establish a more comfortable rapport with a mentor later in the term.

For parents who are wary of their student's ability to drive "into town" or on "the interstate," transportation becomes a main focus. The instructor may be required to place students as close to home as possible. For other parents, the more prestigious the mentor's credentials, the better. The instructor's placement priority may be influenced not only by the students' preferences, but by the parents' as well. The student's placement with a mentor must blend the student's and parents' wishes with the instructor's judgments about the best possible situation for the student's education and well-being.

At the meeting instructors have the chance to seek feedback from parents about their child's needs. Despite the protests of some older high school students, parents can play a pivotal role in garnering the best possible educational experience for their children, and each one should be heard. Figure 6-4 provides one example of a simple questionnaire which parents can complete that may reveal very helpful general data. The purpose of Figure 6-5 is to gain information particularly relevant to a successful *Field Experience.*

As the meeting concludes, parents will inquire about how they can help, so it's good to have several possibilities in mind. Certainly, all parents should receive a list of the program's current needs for mentors and a form they can return with leads. They can list themselves as resources for informational interviews as well as mentorships. Perhaps, a parent or two will be expert in a topic appropriate for *Seminar* and would be willing to serve as a guest speaker. Other parents can serve on the Steering Team or a team sub-committee. Parents might offer to provide other services ranging from clerical and printing work on a newsletter to assisting with photography or organizing a recognition event. Parent involvement provides heartwarming evidence of their support not only for the program but of their children as well.

Fig. 6-4

MENTOR PROGRAM MENTOR SEMINAR PARENTS' COMMENTS

STUDENT'S NAME .... **DATE** ....

INSTRUCTOR .... **PHONE** ....

We welcome your comments and suggestions for working with your child. Please use the following space to provide any information, suggestions, or comments that might assist us in any way as we work with your child.

....

....

....

....

....

....

....

....

....

....

....

....

....

....

Of course, feel free to contact us at any time at .... with any questions or concerns that you may have. We'll also look forward to seeing you at conferences.

Fig. 6-5

PARENTS' COMMENTS

STUDENT'S NAME .... **DATE** ....

PARENT(S) RESPONDING ....

STUDENT'S FIELD(S) FOR STUDY ....

INSTRUCTOR ....

In order to do the best possible job of working with your child, we would appreciate your input here to assist your student and us in deciding with whom or where a good mentor match might be. A mentorship match is made by trying to best align the student's learning and personal needs (such as transportation) with available mentors. Please keep in mind that we cannot control every variable (such as which people or businesses are available in a field, or where they are located).

1. Please describe the setting that you feel would best meet your child's learning needs this semester. If you know a specific firm, location, or person that you wish for us to contact, please note here.

....

....

2. Please describe the skills and personality you believe a mentor should have to best work with your child.

....

....

3. At this meeting, we have discussed several possible difficulties students have experienced. What do you anticipate might be most difficult for your child?

....

....

4. Is there any additional information about your child that would help us to work with him or her in the Mentor Program?

....

....

Thank you for your input! Please feel free to contact us any time at ....
with any questions or concerns you might have.

"The Community of Adults"

The most valuable resources for a mentoring program come from "the community of adults." Without mentors, obviously, there would be no program. Establishing a sound identity and program integrity within the community will result in continued resources and support in the years to come, so they should be carefully cultivated. Identity and integrity result from positive relationships with each professional who has contact with the program in any way and from favorable communications within the community at large.

Establishing a program identity within the community consciousness entails preparing a variety of resources. First, the community at large must perceive a clear definition of what a mentoring program does, the student population it serves, the purpose behind involving professionals, the role of the school in supporting both the student and the program, and the expectations for professionals who agree to participate. Each of these issues should be addressed in a cohesive purpose statement which can be woven into each communication about the program.

As suggested in Chapter 4, it is helpful to have an informal—or formal—media kit. The media kit can include the program purpose statement, a history of the program, the names and backgrounds of instructors and the steering team, an article which can be used in company newsletters to identify prospective mentors, and another that can be used to generally acquaint the community with the program. As the mentoring program becomes operative, photos of students in action and stories of interesting mentorships make wonderful additions to the media kit.

Local media

As the materials generated are released to local press, businesses, parents, and school personnel, a media kit provides the basis for the program's introduction to the community. After introductory articles, local newspapers seem to appreciate stories relating to a nontraditional mentorship like the one pictured on page 111 where a young woman learns airplane mechanics or articles that call attention to program events.

Because a mentoring program emphasizes partnerships among businesses and schools—important community relations commodities—even photographs with seasonal interest may warrant print space. For example, at Thanksgiving one year a *Mentor Program* student was studying bacterial diseases in turkeys at a university veterinary school. The metropolitan paper ran a photo of the student working with the turkeys and a story with the headline "Mentor Takes Student Under His Wing." Similarly, television and radio stations may also become interested in the emphasis on the community working together and the colorful results of a mentoring program. The program staff will want to keep a scrapbook of articles and a collection of photographs or videos to share with prospective mentors, parents, and school personnel.

Introducing a mentoring program to businesses

The significant role of an educational liaison between a business and schools and the information, materials, and methods to acquaint the liaison with a mentoring program were presented in Chapter 4. In obtaining corporate permission for mentor participation or in recruiting prospective mentors, two additional print materials for the media kit have proven very helpful: a brief brochure which introduces professionals to the *Mentor Program* and the concept of becoming a mentor, plus a complete handbook for mentors. Also, a brief videotape can introduce the program and add concrete images to the description.

Program representatives—instructors, team members, students, or mentors—can meet with prospective mentors, corporate educational liaisons, "gatekeepers," professional or civic organizations and clubs, and representatives of higher education. These activities fall in the category of ongoing program development and communications. As is the case with most enterprises, program staff serving on relevant committees or participating in community endeavors can also boost program awareness.

Program integrity

To establish a sense of program integrity, the actions of staff, students, mentors, and the steering team must be consistent with the program purpose statement. Students must be carefully instructed to present themselves and their needs as consistently with the program's purpose as possible. Students who receive support from the community should find ways to return the favor—whether it be through conscientious study, a smile and a thank you, or applying the skills learned to benefit others.

Not only must a mentoring program meet students' learning needs, it must meet the mentors' needs as well. Mentors must be respected and valued, and given an opportunity to obtain the support they need to succeed. An endeavor that attempts to conjoin so many different people in different roles is constantly subject to surveillance; whatever promises are made must be delivered.

To be successful those involved with a mentoring program must recognize the major role each staff member, parent, and mentor plays as a supporter of student development. The steering team functions as an essential unit for the program providing guidance and a forum for pivotal issues. The team unites people representative of those upon whom the program relies: program staff, students, faculty, mentors, parents, and advocates of the program. Through the knowledge and creativity of the steering team, a mentoring program which meets the unique needs of the students and the community it serves can be developed.

Parents should be offered the option of supporting their own student's learning. The parents' meeting provides an efficient mechanism for generating this support and for informing parents about the adventure upon which their children will embark.

A mentoring program can also become part of a community's culture, a team effort to stretch motivated students just a little farther in their learning. The program staff and steering team provide the essential information to generate public awareness and support.

References

Bloom, B. S. (Ed.). (1985). *Developing talent in young people.* New York: Ballantine Books.

Davis, A. D. (1985). Influences on adolescents' educational plans: Some further evidence. *American Journal of Sociology,* <u>87</u>, 363-387.

Burger, C. R., & Schnur, J. O. (1981). The mentoring approach: Something for everyone, especially the gifted. *Roeper Review,* <u>4</u>, 29-31.

Featherstone, B. D, & Reilly, J. M. (1990). *College comes sooner than you think! The essential college planning guide for high school students and their parents.* Dayton, OH: Ohio Psychology Press.

CHAPTER 7

Recognition, Evaluation, and Beyond

Learning is not only a mechanical process.

Relationships are also important to learning.

> — James Comer
> In Gursky, D., "A plan that works."
> *Teacher*

After she completed her mentorship, Shannon, the young woman introduced in Chapter 1, wrote a thank-you note which read in part:

I'm so happy that someone like you cares about young people and their dreams! I know now that I will be able to achieve at least part of my huge dreams because of all your support and help.

Although Bob Hinker had not seen Shannon's thank you note prior to writing a voluntary summative letter to her instructor, he sensed Shannon's new confidence in her ability to realize her dreams. He described the value of her *Mentor Program* experiences as:

> *. . . a fantastic opportunity for high school students. The value of an experience like this should carry far beyond the actual time I spent and I think that Shannon will find this to be the case with her stay here [personal communications, June 7, 1990].*

Hinker continued the letter by describing how a mutual acquaintance had told him that when Shannon talked about Hinker "she bubbled over with real enthusiasm, which makes me feel like I had a positive influence." Hinker also noted how much confidence Shannon had gained and concluded the letter by saying, "So while Shannon will certainly take something, in fact many things, I will also take new, positive things from this experience." Bob Hinker's letter exemplifies the satisfaction mentors can feel from helping mentees live out better lives and obtain their dreams.

Shannon also wrote, "From my experience, I've not only had a mentor, I've made a friend." I remember visiting with Shannon at her graduation party as she anxiously eyed the front door awaiting her mentor's arrival. Other students report similar friendships that last through the years.

A mentoring program, like most educational endeavors, runs in a cycle. It begins at the start of the term and continues until the instructor issues final grades for the year. In order to bring closure to one cycle and return to the next with renewed vigor, those who contribute to the program deserve recognition for their efforts, the students and the program require evaluation, and the instructor and steering team must devise a plan for the next school year. This chapter discusses completing the cycle of one school year and generating a vision for the next.

Recognizing the Work of Mentors, Students, and Steering Team Members

Principles of effective volunteer management—and common sense—demand recognition of the participants. In the case of a mentoring program, the contributions of the mentors must rate high; however, the students also make their contributions.

Initially, students seek assistance from their mentors; as the experience ends, the mentors also should have gained. As touched on in Chapter 5, the students' project should contribute to the mentor's work, and the mentor's relationship with the student should yield additional rewards and satisfaction.

Finally, the steering team members have labored to organize and support the mentoring program. They, too, must receive recognition for their efforts. In a mentoring program, those planning recognition events must consider mentors, students, and the steering team.

What and when?

Mentoring program students may complete their mentorships at the end of a term or continue them all year. The term-end provides an ideal time to hold a recognition event for those completing their mentorships at mid-year. However, the end of the school year signifies a time of closure for all.

Because these are both times of closure during the school year, they lend themselves to two recognition events. Each event might emphasize a different group of contributors, or both may simply honor program graduates. For variety at mid-year, the *Mentor Program* hosts a Steering Team Recognition Luncheon which recognizes the contributions of the team and honors mentors and students completing the program after the first semester.

At the end of the school-year, the *Mentor Program* joins all the mentoring programs in the region as they collaborate on an Annual Dinner and Open House. The Steering Team Recognition Luncheon and the Annual Dinner and Open House provide two recognition options; the imaginations of those involved in a mentoring program may generate many more.

The Steering Team Recognition Luncheon

Besides recognizing the efforts of the steering team, mentors, and students completing their formal mentorships, the Steering Team Recognition Luncheon can provide a more intimate local setting in which students, mentors, and the team can interact. Many programs participate in the end-of-the-year event, so the number of guests swells into the hundreds. The site for the Annual Dinner and Open House also rotates around the region, so guests may travel a much longer distance to participate than they would to attend the Recognition Luncheon. So, while an Annual Dinner and Open House provides an overall perspective and, perhaps, a more gala event, the Steering Team Recognition Luncheon offers the team special recognition, intimacy, and provides closure to some mentoring relationships.

Another learning experience for students

The Steering Team Recognition Luncheon also can serve as an excellent learning experience for students. With coaching prior to the event, students learn how to host their mentors and how to interact with steering team members. Prior to and during the lunch, students can practice points of etiquette. Examples include calling mentors the day before the event to arrange an appointed spot to meet and greet them, applying table etiquette, and maintaining a conversation with adults who have not met before the luncheon. Many students have never functioned as hosts at an adult event.

Students completing their mentorships also create an exhibit to visually depict their learning throughout the course. The exhibits inform guests about the students' learning and provide a final review for students. Each exhibit has a title and table tent with the student's name and the mentor's name and workplace. If the mentoring program serves more than one school, the table tents also show the student's school affiliation. One suggestion: When citing mentor's names, drop titles like "Dr." or "Executive Director" so as not to rank or rankle people.

The students' exhibits may include their projects if they are tangible such as Dave's clay-animated video and his clay figures or a computer running Don's accounting program. Some projects are not as portable, so they require more thought about how to display them. Shannon had a report on her research about the camels, and she taught classes at a nature center—neither of which made a particularly vivid display. However, she exhibited the props she used to teach about tapping a maple tree and photos of her students and herself involved in the lesson. She also had a poster-sized summary of her research results with accompanying charts and tables. On the table she exhibited the actual data-collection sheets and her report.

Katie had worked on a chemical process to create a lighter-weight cast for setting broken bones. She brought a mannequin to the exhibit which she used to demonstrate how the lighter cast compared with heavier ones. She also designed a poster to explain the basic process.

Of course, at any recognition event the hosts find ways to note the accomplishments of those honored. A luncheon program highlights the names of those recognized—mentors, students, and steering team. If within the budget, those honored always appreciate a token of gratitude such as a certificate, mug, T-shirt, plant, key ring, or other imaginative possibilities along with the verbal tributes.

Program instructors may wish to honor the team in conjunction with district officials. Words of recognition from the superintendent feel special. With the instructors' coaching, students can introduce their mentors and express a few words of gratitude as the mentors come forward to receive their awards. This allows one final opportunity for students to gain skills and confidence in public graciousness.

Students with performing talents can provide an interesting and memorable conclusion to the luncheon. They may also consider the performance as part of their project. For example, Jason decided to perform two original compositions on his acoustic guitar.

Because the members have already gathered, the steering team may decide to meet following the luncheon. This provides the chance for the team and mentors to attend the meeting, ask questions, and offer feedback without additional travel.

Annual Dinner and Open House

The Annual Dinner and Open House includes a larger cross section of the community than the Steering Team Luncheon. Students, mentors, steering team members, parents, faculty contacts, school officials, and board members from all mentoring programs across a region are invited to attend. The dinner is by invitation only, but the open house is for the general public, too. Students who have completed the mentoring program or who are completing it may exhibit their accomplishments. In essence, the event compares to a small, one-evening convention.

The agenda

The time sequence for the evening may be scheduled as follows: Between four and five o'clock students arrange their exhibits. Guests arrive at 5:30 p.m. They receive name tags and students and mentors' get a corsage or boutonniere. Students greet their guests and gather them for pre-dinner conversation and punch.

At 6:00 a buffet dinner is served. At 7:00 a brief recognition program begins. After greetings and an annual update on the mentoring programs represented that evening, a student from each program addresses the group. In their informal and often impromptu talks students share their experiences while involved with the mentoring program. Their comments often reveal exceptional insights into the benefits they derived and the challenges they faced. By 7:30, students return to their exhibit areas and guests review the exhibits until 9:00 p.m.

The interactions during an evening like this create strong memories for all who participate. At the Annual Dinner and Open House, parents may meet mentors for the first time. I remember a scientist describing all his mentee's strengths to the young man's parents. The parents reciprocated by sharing the mentee's youthful forays into science and his comments about the mentor. Everyone was misty-eyed by the time they returned to the exhibits.

More learning and a sense of pride

The exhibits allow students to reach closure on their projects and to feel pride in their accomplishments. They also gain practice in communicating about their field at all levels of understanding. During the exhibit review, students remain at their stations and converse with passersby. They meet people who understand absolutely nothing about their fields along with known experts. The students again must meet the challenge of adapting their comments to the listener's level of expertise—more practice for the real world.

● ● ●

Other opportunities for students may also arise during open house. For example, a young writer displayed her young-adult novel. A mentor for another student in the publishing business approached the exhibit. She read a few pages of the novel, found the student's mentor and chatted for a few moments, then returned to offer the young novelist her card. The publisher wanted to meet with this student to further consider her work.

For the record

Instructors will want to photograph exhibits and the evening's events. If students agree, the instructor should retain a few exhibits as examples for the next class. Viewing a few of the more tangible projects also helps other students grasp the course requirements.

Of course, an event of this scale requires substantial space both for exhibits and for meals. It also requires a substantial amount of funding. Some funding possibilities include: each district pays for its own meals; businesses or foundations fund the evening; participants pay for their own meals; or some blending of the these options. Of course, possible funding sources are limited only by the planners' creativity.

Besides the culminating purpose, the Open House initiates the evaluative phase of *Field Experience*. The projects along with the exhibits demonstrate what the students have accomplished. The students' conversations with Open House guests also demand that they show how well they have learned. The Open House leads to a more formal evaluation of the students' work and of the program.

Evaluation of Students' Work and the Program Evaluation

Expectations of students

Research indicates that students perform well when their teachers consistently set high expectations for them (Brophy, 1979; Pollack, Chrispeels, & Watson, 1987). Teachers holding high expectations for their students set higher goals, provide more focus, hold students accountable for work, and offer the same amount of attention and feedback to each student.

In a high school mentoring program, instructors and mentors expect students to meet goals which include standards of learning, responsibility, and social deportment which far exceed the standard demands of the classroom. The students must develop a clear focus prior to placement with mentors, and both instructors and mentors (and sometimes the mentors' colleagues) hold the students accountable for their work. Because the mentor/mentee relationship requires one-on-one time, students naturally receive individual attention and feedback. Everyone expects the students to perform well and successfully.

As an instructor monitors each student's progress, she provides specific and immediate feedback to the student through each week of the *Field Experience*. This helps to ensure that students will successfully meet expectations. For example, the blueprint must meet the mentor's, student's, and the instructor's expectations or the instructor will suggest changes to improve it. If the student is behind schedule, the instructor should call it to the student's attention and watch for him or her to get back on track. If a project lacks quality and the mentor does not require improvements, once again the instructor will. In any of these situations, the student may negotiate a compromise, but the mentor and instructor must be satisfied with the outcome.

Outcome-based assessment

William Spady (1988), a nationally known expert on outcome-based education (OBE), describes it as "a way of defining, designing, developing, delivering and documenting instruction in terms of its intended goals and outcomes" (p. 4). Traits of an outcome-based system occur in the model for the *Mentor Program* presented throughout this book. Nowhere, however, does the model for mentoring coincide more closely with OBE than in the way the student's outcomes are evaluated.

Boston (1976) said that mentees must receive a realistic appraisal of their progress. Before mentors or instructors can appraise a student's progress, they, along with the student, must have a clear definition of the learning goals. "With well structured goals and agreements between parties, programs can create an atmosphere of seriousness and productivity. Unguided experience does not teach," Baird (1982, p. 40) states.

Boston (1976) recommends that evaluation of a mentorship be "done on the basis of assessing competencies as measured by the successful completion of tasks, the mastery of techniques, the ability to structure problems and solve them according to the canons of the tradition being explored" (p. 34).

In a high school mentoring program which strives to develop students' potentials, mentees must demonstrate skill in solving problems "according to the canons of the tradition being explored." They learn about the field. For success in the field, students must also cope effectively with the people and responsibilities accompanying the "tradition" or work environment.

Mastery of these skills is documented by achieving criteria rather than comparing the performance of one student with others. The student's blueprint, or plan, for learning defines the questions the student will answer, the goals for the mentorship, and the project the student will complete to document his or her learning. The classroom preparation during *Mentor Seminar* defines the criteria for responsible and successful interaction with people in the workplace.

In the blueprint, as devised during the first weeks of *Field Experience,* mentor and mentee set the conditions of learning together, and they project a timeline for meeting the criteria. If the projected timeline proves inaccurate, the student, mentor, and instructor may renegotiate the timeline or the parameters of the project according to the student's needs. This allows the students more opportunities to learn well before moving ahead.

In the weekly reports, students and the instructor regularly evaluate the students' ongoing progress. As the mentors read the reports and the instructor's comments, mentors, too, may assess progress. In this way the students receive constant feedback on their learning both between mentor and mentee and between instructor and student. Because learning goals are clearly defined, then documented, decisions can easily be made about whether the student has mastered a skill or concept.

Neither mentors nor the instructor can easily set a single performance norm that applies to all students within a *Field Experience* class.
Don's computer program and Shannon's research on camels do not
readily compare, nor should they. However, the goals and agreements
set by mentor and mentee in the blueprint provide the individual criteria for evaluation. The blueprints also provide the means for account-
ability and evaluation. As the experience ends, have the students met
each of the goals and agreements they developed?

Written evaluations

After the Open House, the instructor mails evaluation forms to
mentors requesting that they evaluate both the student's work and the
program (see Figure 7-1). Mentors consider the quality of the mentees'
work, the mentees' work habits, and the degree of challenge they
believe their mentees experienced through their mentorship work.

Similarly, the instructor asks mentees to evaluate themselves (see
Figure 7-2). Students consider their responses to the same questions
listed for mentors: Rate the quality of your work, the quality of your
work habits, and the degree of challenge you experienced as a mentee.

Both mentor and mentee are asked to rate the overall quality of the
experience for mentees. In addition, mentors rate the overall quality of
their own experience. Students and instructors may also complete a
more extensive rating sheet which lists the skills and behaviors which
Mentor Program students strive to achieve (see Figure 7-3).

When the evaluations have been completed, the instructor schedules an exit conference with each student. Mentors may attend or
schedule a separate exit conference with their mentees. The exit conference allows participants to review the entire experience and to evaluate the students' learning according to the criteria set forth in their
blueprints. Instructors can evaluate the students' overall performance
in interpersonal communications and responsibility by the criteria
established during *Mentor Seminar.*

Program Evaluation

The mentor and student evaluation forms shown in Figures 7-1 and 7-2 also contain sections for overall program evaluation. Students rate the overall experience and the value of various *Seminar* and *Field Experience* activities together, if they are completed as one course. If *Seminar* has been taught separately, then, of course, that phase would be evaluated at its conclusion (see Figure 7-4). Finally, in the closing evaluations students may offer suggestions to improve the program.

Mentors rate their experiences with the program including such pivotal issues as: whether their responsibilities were adequately described, whether their relationships with mentees were meaningful "in terms of discussions held, ideas exchanged, and experience shared," whether the mentors' participation caused a significant inconvenience in terms of time, and whether they would consider being a mentor again.

For the most objective reporting on an evaluation, the data may be analyzed by an independent evaluator. The steering team also may appoint a committee to analyze and compile the information obtained or the program instructors may do this. The results of the evaluations must be included in planning for the following year.

The team will also want to review the program as a group and to generate feedback from the community to continue to improve the program. Each year provides another opportunity to fine-tune and adjust the program through input from the students, mentors, teachers, the team, parents, community businesses and organizations, and administrators.

For example, as instructor I perceived that students were not well prepared for the demands of mentorship after just a few preparatory classes. For a period of two years I carefully noted the difficulties students and their mentors encountered. I also collected information from program evaluations and conversations with students, mentors, and parents. As I developed a list of skills to ease the transition into mentorship, I presented my ideas to the steering team and asked them to check for relevant curriculum offered within their high schools. I hoped to generate new ideas and to avoid duplicating established cur-

Fig. 7-1

MENTOR PROGRAM MENTOR EVALUATION

Please complete this form to evaluate the Mentor Program and student with whom you worked. Your responses to items on the first page will become part of the students' evaluation for credit and grade. The second page items relate to the program mechanics.

MENTOR NAME .... **DATE** ....

STUDENT'S NAME .... **INSTRUCTOR** ....

Please comment and also circle the most accurate description.

1. Comment on the quality of student work on the project.

....

....

....

SURPASSED EXPECTATION   MET EXPECTATION   NOT UP TO EXPECTATION

2. Comment on the work habits that the student exhibited (independence, punctuality, initiative, etc.).

....

....

....

SURPASSED EXPECTATION   MET EXPECTATION   NOT UP TO EXPECTATION

3. Comment on the student's skills employed to communicate about the project.

....

....

....

SURPASSED EXPECTATION   MET EXPECTATION   NOT UP TO EXPECTATION

4. Comment on the learning challenge that the project provided the student. Did it stretch him/her beyond what he/she already knew?

....

....

....

SURPASSED EXPECTATION   MET EXPECTATION   NOT UP TO EXPECTATION

Fig. 7-1 cont'd.

MENTOR PROGRAM MENTOR EVALUATION, cont'd.

5. Check all the items that describe what the student learned.

___ Technical Skills   ___ Independent Work Skills

___ Advanced Research Skills   ___ Advanced Subject Matter

___ Other (specify) _____

6. On a scale of 1–10, how worthwhile was the learning experience for the student?

1	2	3	4	5	6	7	8	9	10

Useless   Useful   Worthwhile

7. Based on your comments above, what grade would you give the student for his/her overall performance at your worksite? (You may use +'s and –'s.)

A Excellent   **B** Good   **C** Average   **D** Below Average

....

1. My responsibilities were described adequately.

STRONGLY DISAGREE   DISAGREE   UNCERTAIN   AGREE   STRONGLY AGREE

....

2. The informational material was helpful.

STRONGLY DISAGREE   DISAGREE   UNCERTAIN   AGREE   STRONGLY AGREE

....

3. The informational meeting(s) was (were) helpful.

STRONGLY DISAGREE   DISAGREE   UNCERTAIN   AGREE   STRONGLY AGREE

....

4. The mentor/student relationship was meaningful in terms of discussions held, ideas exchanged, and experiences shared.

STRONGLY DISAGREE   DISAGREE   UNCERTAIN   AGREE   STRONGLY AGREE

....

5. My participation **did not** cause significant inconvenience in the performance of my job.

STRONGLY DISAGREE   DISAGREE   UNCERTAIN   AGREE   STRONGLY AGREE

....

6. I would consider being a mentor to a future student.

STRONGLY DISAGREE   DISAGREE   UNCERTAIN   AGREE   STRONGLY AGREE

....

• • •

Fig. 7-2

MENTOR PROGRAM STUDENT EVALUATION

Please complete the following items to evaluate both your learning as part of the Mentor Program and the program itself. Your self-evaluation will be added to your mentor's and instructor's evaluations for credit and grade in the Mentor Program. Your evaluation of the program will assist us in making improvements in the future.

STUDENT'S NAME .... DATE ....

MENTOR NAME ....

Please comment and also circle the most accurate description.

1. Comment on the quality of your work on your Mentor Program project.

....

....

....

SURPASSED EXPECTATION   MET EXPECTATION   NOT UP TO EXPECTATION

2. Comment on your work habits during your mentorship (independence, punctuality, initiative, etc.).

....

....

....

SURPASSED EXPECTATION   MET EXPECTATION   NOT UP TO EXPECTATION

3. Comment on degree to which you were challenged by the learning on your mentorship.

....

....

....

SURPASSED EXPECTATION   MET EXPECTATION   NOT UP TO EXPECTATION

4. Check all the items that describe what you learned during your mentorship.

    __ Technical Skills   __ Independent Work Skills

    __ Advanced Research Skills   __ Advanced Subject Matter

    __ Other (specify) _____

Fig. 7-2 cont'd.

5. How many total hours did you spend working with your mentor or on work related to your mentorship?

6. On a scale of 1–10, how would you relate **your learning** as part of the Mentor Program?

1	2	3	4	5	6	7	8	9	10
Poor				OK					Top Quality

7. Rate the following components of the Mentor Program in terms of the value of each to you, personally.

	VALUABLE				OF LITTLE VALUE	
Orientation (advanced level reading to obtain a focus for the mentorship)	5	4	3	2	1	NA

Preparation Lab & Classroom Topics

• Assertiveness	5	4	3	2	1	NA
• Creativity	5	4	3	2	1	NA
• Decision Making	5	4	3	2	1	NA
• Giftedness	5	4	3	2	1	NA
• Interviewing	5	4	3	2	1	NA
• Weekly Letters	5	4	3	2	1	NA
• Oral Communications	5	4	3	2	1	NA
• Questioning Activities	5	4	3	2	1	NA
• Research Skills	5	4	3	2	1	NA
• Resumé Writing	5	4	3	2	1	NA
• Self-Awareness Activities	5	4	3	2	1	NA
• Stress Management	5	4	3	2	1	NA
• Weekly Seminar Discussions	5	4	3	2	1	NA

Mentorship

• Initial Interview	5	4	3	2	1	NA
• Assigned Readings	5	4	3	2	1	NA
• Observation of Mentor's Work	5	4	3	2	1	NA
• Visits with Others at Worksite	5	4	3	2	1	NA
• Your Project Work	5	4	3	2	1	NA
• Conversations with your Mentor	5	4	3	2	1	NA
• Observations of Others' Work	5	4	3	2	1	NA
• Attending Meetings, Etc.	5	4	3	2	1	NA
• Personal Relationship with Mentor	5	4	3	2	1	NA
• Relationship with Others at Site	5	4	3	2	1	NA

Summation

• Prep. of Open House Product	5	4	3	2	1	NA
• Recognition Program/Dinner	5	4	3	2	1	NA
• Open House	5	4	3	2	1	NA

● ● ●

Fig. 7-2 cont'd.

Please respond to the following questions about the entire Mentor Program.

8. What was the most exciting part of your mentorship?

9. What was the toughest part of your mentorship?

10. What recommendations do you have for the designers and implementers of the Mentor Program?

11. Do you anticipate that you will keep in contact with your mentor(s)?

12. On a scale of 1–10, indicate how worthwhile you feel this program was for you.

1	**2**	**3**	**4**	**5**	**6**	**7**	**8**	**9**	**10**
Worthless				OK					Worthwhile

Fig. 7-3

SEM 1 SEM 2
TRI 1 TRI 2 TRI 3

NAME .... ABSENCES ....

SCHOOL .... TARDIES ....

Honestly evaluate yourself on the following criteria, using the rating scale provided. A place has been provided for STUDENT evaluation and for TEACHER evaluation. Please comment or explain when necessary in the spaces provided. You may use the back of the paper if you need more space.

A – Excellent   **B** – Good   **C** – Average   **D** – Fair   **F** – Poor

SURPASSED EXPECTATIONS   MET MINIMUM EXPECTATIONS   LESS THAN MINIMUM

RESPONSIBILITY/ RELIABILITY (35%)

	MID-SEMESTER MID-TRIMESTER		SEMESTER 1 TRIMESTER 1		SEMESTER 2 TRIMESTER 2		TRIMESTER 3	
	S	T	S	T	S	T	S	T
Attendance in class								
Punctuality in class								
Attendance with mentor								
Punctuality with mentor								
Courtesy: called teacher when absent or tardy								
Courtesy: called mentor when absent or tardy								

Hours of mentorship work weekly

A (10 or more hours) **B** (9-10 hours) **C** (8 hours) **D** (7-8 hours) **F** (less than 7 hours)

Comments or explanations for the above:

MID-SEMESTER/TRI
....

SEMESTER/TRI 1
....

SEMESTER/TRI 2
....

TRI 3
....

Weekly letters in								
Weekly letters on time								
Other assign./req. forms in								
Other assign./forms on time								
Make-up work asked for/completed								

Comments or explanations for the above:

MID-SEMESTER/TRI
....

SEMESTER/TRI 1
....

SEMESTER/TRI 2
....

TRI 3
....

• • •
207

Fig. 7-3 cont'd.

MENTOR PROGRAM GRADING AND EVALUATION, cont'd.

QUALITY OF WORK/ PROJECT (35%)	MID-SEMESTER MID-TRIMESTER		SEMESTER 1 TRIMESTER 1		SEMESTER 2 TRIMESTER 2		TRIMESTER 3	
	S	T	S	T	S	T	S	T
Effort focusing/narrowing topic								
Have you been able to focus? (Y/N)								
Describe your progress:								
Effort put into prep lab								
Quantity of research time								
Quality of research time								
Effort put into project								
Quality of project								
Amount of overall learning								
Quality of overall learning								
Effort put into overall learning								
Have you followed your timeline? (Y/N)								

Comments or explanations for the above:

MID-SEMESTER/TRI

SEMESTER/TRI 1

SEMESTER/TRI 2

TRI 3

QUALITY OF INTERPERSONAL COMMUNICATIONS (30%)	MID-SEMESTER MID-TRIMESTER		SEMESTER 1 TRIMESTER 1		SEMESTER 2 TRIMESTER 2		TRIMESTER 3	
	S	T	S	T	S	T	S	T
Weekly letters – Effort								
Are the letters clear and not vague? (Y/N)								
Have you accounted for 8 hours? (Y/N)								
Do the letters tell what you've been doing, learning, studying, etc.? (Y/N)								
Do they tell about your reactions or feelings to what you've been learning? (Y/N)								
Use of verbal communication in class								
Quality of verbal communication								
Effort in practicing verbal and nonverbal skills learned in prep lab								
Effective communication (e.g., Do you inform the teacher honestly regarding problems with mentorship?)								
Growth in effective communications								

Fig. 7-3 cont'd.

MENTOR PROGRAM GRADING AND EVALUATION, con'd.

SUMMARY	MID-SEMESTER MID-TRIMESTER		SEMESTER 1 TRIMESTER 1		SEMESTER 2 TRIMESTER 2		TRIMESTER 3	
	S	T	S	T	S	T	S	T
Overall growth in the program								
How do you feel about yourself in the program?								

Comments or explanations for the above:

MID-SEMESTER/TRI

SEMESTER/TRI 1

SEMESTER/TRI 2

TRI 3

What has been the most valuable learning for you in this program?

MID-SEMESTER/TRI

SEMESTER/TRI 1

SEMESTER/TRI 2

TRI 3

What do/did you need in the Mentor Program that you aren't getting? How could your teacher help you?

MID-SEMESTER/TRI

SEMESTER/TRI 1

SEMESTER/TRI 2

TRI 3

Other comments:

Overall letter grade you have earned this period

MID-SEMESTER/TRI

....
Student Signature   Teacher Signature

SEMESTER/TRI 1

....
Student Signature   Teacher Signature

SEMESTER/TRI 2

....
Student Signature   Teacher Signature

TRI 3

....
Student Signature   Teacher Signature

• • •

Fig. 7-4

MENTOR PROGRAM MENTOR SEMINAR COURSE EVALUATION

Please rate the following portions of the course on a scale of 1–5, with 5 representing the best or highest and 1 the lowest rating. Please include whatever comments you can. Your cooperation is much appreciated.

1. SELF AWARENESS

Includes Myers Briggs, learning styles, hemispheric modes, Strong Campbell, journals, guest speaker on giftedness, and Groton video.

1   2   3   4   5

What, if anything, **must** be kept in this section of the course?

Things I would change or drop from the class. Please be as specific as possible in your recommendations.

2. CAREER AND COLLEGE PLANNING

Includes researching career information, planning for college, and visiting Carleton College.

1   2   3   4   5

What, if anything, **must** be kept in this section of the course?

Things I would change or drop from the class. Please be as specific as possible in your recommendations.

3. RESEARCHING

Includes using professional journals, indices, the University library, and community resources; writing a reference sheet; and researching your project.

1   2   3   4   5

What, if anything, **must** be kept in this section of the course?

Things I would change or drop from the class. Please be as specific as possible in your recommendations.

Fig. 7-4 cont'd.

4. INTERPERSONAL COMMUNICATIONS

Includes nonverbal communications, assertiveness, conflict resolution, introductions, resumés, interviewing skills and video, body language in business.

1   2   3   4   5

What, if anything, **must** be kept in this section of the course?

Things I would change or drop from the class. Please be as specific as possible in your recommendations.

5. VALUING CULTURAL DIVERSITY

Includes handouts and video on cultural diversity, Jose Garcia, parts of Groton video.

1   2   3   4   5

What, if anything, **must** be kept in this section of the course?

Things I would change or drop from the class. Please be as specific as possible in your recommendations.

6. FACULTY CONTACTS, MEETING WITH A PROFESSIONAL, ALL ASPECTS OF THE PROJECT

1   2   3   4   5

What, if anything, **must** be kept in this section of the course?

Things I would change or drop from the class. Please be as specific as possible in your recommendations.

•••

Fig. 7-4 cont'd.

7. If you could give one piece of advice to next year's class, what would it be?

8. Do you plan to complete your field experience winter trimester of next year? If not, please let me know if or when you plan to complete it.

9. If it applies, please describe the kind of mentorship you would like, including names or places of which you might be aware, specific activities with which you would like to be involved, or any other information that would help me place you.

10. Please write any questions you would like answered about the field experience.

Thank you for all your hard work and attentiveness during the course. We value your responses to this questionnaire.

riculum. The chair also requested that the team speak with students and professionals about the preparation most important for successful mentorships. Through this research, the skills necessary for successful mentorships became apparent. Everyone agreed that strong mentorships require substantial preparation. Again, the program evaluation paid off; *Mentor Seminar* became a separate course and a prerequisite to *Field Experience*.

Of course, educational researchers may wish to conduct more formal research into a mentoring program. For example, instruments may be developed to gauge the extent of the students' learning in a field or to measure the social and emotional gains (such as self-confidence or sense of personal fulfillment) they may experience. Similarly, much remains to be researched about the mentors and their roles. The effects of preplacement training (like *Mentor Seminar*) on mentees' performance could also yield interesting data.

Into the New Cycle and Beyond

Implementing recommendations

With the evaluation feedback, instructors and the team know whether to revise curriculum, student requirements, mentor and public relations strategies, or even the evaluation process itself. In this way, the instructor and steering team model the behaviors expected of students. They challenge themselves and the program to grow and evolve along with the students. Goals for the next year can be set, and the team carefully charts a course for the next cycle and beyond.

Student reunion and update

Those associated with a high school mentoring program hear recurring questions about it: What happens for students after they have completed a mentoring program? Do they remain in the same career field? Do they obtain employment with their mentors? Do the students retain friendships with their mentors?

A well-designed program will track students beyond the program's end. This can be accomplished in a variety of ways. For instance, the instructor and steering team might collect important questions then meld them into a periodic survey of past graduates. If the program publishes a newsletter, it can solicit updates on former students. The updates might appear in a regular column. Of course, program graduates would receive the newsletter regularly. A newsletter also helps keep the program staff or a newsletter committee current on subscribers' addresses.

Some students may choose to remain active in the mentoring program through public speaking to groups, serving on the steering team, mentoring students, or providing other valuable services to the program. Contact with graduates also provides a window on the role mentoring can play in a life cycle.

Those affiliated with the *Mentor Program* have especially enjoyed another approach to keeping current, an annual reunion. Each year, all past graduates are invited to a reunion held during the winter holiday break. The date and time remain the same from year to year. It's very informal, and refreshments are potluck. Students who graduated together reunite and meet interesting people from other classes. Thus new connections are forged as old ones are renewed.

Watching graduates of the *Program* converse and hearing their stories and perspectives provide instructors with a sense of who their former students have become. While difficult to analyze, the information generated at the reunion adds new insights to the data collected on the surveys, real life—something paper and pencil cannot relay. The reunion rewards students and instructors as professionals and as people. And the cycle continues.

References

Baird, L. (1982). Fanning the flame. *Journal of Experiential Education,* 5(2), 40-42.

Boston, B. O. (1976). *The sorcerer's apprentice: A case study in the role of the mentor.* Reston, VA: The Council for Exceptional Children.

Brophy, J. (1979). Teacher behavior and its effects. *Journal of Educational Psychology,* 71(6), 735.

Gursky, D. (1990). A plan that works. *Teacher,* June/July, 46-55.

Pollack, S., Chrispeels, J., & Watson, D. L. (1987). *A description of factors and implementation strategies used by schools in becoming effective for all students.* San Diego, CA: San Diego County Office of Education. Paper prepared for presentation at the meeting of the American Educational Research Association, Washington, DC.

Spady, W. G. (1988). Organizing for results: The basis for authentic restructuring and reform. *Educational Leadership,* 46(2), 4-8.

Persuading Others to Get Involved

Do what you can, with what you have, where you are.

— Theodore Roosevelt

Five years ago when James Nelson spoke about architecture to Kurt's high school drafting class, Kurt became intrigued with the profession. The next year while he prepared for *Field Experience,* Kurt recalled his conversation with Nelson and asked his instructor to try to arrange a mentorship with him.

The instructor called Nelson and suggested the possibility. Nelson was pleased that Kurt selected him as a prospective mentor. As the two chatted, Nelson's reasons for becoming a mentor—or at least some of them—surfaced. He expressed interest in helping educate young people; that was the purpose for visiting Kurt's class. He also stated clearly his desire to contribute to the community. In that conversation, the instructor and Nelson also discussed the business's time and staff commitment. It was agreed that Kurt, Nelson, and the instructor would meet to discuss the mentorship further.

Since that time, Nelson has mentored a student each year. The year after he worked with Kurt, he invited me to speak to an organization of professionals within his community. As social action chairperson, Nelson said he hoped that others there would volunteer to mentor. By the next year when a new social action chair was appointed, our program had a membership and occupation roster for the group; when we needed a mentor in a particular field, all we did was call the social action chair. A network had been established and through the initial efforts of one man, many students have been served.

Nelson's efforts provided a model for other organizations to follow. Having one contact who helps identify and recruit mentors saves *Mentor Program* staff time and allows prospective mentors to serve students, their organizations, and the community.

James Nelson's initial involvement with the *Mentor Program* began years of service. As this book was published, he was serving on the program steering team and speaking to prospective mentees and their parents about mentors' role, needs, and desires. One convinced person can contribute immeasurably. The same reasoning that caught Nelson's attention will interest other mentors. One organization's commitment generates support from other groups.

So, it can be worth the time to persuade people to become involved. But before deciding whether a high school mentoring program is worth pursuing, four questions must be answered about the nature of a program and the effects it has on those involved. First, what is high school mentoring? A specific definition of high-school mentoring clarifies the standards by which a program can be judged. This book has presented the definition used by the *Mentor Program,* but the creators of each program, in order to be successful, must define it for themselves. Because mentoring is covered in depth through the book, the definition will not be covered here. Readers can use the information in Chapters 1 through 7 to generate their own definitions.

Second, what are the effects of mentorships on students and the staff and schools serving them? Third, how does mentor participation impact the mentors and the businesses employing them, and does student participation affect businesses in any way?

Finally, because mentorships involve diverse members of the community in an effort to educate high school students, how might the presence of a mentoring program impact the community as a whole?

The answers to these four questions provide a basis for determining the value of a mentoring program and whether such a program will provide a meaningful and beneficial experience for its participants, their schools and businesses, and, perhaps, the community at large. This chapter focuses on some possible answers—powerful communication, I hope, for convincing others of the value of mentorships.

The information provided here is intended to be comprehensive enough to persuade a reluctant mentor, employer, school administrator, teacher, or parent to become involved. If you wish to pursue a mentoring program, you will need to use the information within this book along with knowledge of your own situation and the resources available in your community and, then, to apply them to your best advantage to convince others.

Before you present the idea, it would be best if you drafted a short (i.e., one page) written proposal for a program which includes some of the givens of your situation. For example, you might include which organizations or businesses you *know* would help; the kind of student supervision you know your principal would require; or how you can prove that benefits to students merit the time they invest.

Some of the most common kinds of resistance encountered from mentors and their employers have been discussed in Chapter 4. Teachers' and parents' concerns have been highlighted in Chapter 6. School administrators will most likely weigh practical considerations such as cost, scheduling, and monitoring the students' off-campus activities with the educational benefits to them. In fact, everyone you talk to will weigh the benefits described here in their decision about whether to become involved in developing a mentoring program.

The Value of Mentorships

Mentoring relationships affect and benefit the students and the faculty and schools who serve them in many ways. The effects for students who participate in a mentoring program include honed thinking skills and creativity, increased self-esteem, better developed skills in the field, more clearly defined career options, connections made between work and school, increased motivation to achieve, friendships made with mentors and fellow students, inspiration generated by a role model, matured sense of responsibility and direction, and better understood and developed potentials. The effects on staff who are connected with a mentoring program include increased satisfaction with work roles, additional classroom resources and professional development, and the opportunity to support an enthusiastic student on a one-to-one basis. Schools, of course, benefit directly in any situation which enriches both students and staff.

The literature cites several effects mentors have derived from service to mentees. These effects include a rejuvenated spirit, clarified goals and renewed hope for the future, a changed sense of self, increased opportunities and new ideas, established friendships, new talent assisted to enter the profession, and accomplished goals through the mentee's efforts.

Businesses may achieve some overall corporate goals through their investment of time and resources into a mentoring program. Besides the increased well-being and satisfaction of their employees who choose to mentor, businesses may help to promote educational change, improve the quality of future employees or citizens and contribute to the community through mentoring. Companies also promote good public relations and may generate marketing benefits as well.

So, a mentoring program affects students, faculty, schools, mentors and their businesses, involving both the people and the institutions which comprise a community. When students and workers, schools and businesses unite on the behalf of youth, the community benefits. A mentoring program benefits the community by helping to foster more ethical decision-making skills in the students who participate, to increase interdependent relationships, and to promote cooperative, rather than competitive, ventures.

This chapter provides evidence supporting each of these benefits. The information should prove useful in persuading those who remain unconvinced about the value of mentoring programs to all concerned.

Effects on Students

The following sections describe the documented outcomes for students who participate in mentoring programs compiled from the literature and from the data elicited from the *Mentor Program.*

Increased self-esteem

Moore (1982) and Johnson (1980) both reported that mentoring resulted in strengthened self-esteem and confidence among mentees in academe and business respectively. While strengthened self-esteem and the intrinsic knowledge that one is capable in some area can be elusive to measure, these are extremely valuable outcomes from mentorship. One student wrote in response to an *MPG Survey* question, "I gained a sense of maturity and independence." A young woman who learned about international trade stated,

> *It's wonderful for self-confidence building. I felt I had some very valuable experience that others my age didn't such as meeting with adults, thinking on your feet, and analyzing written business materials. I also felt I gained autonomy and time-management skills.*

A future artificial intelligence expert noted his strengthened self-esteem through growth in "professionalism" and his ability "to present a good, honest picture of who you are to other people and to respect them."

The autumn after completing her mentorship, a budding scientist had to put her newfound confidence to immediate use. She reported:

> *I think learning about people's personalities is the best skill I could have ever learned. (It comes in handy in dealing with people who do not feel that women belong in a science related field.)*

Sometimes, communicating with adults allows students comfort in revealing a bit more of themselves. A *Mentor Program* graduate summarized this idea by stating, "All the communications skills were great. I used to be really shy and the *Mentor Program* kind of opened me up. Thanks."

Booth (1980) noted that the seventh- and eighth-grade students in her school's mentoring program developed a positive self-image. From students' acceptance of larger responsibilities than those that might have been demanded within a self-contained classroom they derived a boost in self esteem. A *Mentor Program* graduate also reflected on the effect of those demands:

> *Learning to be flexible, compromising and organized has helped me in schoolwork, jobs—in almost everything I do! Without flexibility I never would have gotten to Austria or through college registration and schedule changes.*

Finally, Booth (1980) observed that students can learn to look outside of themselves through a mentoring experience. Their feelings of self-worth can grow stronger by contributing to others in the community. A *Mentor Program* graduate echoed this sense of personal empowerment when she commented, "By learning about etiquette and meeting important people, it made me realize that someday I could actually make a difference."

Better developed skills in the field of interest

Of course, confidence can evolve from a vast array of experiences. As the preceding students' comments suggest, developing new skills is one of the most frequently observed sources of esteem in a school-based mentoring program. Edlind and Haensley (1985) have noted that through the "career mentorships" affiliated with Texas A&M University, the high-school-age mentees increase their knowledge and skills both generally and within the field. Phillips (1977) also noted instruction or training as a key benefit to mentees. A *Mentor Program* graduate whose mentor was a journalist with a major metropolitan newspaper concurred. She recounted:

> *I learned that I can find out anything (almost) I want to know just by perseverance (and phone calls and trips to the library). One friend*

was in her junior year of a journalism major before the professor had the students the do same stuff [my mentor] had me doing my senior year in high school! I really do think the best way to learn how to do something is to do it and to be around people that do it as well! Without [the mentor's] help this never would have been possible.

Students need assistance to obtain valuable experiences and to help them build skills otherwise unavailable to them. As one young woman indicated, the *Mentor Program*'s intervention on her behalf made a significant difference in her education:

My mentorship has turned out to be great experience. I've not only learned lab procedures and etiquette, but I've also had the opportunity to meet many people in the field of molecular biology. In general, I'm learning things I could never do in high school.

Students in mentoring programs gain a diversity of skills in a variety of fields. High schools cannot offer such a variety of experiences with real-life emphasis, depth, and sophisticated equipment. The following students responses to the *MPG Survey* suggest just a few of the diverse fields in which students can build applicable skills through a mentorship:

I learned how to work better with special needs children and was given valuable insight into the social work system.

While with my mentor, actually getting acquainted with the aviation "community"; and seeing what a day of operations is like [was most valuable].

I learned about the court system and the necessary official documents used in abuse cases.

Before I did the Mentor Program I had no idea what the "real" duties of a doctor or nurse were. I learned a lot about the everyday activities involved in medicine.

Honed thinking skills and creativity

Isaksen and Treffinger (1985) distinguish between convergent thinking which involves judgment and divergent thinking which requires imagination. In high school mentoring programs, students learn how to think, observe Edlind and Haensley (1985). They use critical thinking skills to analyze problems and to think about themselves.

When asked his most valuable gain, a *Mentor Program* mentee of a recording engineer responded, "Setting goals and following through." He had gained the thinking skills necessary to structure solutions to professional problems and to sequence his work in order to achieve the results he envisioned.

Another insightful student interested in becoming an entrepreneur stated, "Most important to me was just the time given to serious thought about one's self." This multitalented young man needed time to sort his personal priorities and options in order to make decisions about his future.

As Nash and Treffinger (1986) note, "People in mentoring relationships are problem solvers" (p. 20). They consistently confront the unknown and seek answers. In a mentoring situation, mentor and mentee find new ways to respond to problems within the field of mutual interest; they also use these skills in the process of developing their relationship. Boston (1976) observes that a key role of a mentor is to structure the "creative pause." The mentor may devise problems and allow time to teach the process of reflecting and generating solutions to them. Edlind and Haensley (1985) add that students' creative capacities were enhanced within their high school mentorship program. The research suggests, then, that students must apply both convergent and divergent thinking skills in mentoring situations.

Feldhusen and Treffinger (1985) present "the three-stage model" of developing creative thinking and problem-solving. The third and final stage of the model culminates in "developing independence in research and creative production" (p. 15). In this stage students take initiative and the classroom teacher assumes the role of "resource person and guide."

The mentoring process elevates the students' educational outcomes to a level beyond what students and teacher can accomplish together.

Perhaps mentoring adds a "fourth stage" to the creative thinking and problem-solving model where students still take the initiative, the professional mentors act as resource persons and guides, and the teacher provides the "double-mentoring" or additional support.

In completing their mentorship projects, students have considered a wide range of problems: creating an artificial hand with tension adjustment so the user can hammer nails, then adjust the tension to lift a rose without crushing it; planning the optimum time interval to allow between breeding sows; creating and mounting a personal art exhibit; solving the "Saigon tower" problem in robotics; probing the intricacies of genetically engineering the RSV virus associated with AIDS; or planning and managing a fashion show for a local mall. The opportunities to solve problems and use both convergent and divergent thinking are endless.

More clearly defined career options

In a 1990 survey of American teenagers, the University of Michigan's *Journal of Home Economics* found that three of their top ten worries related directly to future careers. Teenagers listed the following career-related concerns in their top ten worries: choosing a career or finding steady work ranked second on the teenagers' list; being successful in a particular line of work ranked third; and making a lot of money was the eighth biggest worry of today's teens (Gelman, 1990). According to this survey, selecting among career options weighs very heavily upon the teenage population.

Among gifted/talented students, selecting career options is no less daunting. Simpson and Kaufman (1981) studied the career choices and relevant histories of 322 Presidential Scholars. They found that on their own gifted children won't necessarily discover the opportunities available to them. They recommended a comprehensive career education program to "provide the guidance needed by gifted children to efficiently develop their potentials."

Simpson and Kaufman also uncovered the feelings of confusion experienced by multitalented people and recommended they be guided to combine their talents in unusual ways. They suggested that multitalented people who had successfully combined occupations and leisure activities could serve as mentors to help gifted students develop successful combinations in their own lives.

Students who apply for mentorships designate an area in which they seek advanced learning. Developmentally, however, high school juniors and seniors also seek direction for their futures. Establishing their identity as individuals and as participants in society is a primary developmental task at this stage of life (Erikson, 1963). Because of their broader range of potentials, gifted students need more information and insights to realize a part of their unique career-development needs (Colangelo & Zaffrann, 1979; Fredrickson, 1979; Herr & Watanabe, 1979). Edlind and Haensley (1985) observed that mentorships help students to combine their talents into successful careers.

Students with talent in a variety of subjects or fields are often told, "You're so lucky! You can do anything you want and you'll be successful." This implies that they do not need help in choosing a career path. Counselors, teachers, and parents may conclude that their attentions should be diverted to those with less choices and opportunities. Unfortunately, these gifted/talented students are left confused with little idea how to sort their talents and apply them to their college or career choices. At the same time, they feel pressure from others' high expectations.

To complicate matters, these students often seek careers that require extensive training—a high cost investment in terms of time, energy, and money. Gifted/talented students may view their career as a means of self-expression or as a life-style because of their heavy investment in reaching a particular career goal. While career education may not rank as the highest priority of school-supported mentoring programs, it should be a component. Students need help and support in evaluating their educational and career options, and mentors are often best equipped to provide that guidance.

Connections made between work and school

The anecdote about Kara which begins Chapter 5 provides an excellent illustration of the impact of making real-life connections with classwork. When she observed veterinarians reconstructing a tail for a peregrine falcon and hematology work in the lab to sex an eagle, she

• • •

realized an application for advanced algebra and trigonometry. The connection inspired her to improve her performance in math class and, ultimately, to realize the importance of classroom instruction.

Increased motivation to achieve

Students who are allowed autonomous behavior—acting with freedom of choice, self-determination, and personal control—respond with high task interest, creativity, cognitive flexibility, positive emotion, and persistence according to a study by Deci and Ryan (1987). A mentoring program allows students autonomous behavior in choosing topics and focus, in selecting a mentor, in working with others, and in completing their individual projects.

That participation in a mentoring program involves a moderate risk is another motivating factor for students (Deci & Porec, 1978; Hartner, 1978; Trope, 1978). According to these studies, moderate risk-taking increases performance, persistence, sense of competence, pride, satisfaction, and self-knowledge.

Clifford (1990) lists four circumstances under which moderate risk is likely to occur:

1. *The success probability for each alternative is clear and unambiguous.*
2. *Imposed external constraints are minimized.*
3. *Variable payoff (the value of success increases as the risk increases) in contrast to fixed payoff.*
4. *The benefits of risk-taking can be anticipated. (p. 24)*

Students in a mentoring program experience all four of the circumstances leading to moderate risk:

1. Students hear what others have achieved and what the mentor has to offer before a mentorship is finalized, so they can anticipate the benefits prior to a commitment.

2. Students determine their own course of study with minimal external constraints. They develop their own

skills for autonomous learning to prepare for a mentorship. The mentors guide students in meeting their own learning needs.

3. Students in a mentoring program leave the security of the classroom and the familiarity of their high schools as they participate in a mentorship on a one-to-one basis. These risks are balanced by the hope of a much greater payoff in personal growth and achievement. Success is not guaranteed, but it is probable.

4. If a student truly desires to learn about a particular field of study, what better way to learn than from a successful practitioner expert with access to the additional resources of a professional environment. The benefits of the risk can easily be anticipated.

Students in a mentoring program are invited to take a risk, to learn tolerance for errors, and to experience the pleasure of succeeding where success is not guaranteed. From the view of the researchers cited above, mentor students are invited to a motivating experience.

Friendships made

In mentoring programs students establish new friendships, according to Edlind and Haensley (1985) and Phillips (1977). Booth (1980) noted that mentees "said they liked having their ideas valued by a specialist from the community" (p. 11). Certainly, the sense of being valued by another contributes to the development of any friendship.

In the *Mentor Program Graduate Survey* (Reilly, 1990), over half (61 percent) of the students completing mentorships reported having continued contact with their mentors. Some also reported that they were employed by their former mentors.

Another form of friendship arises from the bonds formed between students who participate in a mentoring program together. Students tell me that outside of mentor class, they rarely have contact with similarly motivated and independent peers. The program instructors consistently observe that through this common experience, students share resources and ideas, socialize together, and become friends.

One group became such close friends that they always went out for pizza after class. I began to call them the "lunch club;" they, in turn, named themselves the "lunch bunch." Our last class session was conducted in that pizza parlor where I joined them for the first time. The students photographed the event and presented me with the results. Five years later, the enlarged 2' x 3' framed photo still hangs in my office, and they are still in touch with one another.

The inspiration generated by a role model

Phillips (1977) reported that mentors offer their mentees encouragement, advice or counsel, help with career moves, inspiration, and a role model. Phillips (1977) noted another aspect of role modelling in a mentor program is visibility and the excitement of being exposed to powerful people. When asked what her most valuable gain was from the *Mentor Program*, a student studying philosophy and physics at a prestigious national university responded:

> *Inspiration: Had the opportunity to see successful motivated students and adults. I also discovered what people did in my field of interest; learned people skills that few students have and that are so necessary in college and the real world.*

Another student expressed her progress as an "Openness, ease with people in authority: I'm more comfortable with anyone in authority now."

A matured sense of responsibility and direction

Martha Fulbright, director of the mentoring program in Walesco Independent School District in south Texas, reported, "parents perceive an increased responsibility and sense of direction in their children" (Cox and Daniel, 1983, p. 59).

In the *MPG Survey, Mentor Program* graduates expressed similar personal outcomes. One former mentee wrote, "It gave me the freedom to pursue a field which I could not have discovered otherwise." Another observed, "The whole experience has enabled me to deal with difficult situations and to take advantage of my circumstances." A third program graduate stated, "It gave me confidence to go ahead and try new things." In a mentoring program students can also gain an equally valuable sense of direction by ruling out options as by selecting them.

Better understood and developed potentials

Phillips (1977) and Edlind and Haensley (1985) have documented that mentoring programs allow students to develop more fully their recognized talents as well as undiscovered talents. In an *MPG Survey*, a potential lawyer reflected that skills learned during her mentorship with a university law professor carried into her college career:

> *I also got involved in University politics and found I had a flair for it . . . good enough to put me in office. I am currently winding up as President of [my] State University Student Association.*

Faculty, Schools and Mentor Programs

Educators frequently write about the results when students participate in a mentoring program, yet they rarely note the effects on the faculty and the schools which develop and offer this sort of program. Understanding how a school program affects students should certainly be top priority for educators. However, in a thorough examination of a program, the effects on staff and the institution should also be considered. While the literature on the effects of mentoring programs on staff and schools is extremely limited, this section attempts to share the observations that do exist.

Instructor satisfaction

In Chapter 4, two mentoring program instructors described the rejuvenation and excitement they felt about their work. While their words are powerful descriptors, the instructors' actions also eloquently communicate their satisfaction. I have observed instructors literally hopping with joy when they know they've established just the right match between a student's needs and a mentor's capabilities. They can hardly wait to share the student's accomplishments with other instructors, mentors, or parents.

Sometimes the pleasure comes from connecting students with mentors who have rare expertise such as the clay animation specialists who worked with Dave. Other times it is because the student has idolized a particular person for years prior to the mentorship, and then they begin working together. This was the case, for example, with a meteorologist from a national television affiliate and with a freelance environmental promoter who had spoken to her mentee's elementary class years before they ever met. Helping initiate a special relationship also increases instructors' feelings of gratification. I know I felt gratified when I watched Shannon anxiously await Bob Hinker's arrival at her graduation or when Kara's mentor warmly presented her with an elegant book about raptors.

Observing and guiding students as they create meaningful projects adds to an instructor's sense of satisfaction because students have attained greater knowledge and skills or have grown in their personal abilities such as communicating, coping, or being responsible. Instructors also feel great satisfaction when students have helped others through such activities as developing games to meet the special learning needs of twin boys with physical disabilities or supporting battered spouses and children as they rebuild their lives. Speaking from experience, mentoring programs bring instructors each of these joys and more.

Speakers and contacts for teachers in the field

When students interact with both their mentors and their teachers, teachers and mentors connect. A mentoring program steering team which provides guidance and feedback to program staff can also provide a means for teachers and mentors to interact. As a result of this interaction, mentors may volunteer to speak in the classroom; teachers may also request visits with mentors to learn more about their fields of expertise. For example, a biology teacher with a strong background in anatomy was pleased to have the opportunity to visit a cardiologist who operates a national cardiovascular registry. The contact between the school staff and mentors enriches both groups and can have implications for the education of those students who choose not to participate in the mentoring program.

Unexpected payoffs for faculty contacts

When the *Mentor Program* instructors suggested that teachers could provide support and additional educational expertise for *Mentor Seminar* students with interests compatible to their own, the steering team hesitated. Even on an informal basis, this would be an additional duty for teachers within their already hectic schedules. Yet students wanted to share their learning during *Mentor Seminar* and to have someone outside of their mentor site with whom "to speak the language" during *Mentor Field Experience.* It made sense.

The steering team formalized the concept by writing a job description for "faculty contacts" and by voting to sanction the opportunity for all mentees. Next the team explained the possibility to the teachers.

The reports from faculty contacts have been unconditionally positive. They feel stimulated and satisfied by the opportunity to support the learning of a motivated student. The faculty contacts also reported that they had learned from the *Field Experience* students and their mentors; this helped them keep abreast with their fields. For example, I watched one young woman coach her biology teacher on the details of genetic engineering; a nationally respected cardiopathologist invited a science teacher with expertise in human anatomy to visit a cardiac research institute. Sometimes in discussing their learning or their projects, teachers get fresh ideas for class curriculum or projects. Many teachers have received these unexpected payoffs in their roles as faculty contacts. As one faculty contact stated,

> *I enjoyed having one-to-one contact with a motivated student; her enthusiasm was contagious. She was politely assertive and made it [the role of faculty contact] easy for me. I learned, too.*

Benefits for Mentors

This section considers the effects of mentoring on professional mentors.

Rejuvenated spirit

One significant effect of mentoring, a rejuvenated spirit, has been recognized through the work of psychologists, Daniel Levinson and Eric Erickson. Erickson's (1980) theory of "generativity" posits that from the ages forty-five to fifty-five, middle-aged people enter a stage of their development where they feel concern for the upcoming generation of adults. At this developmental stage, adults want to help prepare younger adults for responsibilities of their own middle age. Mentoring another person provides an opportunity to pass along knowledge, skills, attitudes, and values, and satisfies the mentor's internal need to contribute. Levinson et al. (1978) also describe the "self-rejuvenation" that occurs through mentoring another person's professional growth and development. Like Erickson's work, this study revealed the satisfaction people feel from helping others lead better lives and live out their dreams.

Increased opportunity in the profession and new ideas stimulated for mentors

A public relations mentor described his primary reason for mentoring as: "the opportunity to help educate the professional community of tomorrow." Many professionals feel compelled to lend their experiences and efforts to a younger person, to "pass the torch" of the profession to the next generation. They know they can strengthen their fields by developing new talent and derive satisfaction from increasing opportunities within the field.

Developing new and fresh talent carries another reward for those who choose to mentor. The mentors experience the "enthusiasm and fresh new ideas of the student" (Phillips, 1977). As a result, mentors reevaluate the meaning of their work and their standard approaches to it. Often contact with their mentees sparks ideas for mentors. One mentor, an author and editor, gave her mentee a new manuscript to illustrate while a professional artist simultaneously created his interpretations. The mentor used the sketches to spark new ideas for illustrations in the book. Before Dave met them, his mentors concentrated on special effects, limiting their clay animation work. As Dave created his film, his mentors not only advised him, but their own interest in this form of animation resurfaced. They decided to develop their own clay-animation production to attract clients.

Accomplished goals through the mentee's work

Phillips (1977) reported that mentors can achieve vicariously through the mentee's work. They can also earn future credit for services from the mentees. For example, a former Mentor Connection student went into business with his mentor. The mentor later reported:

He helped us get the business started, and now he's off on his own, the president of his own company. He wanted to get into more (theatre) set design. But he was a founding partner of this firm, and it was a good situation for both of us." (Foster, 1990, p. 37TH)

Mentees frequently undertake projects which mentors wish to accomplish, but cannot due to other priorities. For example, a *Mentor Program* student received mentoring from a prosthetist, who creates artificial limbs. The mentor had observed the need to create an artificial hand in which the wearer could adjust the tension instead of changing the prosthesis. With the new prosthesis, a wearer could readily hammer nails, adjust the hand tension, and then, pick up a delicate flower without squashing it—all without changing the hand.

The mentee undertook the project and accomplished it in four months. One of the mentor's clients demonstrated the new prosthesis at the program's end-of-the-year exhibits. Later, the mentor heard from an out-of-state patent attorney whose company had filed a prototype and anticipated a completed product in two years!

Established friendships for mentors

Edlind and Haensly (1985) noted that high-school-age mentees can stimulate new ideas and also help mentors accomplish their work. They also report that the friendships developed are significant to mentors as well as their mentees. As already reported, the *Mentor Program Graduate Survey* found that more than half of the students surveyed (61 percent) maintained contact with their mentors (Reilly, 1990).

However, the program graduates could not report the delight mentors have expressed at maintaining those ties. As instructors place new mentees, experienced mentors frequently tell then about their former mentees or ask if the instructor knows how a former mentee is progressing. Once when I was speaking at a Chamber of Commerce luncheon, a former mentor stood up at question-and-answer time. He explained that he had mentored a student three years ago, then asked: "How do you inform mentors about what has happened to the students with whom they worked? I haven't heard from the young man I mentored in a long time. I'd like to know how he's doing." Despite the mentee's decision not to maintain contact with his mentor during that period of his life, the mentor retained an active interest in his mentee. When I informed him of the younger man's whereabouts and activities, the mentor was obviously pleased.

James Nelson, whose service to the program is documented in the beginning of this chapter, addressed *Mentor Program* students and parents. His aim was to share the essential needs that professionals have in a mentoring relationship. One of the key points this mentor stressed was: "When you have completed your mentorship, don't forget us! We care about you and want to know how you are doing—even if you choose to enter an entirely different field."

Monitored gate to the profession

Phillips (1977) noted another reason for mentoring includes acting as a gatekeeper of inner circles or repaying past favors. Many mentors rigorously screen prospective mentees about their knowledge of the field prior to establishing a relationship. For example, a mentor expert in laser technology demanded that her prospective mentee name the different kinds of lasers and then asked to explain how each one worked. Others demand a letter of inquiry and a complete resumé before they will even consider an initial meeting. What these people want to encourage is "the best and the brightest" young people who aspire to enter the field, so they screen rigorously.

Most people readily recall those who supported their entry into a profession and recognize the value of that assistance. Many mentors clearly state that they become involved to return the favor of mentoring given to them. In Chapter 4, a network news anchor talked about a mentor who helped her break into the field; another mentor, a police chief, valued the guidance he received so greatly that he urged each officer on his city's force to mentor others; and former *Mentor Program* mentees ask to become mentors for the same reason.

Changed sense of self: A risk or a benefit?

Through their decision to open the gates of a profession and their involvement in a mentoring relationship, mentors stake portions of their time, energy, and physical, emotional, and intellectual resources in the student's growth and development. Baird (1982) discusses the effects of mentoring by noting:

> *Perhaps the greatest risk he [the mentor] takes is the risk of changing him[her]self. Those with whom he [she] has volunteered to work also give, share, risk, and sacrifice—on* his [her] *behalf. He [She] needs them as much as they need him [her]. (p. 40)*

Thus mentors and mentees stake portions of their time, energy, and physical, emotional, and intellectual resources in the hope of gaining from a mentorship.

How Businesses Benefit

Along with students, faculty, schools, and mentors, businesses must also stake a significant investment in mentoring programs: They must approve and pay for the time employees contribute to a mentor program, and they often provide resources, materials, and space for the mentee.

Businesses also need to anticipate some return on their investments. The benefits discussed in the previous section which increase the success and well-being of employees have a positive influence on businesses as well. Other gains for businesses may be to promote educational change, to improve the quality of future employees or citizens, to contribute to their community, to promote good public relations, or even to market their product. This section reviews how the literature documents businesses' stake in mentoring programs and the benefits which businesses can expect to obtain from them. How mentoring programs, and therefore involved businesses, may contribute to the community will be discussed in a separate section.

Reversing "a rising tide of mediocrity"

While immediate benefits may be derived from the mentoring experience, the experience also lends itself to a long term benefit which has even greater potential. Mentoring high school students can help solve the problem of mediocrity in education.

In 1983, *A Nation at Risk* alerted the public to "a rising tide of mediocrity" in public schools. In a 1990 report to the National Commission on Children, Marc Tucker, president of the National Center on Education and the Economy, testified that to an employer "a high school diploma means absolutely nothing" (Newlund, 1990, p. 1B). Tucker warned the Commission that America's school system is failing its children, its workforce, and its economy. He suggested that the United States adopt the educational and industrial systems which function successfully in Japan and Europe. In describing his research comparing American education with that of other nations, Tucker said, "The contrast was utterly stunning."

Tucker advocated rigorous vocational training like that offered in Europe and Japan as one antidote for a worthless high school diploma:

> *The standards [in Europe and Japan] are very high. When kids have met them they can be assured that they will be a respected member of society, that they will have accomplished a set of tasks that correspond to what employers want . . . There is nothing like that in this country.* (p. 1B)

Recognizing the severity of the nation's educational problems and their impact on businesses, the business community has recently exerted efforts to influence and change school operations (Perry, 1988). Large corporations such as Exxon and Polaroid have implemented programs that attempt to deal with educational problems which impact directly or indirectly upon business (Mann, 1987; Perry, 1988). However, the motivation to play a role in education may be different for small- and medium-sized companies because they believe they do not have the resources to engage in educational endeavors.

Altruism

The importance of small- and medium-sized companies may be reluctant to extend the leadership for business and school partnerships. They express concern about becoming involved in educational conflict (Salodof, 1989). Mann (1987) found that, according to superintendents, small- and medium-sized businesses more often will support education for altruistic reasons such as civic pride, boosterism, social conscience, and corporate guilt. Regardless of the size of the business or the motivating factors, historically the least exercised option for businesses dissatisfied with education is to form a partnership (Perry, 1988).

While numbers of partnerships are rising, educational problems remain

A 1989 White House survey of business and school partnerships found that the number of school-help "partnerships" more than tripled during the five years previous to that time. In June 1989, Gary Putka reported on the front page of *The Wall Street Journal,* "Business has become one of the radical elements in school reform," although he noted problems on both the business and educational fronts:

> *Sometimes business's commitment evaporates when times get tough or management changes. Other times, school officials aren't willing or able to respond to demands for change. (p. 1A)*

Putka continued by reporting education's skepticism about business' commitment to partnerships :

Educators welcome business help, but they remain skeptical. They say that some business efforts amount to little more than public relations efforts with little lasting effect. What's more, since business' growing involvement in the schools seems directly related to its need for workers, educators wonder whether the business concern is lasting, or whether it will evaporate when the unemployment rate rises. (p. 1A)

Skepticism shared by educators and businesspeople cannot resolve whatever educational needs our communities face. However, working together to resolve those problems may help. The existence of a high school mentoring program depends on a collaborative effort between schools and businesses. Schools must change the way they structure instruction. Businesses must allot precious time, energy, and facilities to accomodate needs that do not directly contribute to the economic goals of the organization. These are substantial, if not drastic, internal changes to accomplish a common mission on behalf of youth—but they can be accomplished!

Mentorships promote change

Whatever questions remain about business and education partnerings, mentoring programs have been shown to offer significant benefits to mentees and their mentors. Further, they afford businesspeople the opportunity to become "insiders" in education and to make a significant contribution to the educational experience of each student. Mentorships also aid the individual's career development as evidenced by the fact that several mentees have obtained employment within their mentor's companies immediately following completion of the *Mentor Program* or Mentor Connection or as they complete their educations.

Recent estimates reveal that business and industry spend over $30 billion a year on education and training. More important than dollars, is the way businesses approach their role in education. John Clendenin (1990), a corporate leader, said:

> *The essential role that business must play is to work closely with educators and clearly articulate the skills, attitudes, behaviors, and dynamics of the workplace. We must do this to help educators devise and implement the appropriate coursework and experiences that allow children to make the successful transition from school to their futures. (p. 20)*

Certainly, mentorships offer one opportunity for business to become directly involved in the quality of education within their communities.

Levinson et al. (1978) observed that both education and businesses provided "mentoring that is generally limited in quantity and poor in quality" (p. 331). While mentoring has become a recognized source of human development, Perry (1988) has simultaneously observed the limited use of business-school partnerships, and therefore mentorships, to improve education. This resonates with Levinson's (1978) claim that the reluctance to form mentorships, "is a waste of talent, a loss to the individuals involved, and an impediment to social change" (p. 334).

Positive public relations

Mentorships also provide excellent public relations opportunities for businesses. The photograph on page 241 shows Dave and his two mentors developing a clay animation film. The photo and an accompanying article circulated across the entire metropolitan area in *The Minneapolis Star and Tribune* (Foster, 1990) generating exposure for their special effects firm.

Although the mentors sought only to support the young man pictured in his desire to create a clay-animated film, the photo was excellent public relations for the firm. As Mann (1987) noted, businesses, like individual mentors, may simply wish to contribute to the community in which they are located. However, exposure and increased public good will toward a company can result, and such benefits should not be overlooked in selling the idea of mentoring to a company or corporation.

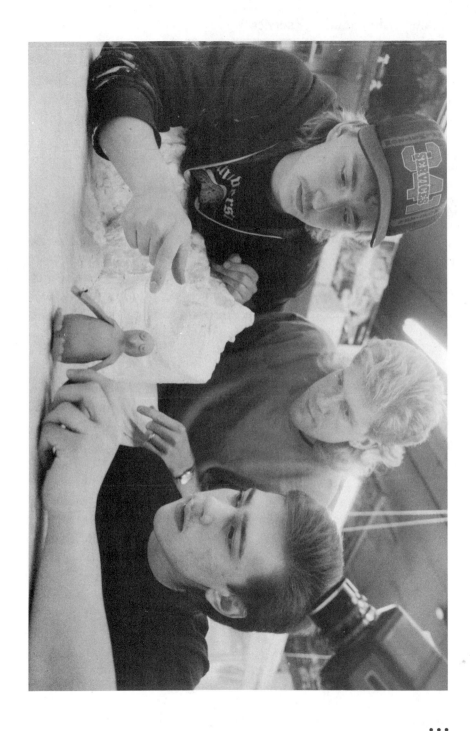

Marketing of products or services

Business infrequently states marketing of their products or services as a reason for becoming involved with a high school mentoring program. Mentoring does not yield high financial returns directly. However, some businesses do admit that through mentoring efforts a segment of the community becomes more aware of a company's products, its reputation, and new clients or customers result. The community it serves, of course, is instrumental to a business's success.

Mentoring Programs Can Benefit the Community

This section examines some possible benefits that a mentoring program might bring to the community as a whole. While it may be more difficult to concretely assess how an entire community benefits from a mentoring program, research implies that the community does gain. The gains include improved values, more interdependent relationships, and increased numbers of cooperative ventures.

The need for valuing citizens

Conversations between neighbors, teachers, people in business, and even between the nation's ethical scholars carry a common theme. A consensus is emerging: Schools must intervene more directly to positively reinforce "a common set of values necessary for responsible citizenship in personal, public, and corporate life" (Useem, 1987, p. 16). Useem (1986) argued that a demand for citizens to positively contribute to society prompted the rapid growth of business/school partnerships during the 1980s. These partnerships were forged as a means to strengthen democratic society. Useem's research also indicated that programs which serve youth cannot succeed without an intrinsic element of individual caring. In youth programs such as mentorships, the adults directly communicate values through their example of altruism, respect, and responsible behavior.

Developing a personal ethic

Caring adults—or mentors—can model positive values. Mentors may also help develop a personal ethic through challenging their mentees. In a study of developing leaders, Moore (1982) reported, "The mentor may stimulate or actively assist the protegees to develop a personal ethic" (p. 26). Mentees may not always agree with their mentors so they must develop their own methods of assessing ideas and situations. A common means for mentees to arrive at a personal ethic is to compare their own principles and beliefs with those of the mentor. Edlind and Haensly (1985) concurred with this observation. Mentees gain the skills to decide their own values and a stronger understanding of them.

Applying values to moral situations

Gaining an understanding of positive values is important for young adults. Yet they also need the skills to decide the appropriate use of their values in a moral situation. Deemer (1989) uncovered additional evidence that mentoring may enhance mentees' ability to apply values to moral situations and to be more successful and satisfied with their careers. In a study of the relationship between students' senses of judgment, fairness, and academic variables, Deemer found that moral development may be associated with different life choices.

From the high school years through the initial phases of career development, prolonged and involved experiences in intellectually stimulating environments—whether in school or in the workplace—were strongly associated with young adults' growth in moral judgment and higher moral judgment scores. The moral advancement gained from these experiences allowed the young adults to be more successful and to derive more personal fulfillment from their careers. If students experience the prolonged intellectually stimulating situation to which a mentoring program aspires, the experience may also affect the students' moral judgment and their career satisfaction.

If mentoring can help young adults develop their ability to form the values necessary for responsible "personal, public, and corporate life" and help them to apply those values, these individuals will be more of an asset to their communities.

Interdependent Relationships

Born of the student's autonomous desire for knowledge, the mentoring relationship begins with the mentee's dependence on the mentor. The mentor fosters decision-making skills and a positive personal ethic which leads to the mentee's increased competence and ability to function independently. Together mentor and mentee strive toward interdependence in their relationship and in the outcomes of their work together. Eventually, mentors and students collaborate on a project that is uniquely the student's, yet requires the mentor's expertise. Mentor and mentee work together for the common good of the profession to which they are both committed.

Even in a highly competitive society, interdependence is an essential "habit of highly effective people," says Covey (1989). He suggests that a person moves up a hierarchy from the "habit" of dependence to autonomy to the most beneficial habit, interdependence. When people are interdependent, they retain their own identities. At the same time, interdependent people are able to help one another and work for the common good. Mentoring can assist young adults to help one another and to work for the common good.

From cooperation to collaboration

On an institutional level, cooperation, rather than competition between schools and businesses also enhances a mentoring program. In fact, a mentoring program demands that schools and businesses work together and pool resources toward the common goal of providing advanced-learning opportunities for students. This effort can enhance community spirit. It can also stretch schools and businesses beyond cooperation to collaboration.

Cook and Cooking (1980) define collaboration as distinct from coordination and cooperation:

> *Collaboration is used to refer to long-term concerted efforts of agencies which labor together, which become interdependent, which are willing to undergo drastic changes internally if need be to better accomplish the common mission which binds them together. (p. 4)*

They plead for agencies to move from the traditional competitive approach to a more collaborative effort in community problem solving.

Mentoring programs require all involved to assign a somewhat lower priority to issues relevant to just the business or just the school. Both institutions must commit in theory and in practice to addressing a larger community need, better education of youth. Through working together, a sense of common mission—a community spirit—can emerge and everyone involved benefits.

Effective mentoring facilitates interdependence

Mentorship programs may provide a unique opportunity for the educational system to become more firmly connected to the rest of the community. Fantini (1981) described American education as being in the very early stages of an important transition from school system to educational system. According to Fantini, an educational system offers more options and alternatives for learning, greater recognition and utilizations of the learner's individual talents as the basis for developing a personalized learning plan, and more extensive use of community resources for educational purposes. A high school mentoring program provides one possible means by which educational changes can be accommodated.

Boston (1976) states that an "educational system exists for the purpose of equipping young people to assume their rightful places in the society and culture" (p. 33). This chapter has addressed the many ways in which mentoring programs help students to bridge their high school experiences into the arena of the workplace and the larger community. As a result of their mentoring experiences, students gain intellectual, cultural, and social skills which can benefit their personal, social, and corporate lives. Mentors also derive important new satisfactions and skills, including a rejuvenated spirit, clarified goals, and renewed hope for the future. Staff who are connected with a mentoring program also feel increased satisfaction with their work roles.

On an institutional level, a mentoring program presents rewards and challenges for the schools and businesses who become partners. When schools and businesses cooperate or collaborate on a high school mentoring program, they both gain. Schools gain better educated students, and schools and businesses increase the well-being and satisfaction of their employees. Ultimately, a high school mentoring program may benefit the community through the changes that result within the individual mentees and mentors and the overall rewards enjoyed by schools and business. Participation in a mentoring program also demands that those involved set a lower priority on competitive values and the need for personal autonomy in order to forge a collaborative, nurturing relationship between mentor and student, business and school. As a result, participants' sense of community, of coming together for a common cause, is strengthened, and urgent educational needs are met.

The next chapter presents perhaps the most persuasive argument of all, one student's experience.

References

Booth, L. (1980). Motivation gifted students through a shared governance apprentice/mentor program. *Roeper Review,* 3, 11-13.

Boston, B. O. (1976). *The sorcerer's apprentice.* Reston, VA: Council for Exceptional Children.

Carnegie Foundation. (1983). *A nation at risk: The imperative for educational reform.* Washington, D.C.: National Commission on Excellence in Education.

Clendenin, J. L. (1990). Reform through human resource planning. *The School Administrator,* April, 20-21.

Clifford, M. M. (1990). Students need challenge, not easy success. *Educational Leadership,* 48(1), 22-25.

Colangelo, N., & Zaffrann, R. T. (1979). *New voices in counseling the gifted.* Dubuque, IA: Kendall/Hunt Publishing Company.

Cook, & Cooking. (1980). Interagency action: Cooperation, coordination, collaboration. *Community Education Journal,* 7(2), 3-4.

Covey, S. R. (1989). *The 7 habits of highly effective people.* NY: Simon & Shuster.

Cox, J., & Daniel, N. (1983). The role of the mentor. *G/C/T,* September/October, 54-61.

Deci, E. L, and Porac, J. (1978). Cognitive evaluation theory and the study of human motivation. In: M.R. Lepper & D. Greene (Eds.). *The hidden costs of reward.* Hillsdale, NJ: Lawrence Erlbaum Associates.

Deemer, D. K. (1989). Moral judgement and life experience. *Moral Education Forum,* 14(2), 11-21.

Edlind, E. P., & Haensly, P. A. (1985). Gifts of mentorship. *Gifted Child Quarterly,* 29(2), 55-60.

Erikson, E. H. (1963). *Childhood and society.* (2nd Ed.) New York: W. W. Norton.

Erikson, E. H. (1980). *Identity and the life cycle.* New York: W. W. Norton.

Fantini, M.D. (1981) Options, alternatives and gifted talented. In W. I. Marks & R. O. Nystrand (Eds.). *Strategies for educational change: Recognizing the gifts and talents of all children.* NY: Macmillan.

Feldhusen, J. F., & Treffinger, D. J. (1985). *Creative thinking and problem solving in gifted education* (3rd Ed.). Dubuque, IA: Kendall/Hunt Publishing Company.

Foster, J. (1990). Mentor program gives students hands-on guidance. *Minneapolis Star Tribune,* January 11, 1Y, 9Y.

Fredrickson, R. H. (1979). Career development and the gifted. In N. Colangelo & R. T. Zaffrann (Eds.). *New voices in counseling the gifted.* Dubuque, IA: Kendall/Hunt Publishing.

Gelman, D. (1990). A much riskier passage. In *Newsweek Special Edition: The new teens. What makes them different?* Summer/Fall, 10-17.

Hartner, S. (1978). Effectance motivation reconsidered: Toward a developmental model. *Human Development,* $\underline{1}$, 401-406.

Herr, E. L, & Watanabe, A. (1979). Counseling the gifted about career development. In N. Colangelo & R. T. Zaffrann (Eds.). *New voices in counseling the gifted.* Dubuque, IA: Kendall/Hunt Publishing.

Isaksen, S. G, & Treffinger, D.J. (1985). *Creative problem solving: The basic course.* Buffalo, NY: Bearly, Ltd.

Johnson, M. C. (1980). Mentors-the key to development and growth. *Training and Development Journal,* $\underline{34}$(7), 55, 57.

Levinson, D. J., Darrow, C. N., Klein, E. B., Levinson, M. H., & McKee, B. (1978). *The seasons of a man's life.* NY: Alfred A. Knopf.

Mann, D. (1987). Business involvement and public school improvement, Part I. *Phi Delta Kappan,* October, 123-128.

Mann, D. (1987). Business involvement and public school improvement, Part II. *Phi Delta Kappan,* November, 228-232

Moore, K. M. (1982). The role of mentors in developing leaders for academe. *Educational Record,* $\underline{63}$(1), 23-28.

Nash, D., & Treffinger, D. (1986). *The mentor.* East Aurora, NY: D.O.K. Publishers.

Newland, S. (1990). U.S. schools failing children, economy, expert says. *Minneapolis Star Tribune,* October 19, 1B.

Perry, N.J. (1988). Saving the schools: How can business help? *Fortune,* November, 42-56.

Phillips, L. L. (1977). *Mentors and proteges: A study of the career development of women managers and executives in business and industry.* Unpublished doctoral dissertation, University of California, Los Angeles.

Putka, G. (1989). Learning curve: Lacking results corporations rethink aid to public schools. *The Wall Street Journal, 70*(178), A1 & A9.

Reilly, J. M. (1990). *Mentor Program Graduates Survey.* Unpublished.

Reilly, J. M. (1991). *Mentor and Student Program Evaluations: 1987-1991.* Unpublished.

Salodorf, J. (1989). Public schools and the business community: An uneasy marriage. *Management Review,* January, 31-37.

Simpson, R., & Kaufman, F. (1981). Career education for the gifted. *Journal of Career Education, 8*(1), 38-45.

Trope, Y. (1979). Uncertainty reducing properties of achievement tasks. *Journal of Personality and Social Psychology, 37*, 1505-1518.

Useem, E. (1986). *Low tech education in high tech world: Corporations and classrooms in the new information society.* New York: The Free Press.

Useem, E. L. (1987). Improving values through school-business alliances. *Curriculum Review, 26*(4), 16-20.

CHAPTER 9

Chris's Experiences with the Mentor Program

As you think you travel; and as you love you attract. You are today

where your thoughts have brought you. You cannot escape the

results of your thoughts, but you can endure and learn.

. . . You will realize the vision (not the idle wish) of your heart, be it

base or beautiful . . . for you will always gravitate towards that

which you, secretly, most love. Whatever your present environment

may be, you will fall, remain or rise with your thoughts, your

vision, your ideal. You will become as small as your controlling

desire; as great as your dominant aspiration.

— James Allen

At the beginning of Chapter 1, Chris was introduced as the intelligent, artistic student for whom school was a game he could play and easily win. If you look at the cover of this book and the design of its pages, you will see Chris Adams's art. As you've probably guessed, both refer to the same person.

I met Chris Adams on a snowy day in early 1988 when as an eleventh grader, he came to my office for an informational meeting about the Mentor Program. Chris was quiet, yet a person of depth; he asked probing questions during the meeting.

Within five days after the meeting, Chris had finished the application process, and the packet was on my desk. His was the first application for the coming year, and the earliest ever received. I immediately appreciated his responsiveness.

Yet after a group interview where Chris observed intensely and said little, I anticipated a hint of turbulence ahead. Would he expect the same responsiveness from me that he demanded of himself? Would he be willing to communicate those underlying "still waters?"

My responses proved to be a good starting point to our relationship, although time added new dimensions to it. Chris became a Mentor Program student and now, at age twenty-one, has become a colleague. He is living testimony to the joys inherent in my position.

Because his presence is so visible throughout the book, the publishers and I asked Chris if he would be willing to share his personal experiences in the Mentor Program. Characteristically addressing the crux of the matter, he shares his insights through the following narrative. Chris chose to use segments of the weekly reports he wrote while in the Mentor Program at age seventeen and his current reflections on the past. The quotations Chris selected from his weekly reports are dated; his text has not been edited except to change the names of the people and companies. I have added the subheadings and comments, in italics, after Chris completed all of his work. They are my recollections and observations as I complete this book. Chris did not see anything I had written when he wrote his own narrative.

Background (Chris Adams)

I never thought of myself as gifted and talented, in the educational sense of the phrase. I was in some gifted classes in junior high (health, social studies, English), and I never really felt that they had a real impact on my life. It seemed like they took themselves a bit too seriously.

School always seemed to be easy. At least, the school work was easy. Growing up is a little different. Classes went by and weeks went by and then years. I hardly ever missed a day. I never skipped. I was only at the principal's office once. I was in elementary school (fourth grade), and I never actually saw the principal.

I wouldn't say I was a "model" student because I enjoyed it. School was never fun. Learning and doing were fun, but never school. I was good because it was easy. And it got results. It wasn't for some time that I began to analyze the system.

Seventh and eighth grades were when I started learning what teachers (parents, adults) wanted to hear, what they wanted me to say. Approval gives everyone a good feeling. It gave me a good feeling, but it also motivated me and taught me. I like to *do* and *use*, not just read about it or write about it. I have many diverse interests, and I tend to become highly involved or interested in things until the novelty or curiousity has passed. Few things are ever completely discarded, mind you, just . . . "put away."

If I would have known these things about myself back in eighth grade, perhaps I might not have been so bored. The boredom, late in eighth grade, became the game.

Boredom. Tiring. A waste of time. All these things became synonymous with "school." The teachers weren't teaching, the classes weren't classy. It was all very frustrating. You'd tell them you understood, but they didn't believe you. So you took a test, then dwelled upon the subject for another week, just to be sure.

Things we learned seemed irrelevant, ill-timed. When do we get to try it? When can we *use* this information or these skills. School was a game and not even a fun one. School required little mental effort, so I began to wonder just *how little*. How much could I get away with, without getting into trouble? Subtlety, of course, was central. It was more fun if the other side didn't even know you were playing.

A New Opportunity

Eventually even the game got boring. After all, I was winning, at least by my own standards. By the end of my junior year, I wasn't sure how much more I could take. I needed something different. Not just a change, but something fundamentally different.

During the registration for twelfth grade, I ran across the course description for the mentoring program. It was tucked away in an obscure portion in the very back of the book, under programs offered by the technical center nearby. Since my father worked there, I asked him to get me more information.

It really seemed too good to be true: You work with a professional in the real world, learning *skills* and applying that knowledge as you go. Plus miss a half-day of school to boot. I began the application proce- dure (believe me, it was a procedure) at once. I had to submit a propos- al of what I planned to do and get recommendations and signatures from school officials I had never even *seen*. Then there were interviews and discussions, and, after much ado, I was accepted. If I make it seem long and arduous, perhaps I'm exaggerating a bit. But at the time, it looked to be a serious step I was taking. Career planning, you know . . .

Yes, and all accomplished in five days!

Mentor Seminar

The mentorship class I was in was held in the local technical insti- tute, so I had to drive to class. Driving was fine with me, since anything that allowed me to leave the confines of the school was nothing short of a blessing. There were about ten other kids in my class, mostly girls. The interests ranged from music and art to veterinary science and chemical engineering.

I was curious what it would be like to have such a small class. My high school class sizes averaged twenty-five. Not only did the smaller size allow for greater support and friendship, but also a sense of confidence that we were a small group that could do big things. We (I) came into the class full of energy and excitement, ready to learn, to experience, to *do* what I wanted to in "commercial art."

Focusing

One of the first things we had to do was *focus*. Focus our interests, narrow them down to one manageable, tangible objective. Easier said than done. I had no idea just how general the term "commercial art" was. Illustration, graphics, advertising, marketing, photography, printing, computer, and dozens of other specialties fell into that category. After much research, trips to the library and calling, I finally decided on graphic design, with an emphasis on corporate identity (logos, brochures, annual reports). It seemed to offer a wide variety of work that still allowed for some creativity. I was to learn later whether or not that was an accurate observation.

As this whole process was going on, another part of the program—classroom training—was also providing me with highly useful tools you use in the "adult world." Telephone skills, interviewing, research, assertiveness, and communication were just a few of the topics we covered. At the time, I thought it was fairly tame material. Who *didn't* know about assertiveness?

However, I was soon proved wrong as I began to realize how powerful some of these commonplace skills can be. We need to be more aware of how we present ourselves and interact with others. One of the differences I recognized in myself was an increase in self-confidence. My ability to communicate my needs clearly, without the whiny undertones of a "kid." We didn't pretend to be grown-up, we just needed to be taken seriously.

I think the way schools are run tends to lead to false perceptions of the adult world. They seem to be authoritarian, always forcing you into one thing or another; or deterrents trying to stop you from having fun. I think all of us in the mentor class were pleasantly surprised at the amount of interest and helpfulness we received from professionals in the field as we researched our topics. They offered suggestions, opinions, alternate courses of action and, ultimately, a chance to share their knowledge and experiences one-on-one.

Finding a mentor

The next step in the process was to actually find a mentor. This proved to be difficult in my case because the smaller agencies don't have time to devote to a student and the large agencies wanted college interns. It took many weeks of calling (on Jill's part) before we found a suitable site. That is, one that met my criteria (type of work, location, etc.), Jill's criteria, and a mentor who was willing to take me on.

I was looking for someone really willing to teach Chris, not simply use him as "extra hands" in exchange for the opportunity to observe. As I made calls and discovered the competitiveness and continuous time crunch in this field, I wondered if that would be possible.

Mentor Field Experience

Meeting a mentor

What I remember most is the first time I met Ann at Graphic Design and Production. It was the first time I had ever *seen* a design studio. The only tools I had ever known were a drafting board, T-square, and triangles, and I think that's what I expected to see. Maybe a small area with a few drafting boards, the general tools. Instead, I found a large office with a lot of equipment I had never seen before, plus a reception area, a conference room, accounting offices, and offices for Ann. It was an exciting atmosphere being downtown in a building with dozens of other design studios. It's not something a senior in high school usually sees.

Chris had done his preliminary work thoroughly. He had almost exhausted the many art courses offered at a high school with a nationally recognized program. Chris's coursework included Art I and II,

Architecture I-IV, Drafting I &II, Graphics, Photography, Commercial Illustration, and Independent Study in Illustration.

*During **Seminar** he had met with a cartoonist, an industrial designer, a full-service printer, and a computer animation designer. The summer prior to this course, Chris had worked in his school district print shop. He also did a considerable amount of preliminary design and reading. Yet he had never really seen a design studio before the meeting with Ann.*

We waited for a while, then met Ann in the conference area. We discussed some of the things I would learn, her expectations, etc. She talked a lot about relating with customers and office relations. But one thing that really stuck out was when she said, "Can you start Monday?" It was Friday afternoon, and she was asking if I could start Monday. "Well sure," I said or something along those lines. It seemed like it was going fast. I had no idea that was to set the pace for the rest of my mentorship at Graphic Design and Production.

Ann reviewed Chris's portfolio and commented on his emerging talent. It was apparent to me that she had a plan already in mind to further develop Chris as an artist and, perhaps, as a person. She outlined her expectations to Chris. Observing his reticence, Ann stressed the need to communicate in the context of office and customer relations. I don't think Chris perceived her comments as directed at his skills, but I did. Yes, Ann was going to teach Chris about art and so much more. As a final bonus—to me at least—she mentioned that she might be interested in Chris as a future employee. Nothing seemed too fast for me; it seemed like an outstanding opportunity for Chris. I was delighted.

Original Letters and Current Reactions

At this point Chris decided to quote directly from his original mentorship reports and then comment.

Getting acquainted

November 16, 1988

So far this week I have put in four hours at my mentor's. It's going pretty good. The first day I helped Ann put together a project for Jones Senior High and also talked to the production artist (key-lining, airbrush, paste-up, camera) and the typographer or typesetter, Tim. Yesterday I put together some folders and did some typing on an IBM-compatible computer.

Mostly I've just been learning how the office runs and getting to know the people. So far, I like what I've seen. The business seems to be pretty tame. I was with an account executive and another illustrator when they were going over preliminary sketches for an assignment. Later this week I'm supposed to learn how to answer the phones and handle customers, and I'd also like to talk with their designer sometime soon.

November 21, 1988

Since I already accounted for Mon./Tues., I'll tell you what happened Thursday and Friday: Not much. On Thursday, there was a business meeting, so I just spent some time looking at their books (some interesting titles) and learning how to use "clip art." It wasn't too hard. On Friday I spent the whole time putting together typeface books. This was boring but I familiarized myself with the various typefaces.

Maybe I didn't enjoy it much at the time, but later I was to realize the importance of typography.

A crisis?

November 28, 1988

Last week I only went to my mentorship for one
day, where I finished putting together typeface
books. I didn't learn much from it and my reaction to it is this: I won't do any more of them.

In order to make up for the day I missed I spent
some time reading the folder she gave me and
specifically a brochure called "Typesetting Spec-
ifications." I learned some of the terms typeset-
ters use and what the different typefaces are
called.

Sometimes we students expect too much. We (I) want to jump right in and try things. But there's something to be said about a solid foundation.

For me, this was the most traumatic moment in Chris's mentorship. He had worked very hard to develop a focus and background awareness. I spent untold hours trying to identify a mentor with the appropriate experiences and interest to work with Chris. Ann had even hinted at the possibility of an ongoing job. The field was important to Chris and the job wouldn't bore him. Yet he was refusing to continue an assignment made by this valued mentor.

My first reaction was to scold Chris. Next, I wondered if the mentorship would be what he really wanted. Then I thought about Ann. She certainly wouldn't ever want another student if in all her wisdom and experience she suggested activities and this seventeen-year-old bluntly refused to do them—in writing no less!

I decided to talk with Chris. I asked him why he disliked the working on the typography books so much. "It's too boring," he said. "I'm not learning anything." I tried to explain as best as I could (with a very limited background in graphic arts) the significance of typography to his work and how becoming familiar with it might be helpful. No dice.

We talked about what Chris did want to do and wrote down possibilities. Chris wanted to draw, and he wanted to use the computer. My next suggestion was for Chris to talk to Ann about what he wanted to do and how he might ready himself for those activities.

I felt uncertain about how Chris would apply his training in assertiveness—usually quiet, would he opt to say nothing or remain intractable? I decided to make a preemptive call to Ann—and not to mail the last letter—so I would understand her expectations better and perhaps smooth the path for both, the old "double mentoring" tactic at work.

When I asked Ann how things were going, she responded positively. Bright student. Hard worker. Seemed a tiny bit frustrated. Perhaps he wanted to start on the computer right now.

Bingo! I agreed that the computer was highly motivating to Chris and asked how and when he might be able to begin a little work on it.

Ann said that not even people with college degrees got to create right away. First they had to survey the basics, get to know the business, become a receptionist, do errands—in short, pay their dues. She added that she understood the impatience of high school students; she had been a foster parent of teenagers. She said she would talk with Chris and make an effort to involve him in his interest areas more.

I told Ann that I had asked Chris to approach her with the issue. Would she wait a few days before she brought it up? Chris did approach Ann on his own, and they left that meeting with a clearer mutual understanding.

• • •

I gained from the experience as well. Although I had encountered it before, I clearly realized that few high school students understand anything about paying their dues. Students come to school expecting a plan, instruction, assignments, assistance, and a grade without substantial demands on them. They rarely seem to "pay dues" for their educations. I resolved to work harder at helping students set appropriate expectations of their mentors and themselves. It was a lesson in balancing perspectives.

Down to business

December 5, 1988

Last week was a great improvement in my mentorship. I was able to do some things with Ann and other people from the firm. On Tuesday, I learned how to do printer estimate requests with Ann and a little bit of cost estimating. I never knew they did that with printers and I also got to see what kind of costs are involved.

On Wednesday, I helped Terry with some photocopying and he told me how he feels about his job (good) and Lori had me type the minutes from the last company meeting (actually the last two). This was interesting because I got to see what they talk about in the meetings and how they interact as a group. On Thursday I did a little bit of design work putting confetti-like images on the background of a thank you card for the university. This was a small step, but I was happy to do some work like that.

This week I hope to learn how to use the camera. (Didn't get to last week because they were too busy.) All in all, it was a much more productive week that the last two!

P.S. I'm not mentioning how much time spent because I go four days a week for two hours each.

I still remember the confetti project. It made me feel really good to be doing something important. A very small gesture on the part of a mentor may not seem so small for the student.

```
December 12, 1988

I had a fairly interesting week. On Tuesday I did
some reorganizing of the type books, and now I'm
completely finished with those. While I was doing
that I talked to Beth about typography. She
loaned me the "Type Directors' Club" typography
annual, which has the best work of the year from
all around the world. I really liked looking at
this book and it gave me some new ideas and new
ways to look at typography.

Wednesday I did some deliveries. I went to Con-
noir Design, which is right down the street, and
the post office. I now know where the post office
is and the library. Thursday I put together
invoices and borrowed another typography annual.
Friday I read an excellent book on typography for
beginners. I learned a lot of terms (kerning,
leading, pica, point, X-height) and some ways to
arrange type (justified, wordspacing, linespac-
ing) and its overall effect on the page. Also,
Ann's husband, Bill, told me he might have a pro-
ject for me in the near future. This week will be
busy because of the open house, so I don't know
what I'll be doing.
```

I began to be very interested in typography, and I still am. It's the basis for much written communication, and I think the raw power and variety of work that could be done was what fascinated me.

```
December 19, 1988

On Wednesday I worked for five hours and learned
many new things about PageMaker such as: how to
use column guides, changing typefaces within a
block of text, how to do manual kerning, and the
```

problems involved when the computer has to bit-
map a typeface for the printer.

Thursday was the open house, which turned out
very well according to Ann. On Friday Bill gave
me a project to work on that is due January 10.
It is a presentation board for a consulting engineer and is to be entered in a statewide competition of the consulting engineers' council. I find
out more details tomorrow, when I meet the guy.
This will probably be taking up all my time until
I finish.

This was the first project that was really mine. It was sort of a test of
my ability at this point.

"The sparkle"

January 9, 1989

These past two weeks have been very exciting. All
of my time has been spent on my project for Mr.
Whay's entry in the consulting engineers' competition. I have probably learned more with this
project than with all my other time spent there.

First of all, I had to deal with an actual client
[not a teacher (no offense!) or an imaginary
business]. This wasn't too difficult because Mr.
Whay provided me with content, but I still had to
pull it together. From what Tim told me, I had it
pretty easy because most clients want a certain
"look" and keep changing their mind about the
design, while Mr. Whay just said, "Do whatever
looks good." I also had to keep in contact with
him and get ideas approved.

Probably the most important thing I learned was
actual production processes. I have never had to
carry through to the production stage. It was
very difficult working that large. I was told

that projects are hardly ever on that scale. In order to see if things fit right, Tim suggested I make a half-scale mock-up before I do the final. I did, and I'm glad I took his advice because I found out how much the type had to be changed.

Getting the type on the board was another problem. Finally we decided to make "matro" letters. These are like press-on letters and we have the capability to make our own so we did the headline and subhead in green, and the body copy and logos in black. I also learned that I had to rely on others a lot and that was an unnecessary burden to them, I think.

Anyway, we finished the project on time. We were extremely pleased with the result, as was Mr. Whay. He said that he feels we have a good chance at winning the competition. It gets judged tomorrow so I've got my fingers crossed!

See how much I learned!?

Chris had worked on the same artistic problems before, but the real-life nature of this project pulled many of the "puzzle pieces" together into a clearer pattern. It also motivated Chris to stretch and meet the challenge. This was the first time I had seen Chris bubble with enthusiasm.

If Chris had not had the opportunity to extend the experience beyond one semester, this would have been his final letter. It takes time for all students to adjust to their mentor site, the staff and facilities. Look what happens next.

Employment, too

January 23, 1989

Last week was very busy. I learned a lot of things. Since I'm working there extra hours, I intended to keep my work hours and mentor hours separate, but they just got jumbled up. So I'm just counting the whole thing as learning.

Ann has given me one big assignment: a national supermarket chain. I'm supposed to be doing something for them, but I haven't got all the details yet. I'm excited about it though.

I finally finished my project for SJ Associates. I got a *lot* of computer time on that and did my first keyline (putting the work on an illustration board, prepared for printing). During the course of the week I also ran deliveries; did computer scans; learned how to use *Lotus 123*— working on the master list of customers, prospects, and employees; learned how to enter work invoices into the computer; helped shoot stats; and helped with payroll.

Ann offered me a part-time job with Graphic Design and Production, and I accepted. From this point on, the learning was greater and I got more responsibility as my skills improved.

Periodically, mentors offer students jobs—especially when their familiarity with the business and their skills become useful. A program's response to this issue can be debated. At the time, Chris was working at a far less satisfying job, was concerned about funds for transportation and for college, and, of course, much preferred Ann's offer. He also needed the stimulation Graphic Design and Production offered him.

Our policy for mixing work with mentorship is that the advanced-level instruction and the follow-through with program goals must continue as planned; the student must continue a minimum of eight hours per week of unpaid instructional time with the mentor (who, as you may remember, receives no pay for this role either). Any time students work beyond the required eight hours they may be paid.

The instructor confirms this arrangement with student and mentor. The mentor literally subtracts eight hours from the total number of hours present before considering pay. In this way students return the volunteer time given to them, and the focus for students and mentors remains on learning for at least eight hours. However, as Chris noted, this arrangement seems to accelerate learning.

It was difficult for Chris to separate mentorship time from work time. I asked only that he note eight hours of solid-learning time each week, which he did faithfully .

Growing confidence

January 30, 1989

Last was a busy week again. Now that I'm working there I seem to be doing a lot more. I've found out about the supermarket account I'm managing. I have put together a marketing project for the deli/bakery departments of the various divisions around the country.

I'm also in charge of an assignment for a sail-boat company. I have to do about 115 illustra-tions on the computer using Aldus Freehand. On Thursday and Friday and Saturday I did camera work shooting screens. That is converting regular 35mm photos into halftones, which is pictures with "dots" (like newspaper pix) so it can be printed. This was pretty interesting. And, finally, Bill gave me another project that I'm getting info on this week.

February 6, 1989

It seems that every week is a good week now! I'm always learning something new and doing different things. Last week I found out what it's like to call a million different places to see if they can do what we need done. (Phone skills [learned in *Seminar*] are coming in handy!)

I got more info on one of my projects so now I can get started. I got done with a good portion of the supermarket account and next week I'll be meeting with the guy from the sailboats company, who I'm doing all the computer illustrations for.

When the mentor is absent

February 13, 1989

I went to see a dealer about new software for one of my accounts, but it didn't look promising. I guess that was basically my new experience for the week. I've almost finished the supermarket job. I did the keyline this week now I have to write a letter to the companies and mail them out. I'm sure I'll have more to do when Ann gets back.

Maybe I was a little dependent on Ann still. But the rest of the employees were probably not yet totally convinced of my ability.

As time goes on, I've become much more strict about students assuming responsibility for things to do. As discussed in Chapter 4, students must tell about plans and activities for the following week as part of their progress report assignments, and they must ask mentors to suggest a few alternative ideas for reading or working at times when emergencies arise. This way there is always something to do.

The "mentor account"

February 27, 1989

These weeks are getting busy! I've got enough things going on now that I don't have to wander around the office begging for things to do. I have quite a bit of news, most of it good. First the poster [requested by the *Mentor Program* steering team to increase students' awareness of the course within the high schools served] is moving along and should be ready to print by Friday!

Ann went to the national headquarters of our supermarket account last week and my promotional letter and timeline were approved the first time around. One of the staff said that I had done well because it's hard to please the people at the supermarket account.

I talked to a client I'm doing a postcard for and he seemed happy with what I proposed and gave me the go-ahead for that project. I also received a letter from Mr. Whay. He complimented me on my good work and said he would like to work with me in the future...He also sent a letter to Bill basically saying he was pleased with the job I did.

I'm meeting tomorrow about the sailboat company illustrations which are due in two weeks... Everything is going smoothly at work and I'm happy with where I'm at. I think things can only get better the more experienced I get.

Our steering team was so taken with Chris's experiences and his growing expertise that when the question of a program poster arose, they requested he do it. We weren't disappointed.

The learning goes on

March 13, 1989

Last week was incredibly busy because I was finishing up the sailboat project. John came in and
made the necessary revisions and about 30 drawings are now complete.

I also found out how to "spec" work for a printer
that involves specifying what colors, sizes,
screens, typefaces, paper, etc. that you wanted
printed. Then I saw a proof of what it looked
like and ok'd the printing. Again, the frustra-
tions I encountered were lack of mechanical
knowledge. I'm going to have to read some more
about printing I think.

March 27, 1989

This past week was pretty good. I'm hopefully
finished with the sailboat project. (Hopefully
because someone else might have made more
changes.) I'm glad it's done because it's been
taking up all my time. Now I can work on other
things. I sent some supermarket stuff to the
printer and the first mailing for deli/bakery
programs will go out next week.

I still get bored with big projects, just because I like to keep moving
on new things. As far as clients who make changes—I'm afraid I'll
never be able to escape them.

Back to the business

April 17, 1989

The past week has been full of some new experiences. I spent several days working in the
accounting area helping Ann straighten out the
accounts. I've never really done that before, so

it was pretty interesting — but I wouldn't want it as a career! I also helped and did something called opaqueing. It covers up little white specks in negatives so the light won't show through.

May 8, 1989

On Wednesday and Thursday I worked our booth at the strictly business expo in the new convention center. That was really fun. There were hundreds of booths about everything from computers to copiers to refreshment machines. I worked as a sort of salesman for our company, telling people about our services, handing out literature, and giving demos. I was surprised how many people aren't familiar with the graphics business. We had lots of people ask about the work we do on the computer.

May 15, 1989

I spent most of the last week doing some work on CAD drawings (computer-aided drafting) for a large biomedical supply company. I like doing work like that on the computer. I also spent some time doing thank you notes and follow-ups on potential clients from the strictly business expo.

The Proof is in the Pudding

The letters ended there, but the learning didn't. I was constantly finding out more about typography, design, production and printing, as well as almost every major program on the Macintosh® computer.

After graduating from high school, I attended an art college, a college devoted entirely to the visual arts. I decided on this course largely because the success of mentorship confirmed my belief that graphic design was what I wanted for a career.

• • •

I chose art school for a simple reason—that's all you do. Art, art, art. Something that would *apply;* something useful for a change.

I did, however, go into it with mixed feelings. I can remember having a conversation with my high school art teacher on the very first day I met him. I was a sophomore, in my first art class in this school, and I assured him I wouldn't be going to college—tech school, maybe, but not college. Even then I thought it would be a waste of time (and money) to study things unrelated to art (physics, biology, etc. . . .). For some people that may not be, but I do a lot of learning on my own and I wanted to *focus.*

As it turned out, college posed many of the same problems high school did—except now it was costing me. I hate to waste time, but I hate to waste money even more. Here I thought I would learn about design, typography, and the business, the real world. Not so. I was put into survey classes that skimmed over subjects briefly and explained little.

Again, I found myself ahead of things. I had been doing full time production work in my mentor's graphic studio for six months, and they were assigning me arts and crafts projects.

There were only two classes in first semester that I felt were any use at all. I spoke with my advisor during registration for second semester and explained my situation. My mentor was a big help again; she advised me of the benefits of preparation and presentation. I went into my advisor's office with a detailed resumé, list of goals, and a patent, reasonable argument of why I wanted my first year credits waived so I could get into second year design classes.

It worked. By the end of the year, I wasn't planning on a degree, but I must say that I learned some things.

After talking with other professionals in the field, I determined that I didn't need a degree in art to be successful in this field. I decided it would be best not to let the job opportunities that were coming my way slip by. As of this writing, I still don't plan on going to school full time. I don't have time or money. But I still have things to learn and may go back for periodic classes. School and I just don't seem to agree.

I left Graphic Design and Production in October 1990. I felt I had grown into my position fairly well, and when the opportunity arose (from Ann) to freelance at another studio, I took it. The freelancing eventually led to a full-time job, which is where I'm at now.

Of course, I felt bad leaving Ann's, and I can never thank her enough for all the time and effort she gave me. I owe her a lot, and I hope some day I can give a young person the same chance she gave me.

Epilogue (Jill Reilly)

The next two school years after Chris graduated, I was editor for *Counseling & Guidance,* the newsletter of the Counseling and Guidance Division of the National Association for Gifted Children. This was a new project for the Division which required "a style." At the same time, Chris was taking a typography course at the college of art and design. Bless him, Chris volunteered to create a newsletter format which he could also use for his class and as a portfolio piece.

When *Counseling & Guidance* profiled Chris to recognize his contributions (Reilly, 1990), we asked him to share his own insights into the social and emotional needs of gifted or talented children. Chris responded in a way which, I believe, reflects aspects of his mentorship experience.

> *It's hard for me to say what those needs are in general, but for me the most frustrating part of the traditional school system was being locked into the same pace as everyone else. I enjoy learning quickly. I need space to move and find some things out on my own. But that doesn't mean I don't need structure or a safety net . . . just let me know you're there and give me a few helpful hints along the way. Or argue some sense into me if that's what it takes.*

In his landmark study of the role of mentors in creative achievement, E. Paul Torrance (1984) found that mentors can make a significant difference in the creative achievements and educational accomplishments of mentees. Ann helped Chris develop his talents and used her influence to help him remain in school. One year after the *Mentor Program* ended for Chris, Ann continued to encourage Chris as an artist, an employee, and as a student. She helped him plan strategies to gain entrance to more advanced college courses. Although Chris left Ann's firm for a new position as a graphic designer, she clearly made a difference in Chris's educational achievements and in his life.

Torrance concludes his study by stating the seven most important things mentors can do for their mentees. All seven relate directly to Chris's experience, but two most closely echo his own perceptions of the experience. Torrance (1984) says that mentors should help mentees to:

> . . . *learn to free themselves from the expectations of others and to walk away from the games that others try to impose on them [and to] free themselves to play their own game in such a way as to make the best use of their strengths and follow their dreams. (p. 57)*

Opinions may vary about Chris's educational choices. If Chris's experiences as described here generate dialogue, both he and I are delighted. However, in the dialogue we ask that you seriously consider the impact of mentoring on Chris's growth and development as a person and as an artist. Think about how this opportunity, or an offshoot of it, might benefit other students you know or will meet in the future and your role in offering it to them. You can realize the vision you form.

References

Reilly, J. (1990). Meet Chris Adams. *Counseling & Guidance,* 1(4), 3-4.

Torrance, E. P. (1984). *Mentor relationships: How they aid creative achievement, endure, change, and die.* Buffalo, NY: Bearly Limited.

ABOUT THE AUTHOR

Jill Reilly, Ed.D. is the Coordinator and Instructor of the Mentor Program at the Intermediate School District #917 in Rosemount, Minnesota. Although this mentorship program focuses on gifted and talented high school students, Dr. Reilly's mentorship techniques have been used successfully with a wide range of students in a variety of settings.

Dr. Reilly has served on the Board of Directors of the Counseling and Guidance Division of the National Association for Gifted Children, as well as on the Education Committee of the Burnsville, Minnesota, Chamber of Commerce. She received her Ed.D. degree from the University of St. Thomas in St. Paul.

Dr. Reilly has conducted hundreds of workshops on high school guidance and college planning. Along with Bonnie Featherstone, she created the Individualized College Planning Seminars and co-authored another widely acclaimed book, *College Comes Sooner Than You Think!: The Essential College Planning Guide for High School Students and Their Families.*

As a parent of three school-age children as well as a teacher, Dr. Reilly has an intimate knowledge of the important dimensions involved in helping youngsters reach their potential.

COLLEGE COMES SOONER THAN YOU THINK!
The Essential Planning Guide for High School Students and
Their Families
by Bonnie D. Featherstone, B.A. and Jill M. Reilly, M.A.
(1990) 175 pages
ISBN: 0-910707-17-0

The first-college planning book written for students and their parents to
use *together*. The entire planning process is a family affair to help each family find the college that's best for everybody concerned.

Easy-to-follow-and-use. Covers all the basics — evaluation of the student's
strengths and weaknesses, likes and dislikes (by both parent and student),
exploration of careers, organization of records, preparation of a first
resume, shopping for colleges, campus visits, planning finances, preparing
for tests, filling out applications, and much more.

Step-by-step planning process with ample room to "fill in the blanks" is
given, along with a complete bibliography for other special areas such as
scholarships. The authors have extensive experience. Both are teachers,
parents, and frequent workshop presenters. This user-friendly book is an
effective tool for communication and decision-making in college planning.

- -

ORDER FORM

COLLEGE COMES SOONER THAN YOU THINK!

Name _____

Street _____

City _____ State _____ Zip _____

Phone _____ ☐ Check ☐ PO # _____

Make checks payable to OPP

☐ ☐ ☐ ☐ ☐ ☐ ☐ ☐ ☐ ☐ ☐ ☐ ☐

☐ VISA ☐ MasterCard Exp. _____ Signature _____

6.5% State sales tax for Ohio residents only.

MAIL TO: Ohio Psychology Press
P.O. Box 90095
Dayton, OH 45490
TO FAX YOUR ORDER: (513) 454-1033

SHIPPING
1 book = $3.00
2 books = $5.00
up to 4 = $7.00
up to 6 = $9.00
up to 7 = $11.00

•••

278

Qty.	Amount
	@ $12.95
Sub Total	
Shipping	
*6.5% tax	
Total	

(PLEASE PHOTO COPY THIS FORM)